READING THE OLD TESTAMENT WITH THE ANCIENT CHURCH

Exploring the Formation of Early Christian Thought

Ronald E. Heine

Baker Academic

Grand Rapids, Michigan

© 2007 by Ronald E. Heine

Published by Baker Academic
a division of Baker Publishing Group
P.O. Box 6287, Grand Rapids, MI 49516-6287
www.bakeracademic.com

Printed in the United States of America

Library of Congress Cataloging-in-Publication Data
Heine, Ronald E.
    Reading the Old Testament with the ancient church : exploring the formation of early Christian thought / Ronald E. Heine.
        p.   cm. — (Evangelical ressourcement)
    Includes bibliographical references and index.
    ISBN 10: 0-8010-2777-2 (pbk.)
    ISBN 978-0-8010-2777-2 (pbk.)
        1. Bible. O.T.—Criticism, interpretation, etc. 2. Christian literature, Early. 3. Theology—History—Early church, ca. 30–600. I. Title.
    BS1171.3.H44 2007
    221.609'015—dc22   2007000485

Reading the Old Testament with the Ancient Church

EVANGELICAL *RESSOURCEMENT*
ANCIENT SOURCES FOR THE CHURCH'S FUTURE

D. H. Williams, series editor

The Evangelical *Ressourcement* series is designed to address the ways in which Christians may draw upon the thought and life of the early church to respond to the challenges facing today's church.

To the memory of my friend and former colleague

Prof. Dr. Otto Betz,
who was a master in using the Old Testament
to interpret the New

"You are not able to enter into the Holy Scriptures without a guide to show you the way."

Jerome, *Epistle* 53.6

CONTENTS

Abbreviations

Modern Sources

ABD	*Anchor Bible Dictionary*
ACW	Ancient Christian Writers
ANF	*The Ante-Nicene Fathers*
BETL	Bibliotheca Ephemeridum Theologicarum Lovaniensium
CCSL	Corpus Christianorum: Series Latina
FC	The Fathers of the Church
JECS	*Journal of Early Christian Studies*
JTS	*The Journal of Theological Studies*
LXX	Septuagint
NIV	New International Version
NPNF	*The Nicene and Post-Nicene Fathers of the Christian Church*, 2 series
NRSV	New Revised Standard Version
OECS	Oxford Early Christian Studies
PG	Migne, *Patrologia Graeca*
WSA	*The Works of Saint Augustine: A Translation for the 21st Century*, 3 parts
ZAC/JAC	*Zeitschrift für antikes Christentum/Journal of Ancient Christianity*

Ancient Christian and Jewish Sources

ComMt ser.	*Origenes Werke* 11 (Die griechischen christlichen Schriftsteller), ed. E. Klostermann, E. Benz, and U. Treu
Exp. Ps	Augustine, *Expositions of the Psalms*

For the other commentary and homiletical literature of the church fathers the following abbreviation system has been used. *Com* (= *Commentary on*) or *Hom* (= *Homilies on*) is joined to a standard abbreviation of the biblical book, so that *ComJn* means *Commentary on John*, and *HomEx* means *Homilies on Exodus*, and so on.

4Q174	*Florilegium*, or *Midrash on the Last Days*
4Q175	*Testimonia*, or *Messianic Anthology*
4Q252	*Commentary on Genesis A*
4Q377	*A Moses Apocryphon^c*
4Q521	*Messianic Apocalypse*
11Q5	*Apocryphal Psalms (1)*

PREFACE

THE EVANGELICAL CHURCH is in danger of having a cut-flower faith. Its message of Jesus is largely severed from its roots in the Old Testament Scriptures. This is more the result of neglect than of intention. I am part of an evangelical tradition that began in the nineteenth century with the dream of restoring the church of the New Testament. The leaders of this tradition placed a great emphasis on the New Testament but neglected the Old. They failed to perceive that the Old Testament was the Bible of the church of the New Testament.[1] Many evangelical communions make that same error. None of them, including my own, would claim that the Old Testament is not Scripture or that it should not be a part of the Christian canon. Its vital connection with the church's gospel of Jesus Christ, however, is rarely understood today and even less frequently taught in the church.

This book examines how the church fathers, the leaders and teachers of the church in the first four centuries, used the Old Testament as Christian Scripture. It is not a book about the methods of interpretation used by the fathers, at least not in the usual sense of such studies. Frances M. Young is correct, I believe, when she discounts the adequacy of the approaches customarily taken in the study of the church fathers' interpretation of the Bible.[2] Their interpretative methods will, of course, sometimes be an unavoidable part of the discussion but the purpose of my study does not lie in this arena. I am interested in examining the central role that the Old Testament played in the formation of Christian

1. See Ronald E. Heine, "Alexander Campbell and the Old Testament," *Stone-Campbell Journal* (2002): 163–81.

2. Frances M. Young, *Biblical Exegesis and the Formation of Christian Culture* (Cambridge: Cambridge University Press, 1997), 2.

thinking and life in the early centuries of the church. I hope to capture the way the fathers regarded the Old Testament and some of the uses to which they put it.

While it was natural that the earliest Christians should take up the Jewish Scriptures as their Scriptures, it was also problematic. How should they, as Christians, relate to the demands of the Jewish law? How could they understand Isaiah 53 to speak of the sufferings of Jesus of Nazareth when the leaders of the synagogue understood it to refer to the sufferings of the Jewish people? Does Isaiah 7:14 refer to a virgin giving birth as the Christians held, or to a young woman giving birth as the Jews argued? These were the kinds of questions forced on the early Christians as they took up the Jewish Scriptures as their Bible.

The Old Testament provided the glasses through which the early Christians looked at Jesus of Nazareth. The doctrines they put forth regarding him and the significance of his life for humanity depend on Old Testament texts that they read in relation to him. There would have been no Christianity without the Old Testament. When the books that make up our New Testament were eventually written and elevated to the status of Scripture alongside the books of the Old Testament, the two testaments together formed the Christian Bible. The Old Testament was as much Christian Scripture as the New and was used in the same way as the New in Christian teaching and preaching. This attitude of the fathers concerning the two testaments continued through the period of the Protestant Reformation. Luther and Calvin considered both testaments to be vital for Christian teaching. It was in the post-Enlightenment period that the New Testament began to be orphaned from the Old. This process reached its climax in the critical studies of the late nineteenth and early twentieth centuries. The end result of this process has been an ambivalence about the use of the Old Testament in the church.

Various organizations and individuals contributed to the writing of this book. Chapters 2 and 3 began as lectures I delivered for the C. H. Phillips Lectures at Puget Sound Christian College in 2002. It was this series of lectures that provided the impetus for me to begin developing the seed idea that had lain dormant in my mind for several years. Chapter 2 was also presented to the Kolloquium für Graduierte at the Eberhard Karls Universität in Tübingen, Germany, in 2004.

A stipend from the Institut zur Erforschung des Urchristentums and the European Evangelistic Society made possible a pleasant summer of research in 2004 in Tübingen on the contents of chapter 4. One of the enjoyable times of that summer was a morning spent sitting at table with Prof. Otto Betz and discussing the messianic understanding in the prophets and the rabbis. I must record here my indebtedness to Prof. Betz for many aspects of my understanding of ancient Judaism. This is not the kind of indebtedness that can be footnoted, for it is not based primarily on the many books and articles that he wrote on this subject. It is the unconscious influence from my experiences with him during the ten years we worked together as co-leaders of the Kolloquium für Graduierte at the University in Tübingen. I must also thank my student assistant at Puget Sound Christian College, Ron Schaffner. He read large portions of the book as it was in preparation and caught several slips in typing and consistency. My friend and pastor, Dr. Milton Jones, read a draft of the book and made many helpful suggestions that have made it more reader friendly. I thank also Dr. D. H. Williams, the series editor, for the invitation to contribute a volume to this series and for his helpful criticisms. I, of course, take full responsibility for the flaws that remain. Finally, my wife Gillian and daughter Katrina have been supportive of and patient with my long hours of isolation with books and a computer.

REH

INTRODUCTION

MAJOR THINGS HAVE happened in Christian history when individuals have rediscovered the Bible. In one sense, it was Martin Luther's "rediscovery" of the Bible that led him to formulate the views that gave birth to the sixteenth-century Protestant Reformation. As a young Augustinian monk, Luther struggled with the concept of the righteousness of God. He understood it to point to God's just condemnation of the sinner. Laboring under the burden of the feeling of condemnation and finding no consolation in the practice of confession and penance, Luther searched the Bible for help. In this search he discovered the loving God who graciously grants his righteousness to the believing sinner. Luther made this discovery in his study of the book of Psalms as well as in his work on the Epistles to the Romans, Galatians, and Hebrews. It was on this biblical foundation that he built the doctrines that shaped the Protestant Reformation.[1]

Karl Barth set theological thinking on a new course in the twentieth century with his "rediscovery" of the Bible. Freshly educated by some of the leading scholars of nineteenth-century liberalism in Germany, Barth became a pastor in the small city of Safenwil, Switzerland. As the young Barth labored over his sermons for his working-class parishioners, he perceived that the theology he had learned in university had little to say to their needs. Barth turned to the Bible and in his study of it discovered what he called a "strange new world" where God held center place, not humanity as nineteenth-century liberals believed.[2] Barth formulated an

---

1. See "Preface to the Complete Edition of Luther's Latin Writings," in *Martin Luther: Selections from His Writings*, ed. J. Dillenberger (New York: Doubleday, 1951), 3–12.
2. Karl Barth, "The Strange New World within the Bible," in *The Word of God and the Word of Man*, trans. D. Horton (New York: Harper & Row, 1957), 28–50.

approach to theology that renewed the place of the Bible in theological work. He understood the church to stand under "the authority of the gospel and the law" and asserted that the proper task of theology is to interpret "the Old and New Testaments."[3]

Few Christians today would doubt the centrality of the Bible for the life of the church. There have been and continue to be, however, significant questions about the role that the Old Testament should, or even can, play in church life. These questions have their home more in the Protestant than in the Roman Catholic Church because the lack of a liturgy in the former leaves the act of integrating the Old Testament into the gospel up to the believer or the pastor. Questions have been raised regarding the validity of the church using the Old Testament as well as the proper way to interpret it so that it speaks to Christians. Writing in the mid-twentieth century, Bernard W. Anderson called attention to the centrality of the question of the Christian use of the Old Testament in the meaning of Christian faith. He noted, however, that the question remained "unanswered" by the church and, more tragically, "often unasked."[4]

The Old Testament constitutes approximately three-fourths of the Christian Bible. It was not composed by Christians but by Jews in the pre-Christian era and was, and continues to be, the Jewish Scriptures. The church, however, from its beginnings has claimed the Old Testament as its own. The body of the present book will examine how the church fathers of the first four centuries AD wrestled with the problem of the Old Testament and the ways in which they used the Old Testament, or read it, as Christian Scripture. Before turning to that subject, however, we will first briefly survey some of the attitudes toward the Old Testament held by key figures in the Protestant tradition, beginning with the period of the Reformation.

Attitudes toward the Old Testament in the Protestant Reformation

Erasmus (1466–1536)

Erasmus of Rotterdam was a contemporary of Martin Luther. He never left the Roman Catholic Church so, strictly speaking, was not a participant in the Reformation. Nevertheless, he shared with Luther the desire to reform Christendom. Erasmus, however, took a different route than Luther in his

---

3. Karl Barth, *God in Action*, trans. E. G. Homrighausen and K. J. Ernst (Manhassett, NY: Round Table), 50, 51.

4. Bernard W. Anderson, *The Old Testament and Christian Faith*, ed. Bernhard W. Anderson (New York: Harper & Row, 1963), 1, 5.

attempts at reform. He was very much a Renaissance man and shared the Renaissance ideal of returning to the ancient sources to revitalize contemporary society. In addition to the Greek and Latin classics, to which all leaders of the Renaissance looked, Erasmus also considered the Bible to be one of those ancient sources to which people needed to return.

Erasmus was an excellent philologist and is known especially for his publication of the first critical edition of the Greek New Testament. His scholarly work was focused not only on the Greek New Testament but also on the Greek and Latin classics and the Greek and Latin church fathers. He never learned the Hebrew language in order to study the Old Testament. Instead, he thought that he could discover the ideals of Christ in the New Testament and that these ideals, combined with the best of the classical Greeks and Romans, would lead to the birth of a kind of Christian classical civilization.

Erasmus did not disregard the Old Testament completely. He recognized that New Testament authors drew on it and that it formed an important backdrop for Christianity. It was not, however, of equal authority with the New Testament. When his friend John Reuchlin, the Hebrew scholar, had to defend rabbinical literature against an attempt to destroy it, Erasmus defended Reuchlin, although he did not defend the Jewish literature. In fact, Erasmus confided to another friend that as long as the New Testament was undisturbed he would prefer to see the Old Testament perish rather than have the peace of the church destroyed over it.[5]

Martin Luther (1483–1546)

Martin Luther had a much more positive attitude toward the Old Testament than did Erasmus. Luther knew Hebrew, as well as Greek and Latin, and included the Old Testament along with the New in his translation of the Bible into the German language. Luther's approach to the Old Testament is complicated, but there is never any doubt that he considered the Old Testament to be the word of God and therefore vitally important to the church. In his "Preface to the Old Testament," written in 1523, Luther refers to the Old Testament as "the swaddling cloths and the manger in which Christ lies."[6] This imagery provides one of the keys to Luther's understanding of the Old Testament. Above all, it is a book about Christ.

5. See John William Aldridge, *The Hermeneutic of Erasmus*, Basil Studies of Theology 2 (Richmond, VA: John Knox, 1966), 46–49; and Roland H. Bainton, *Erasmus of Christendom* (New York: Scribner's Sons, 1969), 143.

6. In *Martin Luther's Basic Theological Writings*, ed. Timothy F. Lull (Minneapolis: Fortress, 1989), 119.

If one wants to interpret Leviticus correctly one should read it with a focus on Christ, "for he is the man to whom it all applies, every bit of it."[7] The presence of promises about Christ in the writings of Moses, such as those in Genesis 3:15, Genesis 22:18, and Deuteronomy 18:15, is a primary reason for Luther's high regard for Moses's writings.[8] Luther finds Christ and his kingdom foreshadowed in the Old Testament monarchy, priesthood, offerings, history of the patriarchs, prophecies of the prophets, and spiritual ideas and images in the Psalms.[9]

However, Luther can also say, "Moses is dead. His rule ended when Christ came. He is of no further service."[10] He considered Moses's law to bind only the Jews. Those laws that Gentiles share with Jews have been written in the Gentiles' hearts and do not derive from Moses. Not even the Ten Commandments apply to the Christian as coming from Moses, for to accept one part of Moses obligates one to keep the whole law. "We will regard Moses as a teacher," Luther says, "but we will not regard him as our lawgiver—unless he agrees with both the New Testament and the natural law."[11]

The law continues to function in the church, however, in Luther's well-known coupling of law and gospel. One cannot hear the gospel and receive its grace and life until one has first been killed by the letter of the law. "Life is a help only to those who are dead," Luther says, "grace only to sin, the Spirit only to the letter. No one can have the one without the other."[12] The law teaches people that they are sinners and that they stand with all humanity under condemnation. Once the law has humbled people by making them aware of their true nature then they are ready to repent and receive the gift of Christ. This action not only grants them forgiveness of their sins but also sets them free from the law, just as "Christ is free from the grave, and Peter from the prison."[13]

Luther considered law to stand side by side with the promises of the gospel in every book in the Bible. The New Testament is referred to as gospel because there is more gospel than law in it, and the Old Testament is called a book of law because there is more law than gospel in

---

7. Ibid., 130.

8. "How Christians Should Regard Moses," in Lull, *Luther's Basic Theological Writings*, 142–43.

9. Heinrich Bornkamm, *Luther und das Alte Testament* (Tübingen: Mohr Siebeck, 1948), 82.

10. "How Christians Should Regard Moses," 139.

11. Ibid.

12. "Concerning the Letter and the Spirit," in Lull, *Luther's Basic Theological Writings*, 85.

13. *Commentary on Galatians*, in Dillenberger, *Luther: Selections from His Writings*, 109–10, 120.

it. The two Testaments are a unity, however, because the totality of the divine Word, both law and gospel, is contained in both.[14]

John Calvin (1509–1564)

John Calvin was the most important biblical exegete of the Reformation. He produced commentaries and homilies on most of the books of the Bible. His views concerning the Old Testament are similar to Luther's, but he gives a broader role to the law in the life of the church than did Luther. Throughout his writings Calvin is especially concerned to show that the revelation found in both Testaments has "the most substantial identity."[15]

Like Luther, Calvin believed that Christ is spoken of and is present in the Old Testament. Commenting on John 5:39, in which Jesus challenges the Jews to "search the Scriptures" because they testify to him, Calvin notes that Christ can be known correctly only in Scripture, and therefore the chief reason for studying Scripture is to acquire knowledge of Christ. He further notes that the word "Scripture" here refers clearly to the Old Testament. From this he argues that Christ does not appear "first in the gospel," but that only after "the witness of the Law and Prophets" does he appear "in the gospel for everyone to see." The whole purpose of God's work through Moses was to call people to Christ. "For the law without Christ has nothing solid about it, and in fact avails us nothing." Further, commenting on 2 Corinthians 3:14–17 Calvin states that while the law "is a source of light," we see "its brightness only when Christ appears to us in it," for "there is no light in the law, or even in the whole Word of God, without Christ who is the Sun of Righteousness."[16]

In his *Institutes of the Christian Religion* Calvin defines the law to be "the whole system of religion delivered by the hand of Moses" (2.7.1).[17] He divides this system into the moral law and the ceremonial law, the latter consisting of the laws regulating the worship of Israel. It is the ceremonial law and not the moral law, therefore, that Calvin thinks Christ eliminated (2.7.13–16).[18] The moral law continues to be valid in the Christian era and functions in three ways. First, it reveals God's

14. Bornkamm, *Luther*, 70–73.

15. Ronald S. Wallace, *Calvin's Doctrine of the Word and Sacrament* (Grand Rapids: Eerdmans, 1957), 27.

16. *Calvin: Commentaries*, ed. Joseph Haroutunian, The Library of Christian Classics Ichthus Edition (Philadelphia: Westminster, 1958), 104–5, 111.

17. John Calvin, *Institutes of the Christian Religion*, trans. H. Beveridge, 2 vols. (Grand Rapids: Eerdmans, 1983 reprint), 1:300.

18. Ibid., 310–12.

righteousness and our unrighteousness. It is a mirror in which we see our dirty faces. A second function of the law is to restrain those who otherwise would have no regard for justice. Finally, the moral law teaches believers what the will of God is and functions as "a whip to the flesh" to urge us to obedience (2.7.12). Calvin closes this part of his discussion of the moral law by saying that "it must ever remain an indubitable truth, that the Law has lost none of its authority, but must always receive from us the same respect and obedience" (2.7.15).[19]

In his *Commentary on Hebrews*, however, Calvin frequently comments on the limits of Moses's ministration and the end of the law. Discussing Hebrews 3:5, Calvin speaks of limits placed on Moses beyond which he could not pass. Here Calvin is referring to the incompleteness of the revelation given through Moses compared with the complete revelation given in the gospel. Moses's ministry, he says in his comments on Hebrews 7:12, was as temporary as that of Aaron and "both were annulled by the coming of Christ." He qualifies this statement, however, by asserting that Christ abolished only that part of the law that pertains to the priesthood and not the parts that teach of faith and the fear of God or instruct us in the "rule of life." When he discusses Hebrews 10:1, Calvin suggests that the gospel is present in the law but in a shadowy, indistinct image, whereas it is present in the New Testament in vivid color and in clear and distinct lines.[20] In his commentary on 2 Corinthians 3:7, he contrasts gospel and law as instruments of life and death. The law diagnoses the disease but can prescribe no cure. The gospel, however, provides the remedy. "For as the law leaves man to himself, it condemns him, of necessity, to death; while the gospel, bringing him to Christ, opens the gate of life." Moses's ministry, moreover, is transient; that of Christ is permanent. Calvin considers Paul in this passage to be referring to the abolition of "the whole of the Old Testament, in so far as it is opposed to the gospel." Paul's intent is to show "how much more powerfully the Spirit of God exercises his power in the gospel, than of old under the law."[21]

When he discusses Romans 3:31, Calvin argues that the whole law, embracing the ceremonial as well as the moral, is both abrogated and confirmed in Christ. Faith in Christ confirms the moral law because its purpose is to lead one to Christ by pointing out one's sin. Without faith in Christ, however, the law is powerless to do anything but condemn. The ceremonial law passes away with the coming of Christ, but because

---

19. Ibid., 304–11.
20. John Calvin, *Commentaries on the Epistle of Paul the Apostle to the Hebrews*, trans. John Owen (Albany, OR: Sage Software, 1996).
21. John Calvin, *Commentary on Corinthians*, vol. 2, from the Calvin Translation Society edition, http://www.ccel.org/c/calvin/comment3/comm_index.htm.

the ceremonies foreshadow Christ in their images they also find their confirmation in him.[22]

Erasmus's view of the Old Testament shows that the Old Testament was sometimes slighted in the Reformation period. The attitudes of both Luther and Calvin, however, show that the Protestant Reformation began with a firm conviction that the Old Testament is the Word of God as much as the New Testament and that both together constitute the Christian Scriptures. Both men recognized that the Mosaic law presented certain problems for the Christian use of the Old Testament, but neither thought these problems called into question the value of the Old Testament for instructing the Christian in the ways and will of God. Perhaps most important, both Luther and Calvin found Christ prefigured in the ceremonies and predicted in the prophecies of the Old Testament. This latter fact made the Old Testament foundational for Christian theology.

Attitudes toward the Old Testament in the Enlightenment and Romantic Periods

The late seventeenth and eighteenth centuries saw the rise of what has been called the Enlightenment. Intoxicated by the numerous scientific discoveries of the seventeenth century and irritated by what they considered to be the oppressions of their governments and the Roman Catholic Church, the intellectuals of Europe pressed for new individual freedoms in all realms of life and thought. The autonomous individual who dared to think on his own was the ideal Enlightenment person. Attitudes toward the Bible changed considerably in this period. Leaders of the Enlightenment did not usually question specifically the Christian use of the Old Testament. What they questioned instead was the whole concept of divine revelation.

English Deists

The church in the age of the Enlightenment lacked any outstanding theologian. There was no Luther or Calvin, no Schleiermacher or Harnack, no Barth or Bultmann. Deism was a popular Enlightenment form of theology, centered primarily in England. The Deists believed that God had created the world but that he did not intervene in it in any way. They had little to say in defense of revelation in general, and considered the Old Testament in particular to be of questionable value. Their religion was a religion of

22. John Calvin, *Commentaries on the Epistle of Paul the Apostle to the Romans*, trans. and ed. John Owen (Grand Rapids: Eerdmans, 1948), 151–52.

reason. In 1730 the Deist Matthew Tindal published *Christianity as Old as the Creation*. This work reflects the typical Deist view of revelation. "True Christianity" is reasonable, Tindal asserts, and consists of truths common to all religions of all times. Revealed religion is to be accepted only to the extent that it conforms to reason. Consequently, the Old Testament is to be "discarded" because it presents numerous "'unreasonable' practices," including circumcision and animal sacrifice, as well as stories of miraculous events and the massacres of peoples.[23] Harnack, who will be considered later, singles out the Deist Thomas Morgan as a follower of Tindal who went further than any other Deist in his objections to the Old Testament. Morgan, in his negative views of the religious teachings put forth in the Old Testament, was strikingly parallel to the second-century heretic Marcion, who totally rejected the Christian use of the Old Testament.[24]

John Locke (1632–1704)

Major philosophers of the Enlightenment who had anything positive to say about Christianity attempted to ground it in reason. In 1695 the English philosopher John Locke published a treatise titled *The Reasonableness of Christianity as Delivered in the Scriptures*, and nearly a century later, in 1793, the German Immanuel Kant published *Religion within the Limits of Reason Alone*.

Locke had a positive view of Christianity and did not deny revelation, believing that revelation involved faith. For Locke, however, there was a contrast between reason and faith. He considered all our information to originate in the perceptions of our senses. Once we have perceived something with our senses we then possess that perception in our minds as an idea. The mind can then reflect on these ideas and draw conclusions. Reason, then, is the mind's way of making deductions from ideas arrived at by our "natural faculties." Faith differs from this only in that it involves accepting propositions that we have not arrived at by means of our natural reason but that derive "from God in some extraordinary way of communication." Locke called this second way of arriving at truth revelation. The acceptance of a proposition attributed to revelation must, however, be reasonable, so that in the final analysis reason controls revelation.[25]

---

23. As cited in Robert M. Grant, *A Short History of the Interpretation of the Bible*, rev. ed. (New York: MacMillan, 1963), 247–48.

24. Adolf von Harnack, *Marcion: The Gospel of the Alien God*, trans. J. E. Steely and L. D. Bierma (Durham, NC: Labyrinth, 1990; German original 1924), 136–37. Marcion will be discussed in chap. 2.

25. *An Essay concerning Human Understanding* 4.18.2 and 4.17.4, cited in John Locke, *The Reasonableness of Christianity*, ed., abr., and intro. I. T. Ramsey (Stanford, CA: Stanford University Press, 1958), 10–11.

It is clear that Locke considers the New Testament to be more important than the Old. The Old Testament, nevertheless, continues to play a role for the Christian by functioning in three ways. First, it provides the necessary presuppositions for understanding the central teachings of the New Testament. No one, Locke argues, could understand the New Testament doctrine of redemption without first being aware of the fall of Adam.[26] Second, the Mosaic law provides the moral guidelines that continue to function for the Christian. Here Locke contrasts the law of faith with the law of works. The latter is the Mosaic law; the former is Paul's doctrine of justification by faith that appears in Romans, which Locke understood as focusing on the belief that Jesus was the Messiah. The ritual and civil parts of the Mosaic law applied only to the Jews. The moral part, however, applies to everyone, everywhere. Christians have the advantage over nonbelievers of also being under the law of faith, which covers their shortcomings in keeping the moral law.[27] Finally, the Old Testament prophecies, along with Jesus's miracles, provide the evidence that makes possible belief that Jesus was the Messiah. This is extremely important, for the latter is the central belief required to "obtain eternal life."[28] There is a very rational element in Locke's understanding of biblical revelation and he subordinates the Old Testament to the New, but he does believe that the Old Testament plays a necessary role in Christian faith.

Immanuel Kant (1724–1804)

For Immanuel Kant ideal religion is morality based on reason without the encumbrances of dogmas, sanctuaries, and priests. Morality based on reason, he thought, was the only pure religious faith. Ecclesiastical faith as a kind of necessary second-best, is the vehicle on which pure religious faith depends. Ecclesiastical faith, however, does not have its basis primarily in reason but in Scripture. The latter is necessary for the preservation of faith and serves as the vehicle for moral doctrine. "How fortunate," Kant says, "when such a book . . . contains, along with its statutes, or laws of faith, the purest moral doctrine of religion in its completeness."[29]

While Kant does not specify that the Scripture behind ecclesiastical faith is the New Testament alone, it is fairly clear that this is what he means. He saw "no essential connection at all" between the Jewish

26. Locke, *Reasonableness of Christianity*, 25.
27. Ibid., 30–31.
28. Ibid., 32–33; cf. 43–44.
29. Immanuel Kant, *Religion within the Limits of Reason Alone*, trans. T. M. Greene and H. H. Hudson (New York: Harper & Row, 1960), 98.

faith and the church. He considered the Jewish faith to consist only of a collection of "statutory laws" that did not govern a religion but a political organization. Judaism, in fact, was not a religion at all but a commonwealth of people who "belonged to a particular stock." The church completely forsook "the Judaism from which it sprang, and grounded upon a wholly new principle, effected a thoroughgoing revolution in doctrines of faith."[30]

Friedrich Schleiermacher (1768–1834)

During the time of the Romantic reaction to the excessive rationalism of the Enlightenment a new major voice emerged in the church. Friedrich Schleiermacher, who is considered to be the father of modern Protestant theology, first became a significant public figure with his *On Religion: Speeches to Its Cultured Despisers*, delivered in Berlin in 1799. In these speeches Schleiermacher defended religion against the criticisms of the Enlightenment. In the spirit of Romanticism, he argued that religion was not a metaphysical or even a dogmatic system but that its true nature resided in an individual's feelings of dependence on an infinite God. While revelation is more important to Schleiermacher than to his Enlightenment predecessors, it is obvious from the foundation on which he places religion that biblical revelation is not the highest priority.

Schleiermacher sets forth a systematic theology in his most important work, *The Christian Faith*, published in 1821. As a Protestant theologian he considers the New Testament to be sufficient "as a norm for Christian Doctrine."[31] The Old Testament has no value for dogmatics. Any doctrine depending solely on the Old Testament for its attestation cannot be considered "a genuinely Christian doctrine."[32] Only the prophetic element in the Old Testament has value for Christian usage because only the most general "religious emotions" can be found there. Distinctively Christian emotions can be found in the Old Testament only by the mental processes of removing much that is there and imagining much that isn't.[33] The Old Testament, for Schleiermacher, does not "share the normative dignity or the inspiration of the New." He recognizes the high regard both Christ and the apostles had for the Old Testament Scriptures and thinks this is the primary reason for the position they have been accorded in the church ever since. He argues, however, that this does not constitute a reason for the continued use of the Old Testament by the church. The

30. Ibid., 116–18.
31. Friedrich Schleiermacher, *The Christian Faith*, trans. H. R. Mackintosh and J. S. Stewart, 2nd German ed. (Philadelphia: Fortress, 1976), 604.
32. Ibid., 115.
33. Ibid., 62.

usage of Christ and the apostles, he thinks, would justify the continued use of only the prophetic books and the Psalms. Schleiermacher would prefer that these be added to the New Testament as an appendix. He could agree to the entire Old Testament being added to the New, but again argues that it should appear as an appendix following rather than a work preceding the New Testament in order.[34]

Biblical revelation, especially that found in the Old Testament, did not fare well in the periods of time we label as the Enlightenment and the Romantic eras. This was the time when modern science was developing. It was a time when the human intellect was feeling new freedom after what was considered to be its long oppression by the medieval church. Kant defined Enlightenment as the courage to throw off the "tutelage" of external authorities and to use one's own reason.[35] Biblical revelation was perceived to be too closely related to the clerical authority of the preceding period. This was the time of the individual, the time when the cherished ideals included the freedom to think, the freedom to feel, and the freedom of self-expression.

Attitudes toward the Old Testament in the Modern Period

A major separation between the Old and New Testaments appeared in the late nineteenth and early twentieth centuries, especially in the academic study of the Bible. R. E. Clements notes that the "primary goal" of applying critical scholarship to the Old Testament in the late nineteenth century "was a historical one, concerned with the recovery of a knowledge of the history of ancient Israel and its religion."[36] Books on the Old Testament published at this time often had the words "the religion of Israel" or "the history of the religion of Israel" in their titles.[37] In the view of many late nineteenth- and early twentieth-century biblical scholars, the Old Testament was about the religion of Israel and the New Testament was about the religion of Christians. The unity of the two testaments that had marked the understanding of Luther and Calvin was no longer considered. In an article published in 1904, the Old Testament scholar Hermann Gunkel argued that the interval of time

34. Ibid., 608–11.

35. Immanuel Kant, "What Is Enlightenment?" (1784), in *The Portable Enlightenment Reader*, ed. Isaac Kramnick (New York: Penguin, 1995), 1.

36. R. E. Clements, *One Hundred Years of Old Testament Interpretation* (Philadelphia: Westminster, 1976), 4.

37. See, for example, the titles appearing in Henning Graf Reventlow, *Problems of Old Testament Theology in the Twentieth Century* (Philadelphia: Fortress, 1985), 5–6.

separating the Old Testament from the twentieth century, and even from the New Testament, precludes its use as a source for Christian doctrine. As an intellectual descendant of Schleiermacher, Gunkel did not think this detrimental in any way, for he considered the center of religion to lie in piety, and doctrine to be only peripheral. The goal of Old Testament exegesis was not to discover the teachings in a writer's words but to discover his personality.[38]

Adolf von Harnack (1851–1930)

Some of the most radical statements against the Old Testament at this time were made by the great German church historian and theologian Adolf von Harnack. Harnack's earliest academic work was an essay on Marcion written in 1870 for a contest sponsored by the "theological faculty of the University of Dorpat," for which he received the prize. The faculty urged him to revise and publish the essay but he did not do so at the time. He did, however, continue to work on it and in 1920 published a totally reworked study titled *Marcion: The Gospel of the Alien God*.[39] This early study of Marcion seems to have had an enduring influence on Harnack's thinking. Marcion became his theological model. He idealized Marcion's approach to Christianity. It is this idealized Marcionism that can be seen lying behind the approach taken in Harnack's monumental *History of Dogma*. Harnack considered a major shift to have occurred when the gospel passed from the early Jewish Christians to the Greeks. Christianity became subordinate to a system of reasoned thought in the Greek world. This demanded classifying and prioritizing what had previously been handed on "simply as divine revelation." The body of divine revelation, however, was unmanageable for such a system. The chief culprit was the mass of material constituting the Old Testament, which was joined with the simple message of Jesus that demanded only acknowledgment of God, following his will, and welcoming his kingdom. It was Marcion, Harnack argued, who cut through the confused mass by casting the Old Testament aside so that he could present the simple and coherent message of Christ. Marcion, in Harnack's view, was the great liberator of Christianity. His program was summed up in the words: "*No syncretism, but simplification, unification, and clarity of what bore the Christian label.*"[40]

Harnack thought that it was not until the appearance of Luther in the sixteenth century that "the Pauline-Marcionite recognition of the

38. Hermann Gunkel, "Ziele und Methoden der Erklärung des Alten Testaments," *Monatschrift für kirchliche Praxis* 4 (1904): 521–40, cited in Reventlow, *Problems of Old Testament Theology*, 7–8.

39. Harnack, *Marcion*, ix–x.

40. Ibid., 5–12.

distinction between law and gospel" was again made a central issue. He laments that Luther does not include the whole Old Testament under the judgment that he passes on the apocryphal books. Luther should have said that the whole is "'good and useful to read,'" but that it does not stand on a par with the New Testament as canon.[41]

In this tradition of Marcion and, in his opinion, also Luther, Harnack boldly proclaims that no equation of the Old Testament with the New Testament can be maintained nor "any authority for the Old Testament in Christianity." Protestant churches have known this for a century, Harnack claims, and it is their duty "to place the Old Testament . . . at the head of the list of books 'which are good and useful to be read' and to maintain in force the knowledge of those parts that are actually edifying but to leave the churches in no doubt about the fact that the Old Testament is *not* a canonical book. But," he sadly concludes, "these churches are crippled."[42]

Karl Barth (1886–1968)

There were a plethora of significant theological voices in the mid-twentieth century, but there is no question about the dominating power of those of Karl Barth and Rudolf Bultmann. Barth's theology gave the Old Testament unquestioned canonical status. In his final series of lectures at Basil after a forty-year career in academia, Barth asserted that the content of the canon of the synagogue was recognized by the early Christians "as authentic, trustworthy, and authoritative testimonies to the Word of God." Contemporary "evangelical theology," he continued, listens to "the Old Testament with the greatest earnestness and not merely as a sort of prelude to the New Testament." He gives his approval to the classical statement that "the New Testament is concealed within the Old, and the Old Testament is revealed by the New." When theology neglected this rule, Barth says, and focused only on the New Testament, "it was continually threatened by a cancer in its very bones." However, there is a necessary focus on the New Testament, for it bears witness to the fulfillment of the prophetic word spoken in the Old Testament and to the attainment of the goal of Israel's history. The Christian communities of the second through the fourth centuries recognized the authenticity of the testimony of the New Testament canon to the history of Jesus while "at the same time taking over, with a remarkable naturalness and ease, the Old Testament canon from the synagogue."[43]

41. Ibid., 134–35.
42. Ibid., 137.
43. Karl Barth, *Evangelical Theology: An Introduction* (New York: Holt, Rinehart and Winston, 1963), 27–30.

Rudolf Bultmann (1884–1976)

Bultmann gives the Old Testament a more tentative role in Christian faith than does Barth. H. G. Reventlow categorizes Bultmann as one who "rejected the Old Testament as a source of revelation" but was "willing to accord it a limited place in the church."[44] Bultmann grounds his view in an existential reading of the Old Testament in which one asks of it not how it may provide the essential historical basis on which Christianity rests but rather to what extent its demands impinge on our lives as divine revelation. He uses Luther's contrast between law and gospel as a framework for this understanding and asserts that in this sense "the Old Testament is the presupposition of the New." This means that knowledge of law must always precede the gospel, for grace is not understandable until one feels the impossibility of the demands of the law. However, law in this sense is not necessarily bound to the Old Testament. It refers to the moral demands found there, but these demands, if they are truly moral, are not valid simply because they are located in the Old Testament. Rather, they are valid because they "are grounded in human relationship itself" and can be known by reflection on this relationship. Consequently, the understanding that one is bound by divine moral demands in relation to one's fellow human beings, which can be derived from the Old Testament, need not be derived from this source. The church uses the Old Testament pedagogically to make these demands known because the Decalogue is their "classical formulation."[45]

Bultmann insists that the Old Testament can be read only literally and, assuming such a reading, that it cannot be revelation for the Christian "as it has been, and still is, for the Jews."[46] The stories found in the Old Testament relate to Israel's history, which "is not our history, and in so far as God has shown his grace in that history, such grace is not meant for us."[47] The only way the Old Testament can function as revelation for Christian faith, Bultmann asserts, is for it to receive validation as such from Christ. In this sense the church has seized the Old Testament and argued that only in reading it in light of Christ is it properly understood. But, he continues, this means that the Old Testament is not God's word in the proper sense but that the church "just finds in it again what is already known from the revelation in Jesus Christ." Bultmann asserts, however, that there is a way in which the Old Testament can be

44. Reventlow, *Problems of Old Testament Theology*, 36.

45. Rudolf Bultmann, "The Significance of the Old Testament for the Christian Faith," trans. B. W. Anderson, in *The Old Testament and Christian Faith*, ed. Bernhard W. Anderson (New York: Harper & Row), 13–17.

46. Ibid., 33, 31.

47. Ibid., 31.

understood as the Word of God. Because it contains many things that correspond with "the Christian understanding of existence"—man as creature under God's claim, the consciousness of sin, and the hope for grace—the Old Testament can serve as a mirror that gives us understanding of our own situation before God and of "the Word of Christ which is spoken into this situation." This is the proper way to understand the Old Testament as prophecy and the New as fulfillment. Bultmann draws only a contingent conclusion in reference to the Christian use of the Old Testament. "If," he says, "the Old Testament is taken up into the Church's proclamation as God's word, then the inviolable conditions are:" (1) that it be read only literally, and (2) that it be adopted only to the extent that it is "preparation for the Christian understanding of existence."[48]

Other Protestant voices would modify the sketch I have drawn in one or another detail, but there can be no doubt that there has been an erosion of the position and authority of the Old Testament in much of Protestant theology since the beginning of the Enlightenment. Protestant theology has not had a consistent position on the role of the Old Testament in the church.

We will see in the chapters that follow that the church fathers never questioned that the Old Testament held a central position in the life of the church. They did not all agree on how it should be read in order to speak to the church but, with the exception of Marcion and perhaps a few Gnostics who were not church fathers, they never thought that it should be dismissed as uncanonical or treated as second-class literature in comparison with the New Testament. Averil Cameron has correctly observed that the energies exerted by the fathers in their explanations of the Old Testament demonstrate "how tenaciously Christians" defended it in spite of the difficulties they often encountered in interpreting it.[49]

48. Ibid., 33–35.
49. Averil Cameron, *Christianity and the Rhetoric of Empire: The Development of Christian Discourse* (Berkeley: University of California Press, 1991), 110.

CHRISTIAN SCRIPTURE BEFORE THE NEW TESTAMENT

"And Philip . . . began from this Scripture and proclaimed Jesus
to him."

Acts 8:35

THE CHURCH HAS never been without Scripture even though the Pauline epistles, the earliest writings that constitute our present New Testament, were not composed for two or more decades after the resurrection of Jesus. The remaining writings that make up our New Testament were written in the second half of the first century, some near the end of that century. It would be at least another century before most of these writings were placed together to constitute a recognized canon of Scripture in the church. Yet the writings we call the New Testament, which are our source of information about the beginnings of the Christian movement, indicate that the apostles and evangelists regularly appealed to Scripture to substantiate their teachings about Jesus of Nazareth and other subjects of vital importance to their faith. These references to Scripture are all to what we call the Old Testament, which the early church referred to simply as the "Scriptures."[1] This chapter will briefly examine these early Christian references to the Scriptures. In addition, it will survey the translations in which the early Christians read their Scripture.

The Scripture of Christians in the First Century AD

The very earliest Christians were Jews by birth. Their Scripture had always been what we call the Old Testament or the Hebrew Bible. When they became Christians they continued to use these writings as their Scripture. They did not consider following Jesus to conflict with the faith they had learned from the Old Testament. Jesus was the fulfillment of the hopes they found expressed there.

All references to Scripture in the New Testament are to the Old Testament.[2] When Paul says that "Christ died on behalf of our sins in accordance with the Scriptures, and that he was buried, and was raised on the third day in accordance with the Scriptures," he means in accordance with what the Old Testament Scriptures say about the Messiah (1 Cor. 15:3–4).[3] When Luke says that Paul entered the synagogue in Thessalonica and "reasoned with them from the Scriptures, explaining and declaring that the Christ must suffer and rise from the dead," he means that Paul reasoned from the Old Testament Scriptures (Acts 17:2–3). The same is true in Luke's report that Apollos refuted the Jews in Achaia by "demonstrating from the Scriptures that Jesus is the Christ" (Acts 18:28). And when Paul reminds Timothy that he has known from childhood the sacred writings that can instruct him for salvation through faith in Christ Jesus and then adds, "All Scripture is inspired of God and is useful for teaching, for reproof, for correction, and for instruction in righteousness," he is talking about the Old Testament (2 Tim. 3:15–16).

The phrase "it is written," which appears so often throughout the New Testament to introduce Scripture, always introduces statements from the Old Testament. It appears frequently in the four Gospels to show the connection between particular aspects of Jesus's ministry and words found in the Old Testament. These connections range from statements regarding the place of Jesus's birth, through specific deeds during

---

1. Melito, bishop of Sardis in the late second century, appears to have been the first to have applied the expression "Old Testament" to the books of the Hebrew Bible (Eusebius, *Ecclesiastical History* 4.26).

2. The one possible exception to this statement is found in 2 Pet. 3:16, in which Paul's letters may be included with the Old Testament under the term "Scriptures."

3. Biblical quotations are my translations unless the New Revised Standard Version (NRSV) is indicated along with the reference.

his ministry, to his final suffering on the cross. Luke uses the phrase to introduce a statement from the Psalms justifying the choosing of an apostolic replacement for Judas after the latter's suicide (Acts 1:20). Luke indicates that Paul used the phrase to connect the second Psalm with the resurrection of Jesus in his sermon at Antioch of Pisidia (Acts 13:33). Paul grounds many of his most characteristic doctrines in Old Testament Scripture joined with his understanding of God's action in Christ. These doctrines include the bondage of all humanity to sin (Rom. 3:10–20), the importance of faith in salvation (Rom. 1:17), justification through faith (Romans 4), the stumbling of the Jews and the salvation of the Gentiles (Rom. 9:33; 10:15–21), and his doctrine of the two Adams (1 Cor. 15:45). Paul thought that the events narrated in the Old Testament were recorded to instruct and encourage Christians (Rom. 15:4; 1 Cor. 10:11).

Luke asserts that it was Jesus who taught his followers that the Old Testament was a book about himself. At the end of his Gospel, Luke reports that the risen Jesus walked with two disciples on the road to Emmaus and "interpreted for them what was written about himself in all the Scriptures," meaning, of course, the Old Testament Scriptures (Luke 24:27). Just before his account of the ascension, Luke again relates that Jesus taught his disciples that the law, the prophets, and the psalms all contained material about himself. This final instruction that Jesus gave to his disciples, according to Luke, states that the suffering and resurrection of the Messiah were related in the Old Testament. It also asserts that the Old Testament contains the announcement that the message of repentance and forgiveness of sins was to be proclaimed "to all nations" in Jesus's name (Luke 24:44–47).

There can be no question that the Old Testament was the Scripture of the earliest Christians and that they read it in terms of Christ. This was completely natural for them because they did not consider themselves to be distinct from the Jews. They believed that Jesus was the fulfillment of the promises made to the fathers in the Old Testament; therefore, their beliefs about him were completely compatible with their Jewish faith. When Philip heard the Ethiopian reading from the fifty-third chapter of Isaiah, Luke says that Philip started "from this Scripture," that is Isaiah 53, and "proclaimed Jesus to him" (Acts 8:35). Paul declared to the Roman Christians that the gospel he preached had been "proclaimed in advance through" the "prophets in the holy Scriptures" (Rom. 1:2). The writings of the Old Testament were joined with the Christian message in a seamless connection in the minds of the earliest Christians. They could not have conceived of the possibility of Christian faith without the Old Testament. It was essential to their understanding of who Jesus was, what his life, death, and resurrection had been about, and what he wanted them to do as his followers.

Christian Scripture in the First Half of the Second Century AD

The use of the Old Testament as the only Scripture of the church continued throughout the first half of the second century. The books that make up our New Testament had all been written by this time, but there was as yet no definitive list of which books and letters would constitute what we call the New Testament canon. What Christians of the first half of the second century looked to as authoritative Scripture was still the Old Testament.

The Apostolic Fathers

The writings called the Apostolic Fathers, which include the works of Ignatius, Barnabas, Polycarp, Clement, and the *Didache* use the term "Scripture" almost exclusively in reference to the Old Testament. These documents show awareness of most of the writings that were later included in the New Testament. Statements or phrases are drawn from works that later formed the New Testament, but, with two exceptions, no New Testament writing is referred to as Scripture or put on the same level with Old Testament Scripture in the Apostolic Fathers. A similar phenomenon is found in the works of Justin Martyr, who wrote in the middle of the second century.

The two passages in the Apostolic Fathers where the term "Scripture" is used in reference to a statement found in the New Testament appear in the writings known as *2 Clement* and Polycarp's *Epistle to the Philippians*. *Second Clement*, which may have been written in the middle of the second century or slightly later, refers to Jesus's statement that he came to call sinners rather than the righteous (Matt. 9:13 and parallels) as Scripture. The saying follows a citation from Isaiah and is introduced as "another Scripture." The exegetical remarks concerning the passage in Matthew are introduced with the same formula that introduces those following the Isaiah citation. The two citations are treated as standing on the same level. The fact that the statement in question is a saying of Jesus may account for this (*2 Clement* 2.4). Polycarp's *Epistle to the Philippians*, the other writing among the Apostolic Fathers using the term "Scripture" of something in the New Testament, is dated around AD 135. In this epistle Polycarp joins Psalm 4:5 and Ephesians 4:26 and refers to the two as "these Scriptures" (*Epistle to the Philippians* 12.1).

The writing known as *1 Clement*, which may date from the last decade of the first century, quotes from the words of Jesus twice, introducing them simply as "the words of the Lord Jesus" (*1 Clement* 13.1–2; 46.7–8). The same document paraphrases the words of 1 Corinthians 1:10–13 and identifies them as coming from "the epistle of the blessed Paul the apostle" (*1 Clement* 47.1–3). The author also imitates 1 Corinthians 13 with phrases and ideas drawn from this text without giving any indication of his source (*1 Clement* 49). Ignatius, bishop of Antioch of Syria in the first quarter of the second century, certainly knew at least some of the Pauline epistles. In his own *Epistle to the Ephesians* he refers to the Ephesians as "initiates along with Paul . . . who mentions you in Christ Jesus in every epistle" (*Epistle to the Ephesians* 12.2). In other places Ignatius draws phrases from various New Testament writings, predominantly Pauline epistles, but gives no indication that he is drawing the phrases from these documents.[4]

Much of Polycarp's *Epistle to the Philippians*, which was written a few years after Ignatius's letters, is a collage of phrases drawn from writings found in the New Testament. The source of the phrases, however, is never mentioned. Polycarp knows that Paul had written a letter to the Philippians, for he notes that Paul had labored among them and had praised them "in the beginning of his epistle" (*Epistle to the Philippians* 11.3). As I noted above, Polycarp also quotes a part of Ephesians 4:26 and refers to it as "Scripture."

The *Didache*, which should probably be dated near the end of the first century or early in the second, presents an interesting phenomenon. It appears to draw heavily on the Gospel of Matthew,[5] but never mentions Matthew. The introductory formulas, "Scripture says" or "it is written," do not appear in the document even though there are a few quotations from the Old Testament. The one formal introduction of an Old Testament quotation is, "This was spoken by the Lord," which introduces a quotation from Malachi (*Didache* 14.3). Phrases and statements drawn from writings that make up our New Testament outnumber those taken from the Old Testament in the document. This may be because the document claims to be the "teaching of the twelve apostles," and the New Testament writings were considered to be the works of the apostles.

These Christian documents from the first half of the second century all show clear evidence of knowledge of most of the writings that would form the New Testament. There is an apparent general reluctance, however, to place these writings, which were considered to come from the apostles, on the same level with Old Testament Scripture. *Second Clement*, which, as I noted above, introduces a saying of Jesus found in our Gospels as "Scripture," may indicate a moving away from this reluctance in the mid-second century. The author supports one of his

---

4. See, for example, *Epistle to the Philippians* 17.2–18.1, where phrases are taken from 1 Cor. 1:18–20.

5. For a different view of the relation of the *Didache* to Matthew, see Aaron Milavec, "Synoptic Tradition in the Didache Revisited," *JECS* (2003): 443–80.

teachings by saying that it is declared by "the books and the apostles" (*2 Clement* 14.2). The "books" would appear to refer to the writings of the Old Testament and the "apostles" to either writings or oral traditions stemming from the apostles.

The Old Testament still holds the privileged position of Scripture in the writings of Christians in the first half of the second century. When Clement writes to the Corinthians, he refers to their study of the "sacred Scriptures." These, he says, are "true" and come "through the Holy Spirit." The examples he then calls to the attention of the Corinthian church from these "sacred Scriptures" are all from the book of Daniel (*1 Clement* 45). He does something similar a little later, again referring to "the sacred Scriptures" and "the oracles of God." The specific passages he points to in this instance come from Exodus and Deuteronomy (*1 Clement* 53). It has been noted that Ignatius shows little interest in the Old Testament, quoting it only three times.[6] Nevertheless, two of the three quotations are introduced by the traditional formula "it is written," which was used for introducing Scripture. The *Epistle of Barnabas* is saturated with quotations from the Old Testament. These quotations are sometimes introduced by such formulas as "the prophet says" (*Epistle of Barnabas* 6.2), or "Moses said" (*Epistle of Barnabas* 10.1). The traditional formulas, "it is written" (*Epistle of Barnabas* 5.2; 15.1) and "Scripture says" (*Epistle of Barnabas* 4.7; 5.4), are also found throughout the epistle introducing Old Testament quotations. Barnabas appears to have considered *1 Enoch* as Scripture also, for he once introduces a quotation from this book with the "Scripture says" formula (*Epistle of Barnabas* 16.5).[7]

Justin Martyr

The status of the New Testament writings in relation to the concept of Old Testament Scripture is the same in Justin as it is in the Apostolic Fathers. Justin, however, wrote in the mid-second century.

While Justin alludes to numerous writings found in the New Testament he does not mention any by name. He attaches the apostle John's name to what he refers to as a revelation prophesying that those who believe in Christ will celebrate a millennial reign in Jerusalem (*Dialogue* 81.4). This is probably a reference to our book of Revelation. Justin refers several times to what he calls the "memoirs of the apostles." His quotations from these memoirs are usually parallel to material found in the Gospels of Matthew and Luke. He states that the memoirs are called Gospels and that they are read *along with the prophets in Chris-*

6. See William R. Schoedel, *Ignatius of Antioch*, Hermeneia (Philadelphia: Fortress, 1985), 9.

7. *1 Enoch* is also cited in the New Testament epistle of Jude (vv. 14–15).

tian worship (*1 Apology* 66.3; 67.3). I noted above that a saying of Jesus was treated on a par with Old Testament Scripture in *2 Clement*, which probably is to be dated from the mid-second century. Justin's statement that readings from the memoirs were included along with readings from the Old Testament prophets in worship also shows that material that makes up our present Gospels appears to have been considered equal in status to Old Testament Scripture by the mid-second century.

When Justin speaks of Scripture, however, he means the Old Testament, as numerous passages in his *Dialogue with Trypho* demonstrate (e.g., *Dialogue* 23.4; 37.4). He asserts that Trypho refuses to confess that Jesus is the Messiah, "as the Scriptures demonstrate" (*Dialogue* 39.6). In another passage he claims that the Old Testament Scriptures belong more truly to the Christians than to the Jews because "we obey them," he says, "but you read them and do not understand their meaning" (*Dialogue* 29.2). Justin claims to find the entire Christian message about Christ in the Old Testament Scriptures. "For I have demonstrated," he says, "how Christ has been proclaimed by all the Scriptures as king, and priest, and God, and Lord, and angel, and man, and chief in command, and stone, and child who has been born, and one who has first suffered, then ascended into heaven, and who is coming again in glory in possession of an eternal kingdom" (*Dialogue* 34.2).

The Version of Scripture Read by the Early Church

The Septuagint

The Scripture read by the majority of early Christians was a Greek translation of the Hebrew Old Testament known as the Septuagint. Very few Christians of the first four centuries read the Old Testament in the Hebrew language in which it had been written. The Hebrew language was spoken only in the environs of Jerusalem in the earliest Christian period. In the remainder of Palestine, Aramaic, the language the Jews had spoken in captivity in Babylon, was used. It is likely that Greek was also widely spoken in Galilee. Certainly most of the non-Jewish converts to Christianity outside Palestine spoke Greek. Of the authors of the New Testament writings, Paul, Mark, Matthew, and John show evidence of knowledge of the Old Testament in Hebrew, though their quotations tend to follow the Septuagint.[8]

Among the church fathers, only the Greek-speaking father Origen, in the third century, and the Latin-speaking father Jerome, in the fourth century,

8. See Martin Hengel, *The Septuagint as Christian Scripture*, trans. M. E. Biddle (Edinburgh: T&T Clark, 2002; repr. Grand Rapids: Baker Academic, 2004), 102.

learned Hebrew in order to work with the Hebrew text of the Old Testament. Nevertheless, Origen's numerous exegetical and homiletical works on the Old Testament depend on the Septuagint version. He produced a massive scholarly work on the text of the Septuagint called the Hexapla. In this work Origen placed in six parallel columns the Greek text of the Septuagint, three other later translations of the Old Testament into Greek, the text of the Hebrew Scriptures, and a transcription of the Hebrew Scriptures into the corresponding sounds in the Greek language. In the column containing the Septuagint, Origen inserted an asterisk (*) to show where the Septuagint lacked something that was in the Hebrew text and an obelus (†) before words that did not appear in the Hebrew text. When Jerome produced his new Latin translation of the Old Testament based on the Hebrew text, the older Latin versions that were based on the Septuagint continued to be preferred by most in the church. Jerome himself seems to have done much of his translation of the Hebrew, with the text of the Septuagint, as revised by Origen in his Hexapla, close at hand.

The Septuagint was to the early church what the King James Version of the Bible was to the English-speaking Protestant church from the middle of the seventeenth century to well into the second half of the twentieth century. It was the version read in the services of the church; it was the version from which those who were candidates for baptism were instructed; and it was the version on which the studies and debates of the church's scholars were based. It was, in short, the church's Bible. The Septuagint was not, however, a translation produced by the Christians. It was a translation done by the Jews prior to the Christian era to provide an understandable text of Scripture for those multitudes of Jews whose mother tongue was Greek.

The Origin of the Septuagint

We know very little about the origin of the Septuagint. The earliest account of its genesis is given in the Jewish treatise *The Letter of Aristeas*, which claims that the translation was done in Alexandria in the third century BC so that the books of the Jewish law might be added to the great library there. The story states that King Ptolemy II asked the high priest in Jerusalem to send translators to Alexandria to translate the Hebrew books. The high priest responded by sending seventy-two translators, six from each of the twelve tribes, each of whom, it is said, was skilled in both Hebrew and Greek. It is the number of translators that, rounded off to seventy, provides the name for the translation: *Septuagint*, which means seventy in Greek.

Most of *The Letter of Aristeas* is an apology for the Jewish people. It describes the temple, Jerusalem, Palestine, and the Jewish law, praises the wisdom of the elders sent to Alexandria to translate the Jewish books, and shows the great respect in which King Ptolemy II held the Jewish people and their laws. The actual work of translation is described in a very brief passage. It indicates that the translators worked separately on their individual assignments and then came together, compared their results, and worked out a common version on which they could agree. Demetrius, the librarian in Alexandria, then made a copy based on the revised version that the translators had accepted (*Letter of Aristeas* 302–7). The whole process, it is said, took seventy-two days, the same as the number of translators.

It is widely agreed that much of the story in *The Letter of Aristeas* is legendary. Scholars no longer think that the translation was an official act done at the request of the king to add the Jewish books of law to the Alexandrian library. It is believed, however, that the version was probably made in Alexandria by Jews who needed a version of the law in the language they spoke, and that this was done sometime in the last two or three centuries BC. Josephus, the Jewish historian who lived in Palestine in the first century AD, repeats the story of Aristeas in a lengthy paraphrase of the document. He says nothing, however, of the actual method followed by the translators in their work, mentioning only the way their workdays were divided up and that the work was completed in seventy-two days (*Jewish Antiquities* 12.12–12.118). He repeats the assertion made in *The Letter of Aristeas* (311) that the completed translation was read to an assembly of the Jewish community in Alexandria. The assembly approved the translation and solemnly swore that it should never be altered in any way (*Jewish Antiquities* 12.109).

Philo, the first-century Jewish philosopher of Alexandria, relates an abbreviated account of the story of the translation of the law into Greek, which follows closely the account in *The Letter of Aristeas*. He gives a different explanation, however, of how the translators produced a common copy. They worked under the influence of inspiration, Philo asserts, and produced their translation as if it had been dictated to them. No comparison of texts was needed, therefore, to reach agreement between the various translators, as Aristeas says happened. Instead, each scribe produced exactly the same translation. Moreover, Philo says, the Greek translation represented the Hebrew text perfectly (*Life of Moses* 2.37–40). Philo's exaggerated remarks do indicate, at least, that the Septuagint translation was held in very high regard by the Jewish community in Alexandria in the first century AD. Most of the early Christians held Philo's view of the divine guidance of the production of the text of the Septuagint. Jerome, in the fourth century AD, however, was very critical of it and accepted the story as told by Aristeas and repeated by Josephus (Jerome, *Apology* 2.25).

The Letter of Aristeas refers only to the translation of the Jewish law. It says nothing about the translation of the other books of the Old Testament. When these other books were translated is not known, though most of them had certainly been translated before the Christian era. Philo and Josephus, both first-century AD Jewish authors, know and use the Septuagint and quote from many of its books. Later Christians overlooked the fact that reference is made only to the translation of the law by the seventy-two translators. They considered the entire Greek Old Testament to have been produced at Alexandria at one time and referred to the whole as the Septuagint.

Differences between the Septuagint and the Hebrew Bible

There are two major differences between the Septuagint and the Hebrew Bible as we have the two texts today. The first and most obvious difference is that the Septuagint has always included the additional fifteen books that Protestants refer to as the apocryphal books of the Old Testament. The oldest and most authoritative manuscripts of the complete Greek Bible, dating from the fourth and fifth centuries AD, position the apocryphal books among the books of the Greek Old Testament, followed by the Greek New Testament. The status of these additional books in the minds of the early Christians is difficult to determine with precision. They do not appear to have been accepted in the Hebrew Bible recognized by the Jews, and what their status may have been in the Greek-speaking Alexandrian Jewish community is not known. The old Greek manuscripts referred to above are clearly Christian manuscripts because they contain the New Testament as well as the Septuagint.

The early church does not appear to have considered the apocryphal books to be on the same level as the books that constitute the Hebrew canon. Melito, who was bishop of Sardis in the late second century, gives a list of books that were recognized as the Old Testament by the Eastern Greek-speaking church at that time (Eusebius, *Ecclesiastical History* 4.26.12–14). To a large extent his list corresponds with the Old Testament used in the Protestant church today. It lacks Esther and Lamentations, and includes the Wisdom of Solomon from the apocryphal books. This is our earliest Christian list of Old Testament books and shows that most of the apocryphal books were not included in the Old Testament recognized at that time. The apocryphal books are largely ignored by the Christian writings of the second century and are only selectively cited by Christian authors of the third century.[9] Origen defended the genuineness of the book known as Susanna, and he and others made ample use

9. Ibid., 66–67.

of the Wisdom of Solomon. No church father in the first four centuries AD, however, wrote a commentary on any of the apocryphal books or used a text from one of these books for a sermon.[10] They do, however, occasionally cite apocryphal texts without reference to their status.

The other major difference between the Septuagint and the Hebrew text that we possess today is the considerable divergences that exist between these two texts in some of the Old Testament books. Job and Jeremiah, for example, are shorter in the Septuagint than in the Hebrew text. There are also numerous variations in the books of Joshua, 1 Samuel, 1 Kings, Proverbs, and Esther. In addition, there are minor textual differences between the Septuagint and our current Hebrew Old Testament text scattered throughout the other books. It is not possible to explain these differences with certainty. One thing that has become apparent since the discovery of the numerous fragments of Hebrew biblical manuscripts at Qumran is that there was not a single, standardized text of the Hebrew Bible in the early Christian period.[11] The Hebrew text on which current English Bibles are based is known as the Masoretic text. This text was finalized by the Jews later in the Christian era (late first, mid second century AD).[12] It has always been considered possible, but now much more probable, that the Septuagint may, in many of these points of difference, represent a Hebrew reading that is more ancient than that of the Masoretic text.

Other Versions of the Old Testament in the Early Christian Era

It is fundamental to understand that the early Christians read a text of the Old Testament that differed in some points from the text that we read in our English versions today. Some of these differences are important and some are insignificant. Biblical exegesis then, even more than now, often focused on individual words in the text. If one is unaware that the word differs between the versions being read, or is even absent in one of the versions, then the comments being made on the text will be meaningless.

It is also important to understand that the differences between versions existed in the early Christian world as well. Christians of the first four centuries read the Old Testament either in the Septuagint version

10. Ibid., 68.

11. These biblical texts from Qumran can be read in English translation in *The Dead Sea Scrolls Bible*, trans. Martin Abegg Jr., Peter Flint, and Eugene Ulrich (San Francisco: HarperSanFrancisco, 1999).

12. Hengel, *Septuagint as Christian Scripture*, 44.

or in translations made largely from the Septuagint. The Jews, however, with whom the Christians were often in debate about Scripture and its meaning in those centuries, read their Scriptures in other versions. Because the Septuagint became so closely identified with the Christians in the first and second centuries AD, the Jews largely ceased using it. If they were Greek-speaking, they used one of the Greek versions made by Jewish translators in the second century. If they lived in areas where Aramaic was their native language, they used Aramaic translations and paraphrases called Targumim. The more scholarly members of the Jewish community read the Hebrew text of the Old Testament. Differences between each of these versions and the Septuagint, which was used by the Christians, come into play in conflicts between Christians and Jews about the meaning of crucial texts. We will discuss these disputes in the chapters that follow.

Christians too, however, often made use of these alternative Greek translations of the Old Testament to help them understand the text of the Septuagint, which could be as obscure to a Greek-speaking Christian as the text of the King James Bible often is to a modern teenager. The alternative Greek translations were frequently cited in early Christian biblical commentaries to show what another scholar, who could read the Hebrew text, understood the meaning of the text to be. There were also, of course, Christian communities where Greek was not spoken. The earliest and largest of these communities were in North Africa and Europe where Latin was spoken, and in the regions of modern Syria, Iraq, and Iran where Syriac was spoken. Each of these communities used translations of the Old Testament made in their respective languages. Knowing the particular words on which an ancient Christian commentator or preacher is reflecting can be a major factor in understanding his comments. The following sections will briefly describe these alternative translations of the Old Testament, for they all appear in the chapters that follow.

Greek Versions

Three additional translations of the Old Testament into Greek were produced by Jews in the second century AD. The first of these was produced by a Jew named Aquila near the end of the first quarter of the second century. Aquila made a very literal translation of the Hebrew text, ignoring Greek idiom. He carried his literalism so far that he even translated the Hebrew word *eth*, which serves as a marker for the direct object of the verb in Hebrew, with the Greek preposition *syn*, which means "with" in Greek. This obviously resulted in a curious text at best. Aquila's text has been lost, except for a few citations in the church fathers.

The second translation was made by a proselyte to Judaism named Theodotion. Theodotion seems to have revised the text of the Septuagint on the basis of the Hebrew text. We know more of Theodotion's text than of Aquila's because his translation of Daniel supplanted that of the Septuagint and became the text of Daniel copied in manuscripts of the Septuagint. Finally, near the end of the second century, Symmachus, a Jewish Christian of the sect known as the Ebionites, produced a translation of the Old Testament into Greek. Little is known about the Ebionites except that they were considered heretical by the larger church. Symmachus followed the Hebrew text closely but rendered it into idiomatic Greek. All three of these second-century AD translations of the Old Testament into Greek have perished. Origen copied them, each in its own column, in his Hexapla, but this too has perished except for a few fragments.

Greek translations were also made of individual books or sections of the Old Testament by other unknown translators before the third century AD. Origen had found the text of two, and perhaps three, additional Greek translations of parts of the Old Testament and included them in his Hexapla. Our knowledge of all the translations of the Old Testament into Greek, except for the Septuagint, is based on the citations that appear in some of the church fathers, especially in the works of Origen, Eusebius, and Jerome.

Latin Versions

The most important version of Scripture after the Greek versions, for our purposes, is the translation into Latin. Jerome's name is connected with the translation of the Bible into Latin, but there were Latin translations, perhaps of the entire Christian Bible, before Jerome's, which was known as the Vulgate. These earlier translations are referred to as the Old Latin versions. They probably first emerged in North Africa and in areas of Europe where Greek was not spoken. These Old Latin translations were made from the Septuagint and, later, from other Latin versions. They have left their traces in the biblical citations of most of the Latin-speaking church fathers, especially in the earlier fathers such as Tertullian and Cyprian.

Near the end of the fourth century AD Jerome began his project of translating the Hebrew Old Testament into Latin. He had become convinced that the Hebrew text, as opposed to the Septuagint, represented the correct text of the Old Testament. He thought, therefore, that the Hebrew was the only valid basis for a translation of these books. This acceptance of the Hebrew text as the correct text meant that he also rejected the apocryphal books contained in the Septuagint because they were not a part of the Hebrew Bible. Jerome's translation would eventually become the accepted text of the Latin-speaking church, but with the apocryphal books added. The Council of Trent in 1546 would pronounce it the official text to be used by the church. However, it was not accepted in Jerome's lifetime. Its general acceptance and use lies largely beyond the period of the church fathers considered in this book. Most of the Latin Fathers who will be cited here used the Septuagint-based Old Latin translations.

The Syriac Peshitta

There was also a translation of the Old Testament in the Syriac language known as the Peshitta, parts of which may date from the second century AD. The translation was made from the Hebrew text, not from the Septuagint. It is not known whether the translators were Jews or Christians,[13] but it was this version of the Old Testament that the fourth-century Syriac-speaking church fathers Aphraat and Ephrem used.

The Targumim

Finally, we must mention the translation of the Old Testament into the Aramaic language known as the targum, or in the plural targumim. This was not a version of the Old Testament that the church fathers used. The translations of the targumim were used, however, by a large number of Jews. Readings from the various targumim will be cited occasionally to show the Jewish understanding of particular Old Testament texts in relation to the Christian understanding.

The practice of translating the reading of the Hebrew Scriptures into Aramaic originated in the worship of the synagogue in the postexilic pre-Christian period. Aramaic had been the official language of the Persian empire, and as a result of the captivity, a large portion of the Jewish community spoke Aramaic rather than Hebrew. The translations were first simply oral translations of the readings done in the synagogue service. They were usually not literal Aramaic translations of the Hebrew, but were paraphrastic and highly interpretive. Later, written versions of the targumim were made. Two of these collections are of importance for the concerns of this book. The first is known as the *Targum Onqelos* on the Pentateuch. The other is the *Targum Jonathan* on the Prophets. These were official targumim produced by the Jewish community. Their final, definitive wording was established in Babylon in the fifth cen-

13. Sebastian P. Brock, "The Earliest Syriac Literature," in *The Cambridge History of Early Christian Literature*, ed. Frances Young, Lewis Ayres, and Andrew Louth (Cambridge: Cambridge University Press, 2004), 163.

tury AD. *Targum Onqelos* may have originated, however, in Palestine as early as the late first or early second century AD. Like *Targum Onqelos*, *Targum Jonathan* seems also to have originated in Palestine prior to its final editing in Babylon.[14] There is, however, no generally accepted date for this Palestinian version.

The Earliest Christian Bible: Summing Up

The Christians of the first century and the first half of the second had no question that the Old Testament was their Scripture. As the apostolic writings began to make their appearance, they were held in high regard. This was especially true of the Gospels. The Old Testament, however, continued to hold the undisputed position of Scripture in the minds of the Christians. Gradually, the Gospels appear to have been elevated to a status of equal authority with the Old Testament in Christian worship because they contained the words of Jesus. Nevertheless, it was the Old Testament that gave significance to the story of Jesus in the minds of the early Christians, and they continued to turn to it both to define and to justify their faith in him.

The Old Testament was read primarily in translation, however, by both the Christians and the Jews in the age of the church fathers. The majority of the Christians knew it in the Greek translation called the Septuagint, or in one of the old Latin translations. The larger Jewish community scattered throughout the world knew the Old Testament either in the Greek translations of Aquila, Symmachus, or Theodotion, or in the Aramaic targumim.

Translations always involve a certain amount of interpretation as the thought of one language is put into that of another. Translators of theological texts bring theological viewpoints to their work. Their translations, therefore, have particular theological slants, whether they are intended or not. All the Greek translations mentioned in this chapter had been done by Jews. Only the translation of the Septuagint, however, predated the Christian era. The Christians were adamant that the Septuagint was the trustworthy text of Scripture. The Jews, as noted above, had abandoned the use of the Septuagint and considered more recently made translations to be more accurate. To what extent this attitude reflected their rejection of Christian interpretations of the Septuagint is impossible to estimate. Nevertheless, that Christians co-opted the Septuagint for their own use was surely a factor in the Jews' view. Many arguments

14. On the targumim, see Ernst Würthwein, *The Text of the Old Testament* (New York: Macmillan, 1957), 56–59; and Philip S. Alexander, "Targum, Targumim," in *ABD* 6, ed. David Noel Freedman, Gary A. Herion, David F. Graf, and John David Pleins (New York: Doubleday, 1992), 320–31.

between Christians and Jews had their basis in the different readings that could be found in the various versions used. As will be noted later in this book, there were intense debates between Jews and Christians over the different translations of Isaiah 7:14 found in the Septuagint and in the later versions of Aquila, Symmachus, and Theodotion. Differences between Christian and Jewish views of the Messiah sometimes hinged on the different ways that a specific text had been translated, or on the difference between the Septuagint and the Hebrew Masoretic Text.[15]

In the chapters that follow, I will occasionally go into detail concerning some of the differences in significant messianic texts between the reading of the Septuagint and that of the considerably later Masoretic Text of the Hebrew Bible used by the rabbis. Whether the Greek translation of the Septuagint or the Hebrew of the Masoretic Text more faithfully represents the reading of the ancient Hebrew Bible in those texts where there are differences is the subject of continuing scholarly debate. It is clear, however, that the Septuagint deserves much more serious consideration in attempts to understand Christian origins and to be faithful to those origins than it has enjoyed in the past.[16]

The Old Testament had a tremendous influence on the making of the early Christian mind; it was Scripture for the earliest Christians even before the Gospels were considered to be Scripture. According to the accounts given in the New Testament, the Old Testament was the earliest means for telling the story of Jesus. When we Christians think of returning to the sources of our faith, this earliest Christian Bible must head the list of those sources or we will misunderstand and misrepresent our origins.

15. See the examples in chap. 4 below.

16. See the recent book by R. Timothy McLay, *The Use of the Septuagint in New Testament Research* (Grand Rapids: Eerdmans, 2003); and Hengel, *Septuagint as Christian Scripture*.

The Struggle concerning the Law in the Second Century

"For Christ is the end of the law . . ."

Romans 10:4

THE PROBLEM CONCERNING the use of the Old Testament by the church came into special prominence in the mid-second century when the church was disengaged from Judaism and had become predominantly Gentile. In what way could Christians, who were not Jews, claim that the Jewish Bible was their Scripture when they understood it so differently from the Jews? On what grounds could Christians ignore the law, which was the most important part of the Old Testament for the Jews, and still claim the Old Testament as their Scripture? There were some within the church who argued that the law could not be accommodated to Christian usage.

The church in the second century had to justify its use of the Old Testament against three specific groups. Each had its own set of objections to the Christian use of the Old Testament, though there was common ground among them. The Jews denied that the Christian understanding of the Old Testament was correct. They were especially concerned about the Christians' claim to worship the God of Abraham and Moses while they neglected the law of Moses.

Gnostics constituted a second group who questioned the Christian use of the Old Testament. The term Gnostic, like the term Protestant today, covered a diverse group of people who shared some basic views but differed on many others.[1] The Gnostics mingled aspects of Christian faith with beliefs drawn from various religious and philosophical teachings in the Greco-Roman world. Some Gnostic groups rejected the entirety of the Old Testament; others rejected large portions of it and radically reinterpreted the parts they maintained. The most disturbing aspect of the Gnostics' reinterpretation was their assertion that the creator God who speaks and acts in the Old Testament was not the true God but an inferior deity who acted and spoke out of ignorance.

Marcion and his followers made up the third group against which the church had to justify its use of the Old Testament. Marcion's writings have perished, so our knowledge of his views comes from those church fathers who wrote treatises against him. On the basis of these hostile sources, it seems that the Marcionites completely eliminated the use of the Old Testament in their churches. Somewhat like the Gnostics, Marcion thought the God revealed in the Old Testament was not the God revealed in Christ. He thought the God of the Old Testament was limited in his knowledge, and that he was just, but not loving, in his actions. Marcion believed that the Old Testament was a strictly Jewish document applicable only to the Jewish people.

The question of the law was not the only issue debated between the church and these dissenting groups, but it was a major issue. This chapter will treat these three areas of tension that arose in the second century.

Justin's *Dialogue with Trypho the Jew* and the Jewish Objection to the Christian Understanding of the Law

In the middle of the second century a Christian apologist named Justin composed a work titled *Dialogue with Trypho the Jew*. Nothing is known of Trypho beyond what Justin tells us in the *Dialogue*. The setting of the *Dialogue* is a chance meeting between Justin and Trypho in Ephesus. Justin, who had converted to Christianity from a philosophical background, was out for a walk dressed as a philosopher. He was greeted by Trypho, who was accompanied by a group of friends, and they fell into conversation as they walked. Trypho identified himself as a Hebrew who had fled Palestine because of the recent war there between the Romans and the Jews. This would have been Hadrian's war against the Bar

---

1. See Michael Allen Williams, *Rethinking "Gnosticism"* (Princeton, NJ: Princeton University Press, 1996).

Cochba-led Jewish revolt in AD 135. Other indicators in the *Dialogue* show that it was probably written in its present form sometime after AD 160. Justin located the discussion, however, in the earlier period.

Justin relates to Trypho how he had been converted from philosophy to Christianity. An anonymous Christian had told him about the Hebrew prophets, who "both glorified the creator of all things as God and Father and proclaimed his Son, the Christ" (*Dialogue* 7.3). When the anonymous Christian had completed his discussion with Justin, Justin says he found his soul aflame with a love for the prophets and for "the friends of Christ" (*Dialogue* 8.1). He then suggests that Trypho might want to follow the path to salvation that he has followed himself. Trypho replies that Justin would have been better off remaining a philosopher. He then advises Justin that if he wants to find favor with God he should be circumcised, keep the Sabbath and the feast days, and, in short, observe all the laws found in the Old Testament (*Dialogue* 8.3–4). Trypho's response sets the program for a large portion of the *Dialogue*.

Justin's Defense of the Christian Use of the Old Testament

Justin must defend the Christians' claim that the Old Testament sets forth their religion while they, nevertheless, do not obey the religious laws found there. The Jews' objection, Justin says, is that Christians do not practice circumcision, do not keep the Sabbath, and do not observe the feast days. In fact, Trypho complains, the Christian lifestyle appears very similar to that of the Gentiles or the heathen. Christians are not separated from the Gentiles in any obvious way as the Jews are. Trypho claims that Christians despise the old covenant, reject its duties, and yet claim to know the God of the Old Testament. He challenges Justin to defend how he can hope for anything when he does not observe the law (*Dialogue* 10).

Trypho insists that the Old Testament must be taken as a whole and that the law, especially, must be read and obeyed literally. Christians, however, ignore the literal meaning of the law and claim that the Old Testament is a book about Christ and Christianity. It should be noted here that the Jews in the second century, no more than the Christians, observed all the Old Testament laws literally. No sacrifices had been offered since the destruction of the temple in AD 70. After the second defeat of the Jews by the Romans in AD 135 all hope of Jewish sacrifices being offered again in Jerusalem must have been completely shattered. The literal keeping of the law had, in other words, been rather severely curtailed even for the Jews in the second century.[2]

2. See Marcel Simon, *Verus Israel*, trans. H. McKeating (Oxford: Oxford University Press, 1986; first published in Paris, 1948), 12–50.

The Old and the New Law

Justin begins his defense by arguing that the God of the Old Testament and the God of the Christians is the same God. He maintains strongly that Christians and Jews worship the same God. That common God is the God of Abraham, Isaac, and Jacob—the God of the Old Testament. But, Justin continues, Christians do not hope in Moses or in the law of Moses, for then they would be the same as the Jews. The law given through Moses on Sinai has become old, he says, and is exclusively for the Jews. The Old Testament itself anticipates a new covenant. Justin appeals to Jeremiah 31:31–32, where God had promised to make a new covenant with the house of Israel that would be different from the one he had made earlier when he brought them out of Egypt (*Dialogue* 11). Consequently, Justin argues, there is a new law that has canceled the old one.

The new law is eternal and not limited to a particular race of people. The new law, Justin adds, is Christ. He appeals to Isaiah 51:4, where the Greek translation of the Old Testament known as the Septuagint—the Bible that Justin read—says that a law will go forth from God that will be a light to the nations. The Greek word translated "nations" throughout the Septuagint is the same word that is also translated "Gentiles." So, Justin reasons, this new law from God will be a light to the Gentiles. Finally, Justin asserts that the followers of Christ are the true Israel and true descendants of Abraham. The latter received both testimony and blessing from God before he was circumcised and was promised that he would be the father of "many nations" (Gen. 17:4; *Dialogue* 11). Justin's argument, to this point, dismisses the law as antiquated since the coming of Christ, who inaugurated a new covenant. Christ, he argues further, is the new covenant of which the Old Testament prophets had spoken.

Distinctions in the Old Law

Justin must also show, however, how Christians actually understood the law, for it formed a considerable portion of the Scripture that they had taken over from the Jews. In fact, the Christians did use numerous passages in the law for Christian purposes. On what basis could Christians not do what the law demanded and yet continue to claim that it was a part of their Scripture in order to make use of it? This remains one of the enduring questions Christians have faced. Justin's answer has also continued to be one of the ways Christians have dealt with the issue.

Justin approaches this problem by introducing a distinction into the law. He divides the law into two categories. The first may be referred to broadly as the moral law, though Justin does not give it a name.

This law refers to the worship of God and to righteous living. It is universal and eternal and probably to be identified primarily with the Decalogue, though Justin never makes that identification explicit. In fact, he does not say much about this law at all. This was not the part of the law under discussion for Trypho and him. Justin divides his second category of the law into two further parts. One part relates to what he calls "the mystery of Christ." This he calls a prophetic element in the law. The other part, Justin argues, is the law that was given to the Hebrews "because of the hardness of their heart" (*Dialogue* 44.2). By this second part he means what we refer to as the ritual or ceremonial law.[3] It was this latter category of law over which Christians and Jews differed.

The prophetic part of the law consists of those laws that Justin considers to be types of higher spiritual meanings. These do not, however, appear to be a different set of laws than the ritual laws. They are, rather, those ritual laws in which he finds a latent spiritual meaning. He considers the law of circumcision, for example, to be a type of the true spiritual circumcision. Justin does not consider either the moral law or the prophetic element in the law to have been nullified by the new law that he identifies with Christ. It is the ritual law understood literally, consisting of circumcision, the keeping of special days, sacrifices, food laws, and purity laws, that Justin considers to be nullified by Christ. These laws, he argues, pertained only to the Jewish nation and the dispensation that was inaugurated by Moses. Furthermore, Justin considered these laws to have been given only because of the Hebrews' obstinacy.

The Limited Validity of the Ritual Law

Justin presses the argument that the ritual law was given because of the Hebrews' obstinacy and is not, consequently, of universal validity. We Christians also, he says, would observe circumcision, Sabbaths, and the feast days "if we did not know why you were given these commands, namely because of your lawless deeds and your hardness of heart" (*Dialogue* 18.2; cf. 43.1). Circumcision, Justin argues, is not necessary for pleasing God because God approved of many uncircumcised men before circumcision was introduced. He mentions Adam, who, he says, would not have been made uncircumcised if it was a necessity, and then refers to Abel, Enoch, Lot, Noah, and Melchizedek. This same group of men observed no Sabbaths, nor did Abraham or any of his descendants

3. On Justin's divisions of the law, see Theodore Stylianopoulos, *Justin Martyr and the Mosaic Law*, Dissertation Series 20 (Missoula, MT: Scholars Press, 1975), 51–68; Willis A. Shotwell, *The Biblical Exegesis of Justin Martyr* (London: SPCK, 1965), 8–9.

prior to Moses. The sacrificial system, Justin asserts, was instituted to prevent the Jews from worshiping idols, and the purpose of the Sabbath was to keep them from forgetting God. The food laws, too, were intended to keep God before their minds while they ate because they were prone to join sinning with eating (*Dialogue* 18–20). Justin does allow converts to Christianity from Judaism to continue to observe the ritual law as long as they recognize that their salvation is in Christ and not in the keeping of the law, as long as they do not attempt to convince Gentile Christians that they too need to observe the ritual law, and as long as they maintain normal fellowship with the church in general and do not withdraw to themselves (*Dialogue* 46–47).

Justin insists that the cancellation of the ritual law by Christ does not mean that Christians do not take the Old Testament seriously. In fact, Justin asserts that the Old Testament can be said to belong more to Christians than to Jews, because Christians obey the writings of the Old Testament whereas the Jews read them but do not understand their true meaning (*Dialogue* 29). The Christian reading, he says, sees the Old Testament as a series of prophecies and types that have their fulfillment in Christ and the church. He defines prophecies as verbal statements of the Holy Spirit concerning what was to come. Types, he says, resulted from the Holy Spirit causing something to be done in the history of Israel that was a representation of something that was to happen later (*Dialogue* 114.1).

Justin has argued that the ritual law found in the Old Testament is not to be obeyed in its literal sense by anyone but the Jews. This is true because of the limited audience to whom it was originally given, because of the special circumstances under which it was given (Jewish hardness of heart), and because it has been superseded by Christ, who has brought in the new law that is for all people. This new law had been announced already through the Hebrew prophets. The ritual laws do, however, continue to have prophetic significance for Christians as they point symbolically to aspects of the Christian dispensation.

There is, moreover, a moral law in the Old Testament that has eternal validity for Christians as well as Jews. Justin defended the Christian understanding of the law by introducing these various distinctions. This approach "allowed," as one scholar says, "all the ordinances to be good in their time."[4] Other Christians in the late second and early third centuries, such as Barnabas and Melito, took a less-nuanced approached to the question of the law than Justin did.

4. William Horbury, "Old Testament Interpretation in the Writings of the Church Fathers," in *Mikra*, ed. Martin Jan Mulder and Harry Sysling, Compendia Rerum Iudaicarum ad Novum Testamentum 2.1 (Minneapolis: Fortress, 1990), 761.

Barnabas, Melito, and Origen on the Christian versus the Jewish Interpretation of the Law

The Epistle of Barnabas

The *Epistle of Barnabas* probably predates the writing of Justin's *Dialogue with Trypho*. It is neither an epistle in the proper sense nor the work of the Barnabas who was a companion of the apostle Paul. The only reference to the author's name occurs at the end of the document as a subscript that reads, "Epistle of Barnabas." The assumption by the early church that it was the work of Paul's companion led some to regard it as directly connected with the apostles. It was copied with the writings of the canonical New Testament in the fourth-century manuscript known as *Codex Sinaiticus* and was highly regarded by both Clement of Alexandria and Origen in the third century. While Eusebius lists it among the "spurious books" in his discussion of the New Testament canon, the fact that he mentions it at all shows that it was a work that had been considered canonical by some in the early church (*Ecclesiastical History* 3.25). We do not know who the author was, to whom the writing was addressed (except to fellow Christians), or the precise date it was written. Its composition probably falls sometime in the first half of the second century and perhaps in the earlier portion of that half.

The larger part of the *Epistle of Barnabas* (chaps. 2–17) treats the subject of the proper understanding of the Old Testament. The question of whether the covenant is for Jews or Christians is raised twice in this section and is answered both times by a discussion of the same passages of Scripture in Exodus (*Epistle of Barnabas* 4.6–8; 13.1; 14.1–4).[5] While the two passages do not appear at precisely the beginning and end of the discussion of the Old Testament, they are near enough and repetitive enough to see them as bracketing the central subject of concern in the section. Barnabas's answer to the question is that the covenant was originally given to the Jews through Moses at Mount Sinai but was immediately taken from them when Moses broke the stone tablets because he found the Israelites worshiping the golden calf. Consequently, everything in the Old Testament, including the law, points forward to Jesus, who inherits the covenant and confers it on the Christians whom he has redeemed from darkness (*Epistle of Barnabas* 14.4–7; 4.6–8).

Therefore, nothing in the law of Moses is to be understood or observed literally. It was never intended to be so understood. Moses was a prophet and spoke in parables.[6] His words should be understood as

---

5. The second passage considers additional Scriptures beyond the Exodus passages.

6. See Ferdinand R. Prostmeier, "Antijudaismus im Rahmen christlicher Hermeneutik," *ZAC/JAC* (2002): 40–44.

parables referring to Christ and the kingdom he inaugurated (*Epistle of Barnabas* 6.8–19). The law of circumcision was intended to apply to our hearing and our hearts, but the Jews misunderstood it because an evil angel misled them (*Epistle of Barnabas* 9.1–6). Moses spoke in the spirit when he delivered the laws concerning food. The Jews, however, misunderstood them to refer to literal food (*Epistle of Barnabas* 10.9). In the same way, the law of the Sabbath does not refer to the literal seventh day of the week but points to the end of the world that will occur after six thousand years, calculated in accordance with the biblical statement that one day with the Lord means a thousand years. After six thousand years have passed, the Lord will return, judge the godless, and enjoy true Sabbath rest (*Epistle of Barnabas* 15.1–7).

In contrast to Justin, who allowed a period of time when the ritual law was applicable to the Jewish people in its literal sense, Barnabas has no room for a literal understanding of the law at all. Barnabas's approach gives universal validity to the entire law but only by understanding it figuratively. The two approaches represented by Justin and Barnabas set the pattern for the two ways of appropriating the law by the church. Justin would be followed by Irenaeus, who will be considered later in this chapter, and Barnabas's approach was to be taken up by Melito and Origen, who will be considered next.[7]

Melito of Sardis

Melito was bishop of the ancient city of Sardis in Asia Minor during the third quarter of the second century. Eusebius includes his name, along with those of Philip, John, Polycarp, and others, in a list of "great luminaries" who were buried in Asia Minor (*Ecclesiastical History* 5.24.5). All of these, according to Eusebius's source, observed the Paschal festival on the fourteenth day of the month, which means they celebrated Easter on the day of the Jewish Passover. Little more is known of Melito's life. His writings have been preserved only fragmentarily. However, a nearly complete Greek text of a homily he delivered on the Pascha was discovered among the Bodmer papyri.[8] This homily allows us to see Melito's approach to the Old Testament law.

7. See William Horbury, "Jewish-Christian Relations in Barnabas and Justin Martyr," in *Jews and Christians: The Parting of the Ways, A.D. 70 to 135*, ed. J. D. G. Dunn (Tübingen: Mohr Siebeck, 1992; repr., Grand Rapids: Eerdmans, 1999), 329–30.

8. See M. Testuz, ed., *Papyrus Bodmer XIII, Méliton de Sardes Homélie sur la Pâque* (Geneva: Bodmer, 1960). The homily can be read in English in *Melito of Sardis: On Pascha and Fragments*, ed. and trans. S. G. Hall (Oxford: Clarendon, 1979), or in the more recent translation by Alistair Stewart-Sykes, *Melito of Sardis: On Pascha* (Crestwood, NY: St. Vladimir's Seminary Press, 2001).

Melito's approach to the law might appear to be nearer to that of Justin than to that of Barnabas. He does not deny that the law had a significant function in its literal sense, nor does he insist, as Barnabas does, that the Jews consistently misunderstood the law. Melito sees the law along with all the other elements of the Old Testament revelation to have been a type whose fulfillment is found in the events and teachings related in the gospel. The type functioned like a pattern or model that a sculptor makes before he creates his intended and real work of art. The model has a preliminary value, but once the statue has been created, the model is useless (*On Pascha* 35–37).[9] Judith Lieu has called Melito's interpretation of the Old Testament a "replacement theology." The value of the old lies in the model of the new that it contains. When the new appears, however, "the model has lost all intrinsic value."[10]

Melito's proximity to the *Epistle of Barnabas* can be seen especially in the use he makes of the concept of parable in relation to the law. Barnabas, as noted above, asserted that Moses spoke in parables. Consequently, all of Moses's words must be treated figuratively. Melito asserts that "the people [of Israel] were a pattern of the church and the law was a parabolic writing" (*On Pascha* 40). The gospel sets forth the meaning of the law and is its fulfillment. In contrast to Israel, which is the "pattern," the church "is the repository of the truth." Before the truth appeared "the type was highly honored," as was the "parable" before its "interpretation" (i.e., the gospel) was revealed. But once "the type had transmitted its pattern to the true essence" and the "parables" had been "explained by the interpretation," the type was "rendered void" and the "parables" "fulfilled." "Today," Melito concludes, "those things once highly honored have become insignificant because the things which are highly honored in their essence have been made manifest" (*On Pascha* 40–43). Melito recognizes that the type "had its own proper time" (*On Pascha* 38), and in that respect he shares something with Justin's approach to the law. Overall, however, he is nearer to the approach taken by Barnabas, for, unlike Justin, nothing in the law has abiding value once the gospel has come.

Origen

Origen of Alexandria was the most significant theologian of the third century and certainly the most prolific early Christian writer. He composed commentaries and homilies on most of the books of the Bible and treatises on numerous theological subjects. Among his extant homilies

9. See Stewart-Sykes, *Melito of Sardis*, 32.

10. Judith M. Lieu, *Image and Reality: The Jews in the World of the Christians in the Second Century* (Edinburgh: T&T Clark, 1996), 216–17.

are those on Genesis, Exodus, Leviticus, and Numbers. His life as a Christian theologian spans the first half of the third century. His writings were so diverse and influential that he will figure prominently in various chapters in this book. Likewise, his approach to the writings of Moses will be treated in more detail in chapter 3.

Origen was deeply aware of the inherent confusion, even potential repulsiveness, that the law posed for Gentile Christian converts. He compared the acceptance of the law by the church to the daughter of pharaoh taking up the baby Moses from the Nile. The church takes up "Moses" at the waters of baptism, but he is found lying in a rough-made, unattractive basket smeared with pitch. In such circumstances the law is powerless. These unattractive trappings of the law are the literal interpretations given to it by the Jews. When Moses enters the church, he finds his true strength in the spiritual understanding given to the law (*HomEx* 2.4). Origen considered himself to be following the example of the apostle Paul in interpreting the law. The Jews' way of reading the law, he argues, led them to misunderstand it and to reject Christ. Paul's way of understanding the law, shown for example in 1 Corinthians 10:1–4, was a spiritual reading of the law and pointed those who so read it directly to Christ (*HomEx* 5.1).

In a more profound analogy Origen compares the literal reading of the law to the bitter water the Israelites discovered at Marah. People newly converted from sacrificing to idols will not be able to drink from the law if they read it as a manual for sacrifices. Origen understands this to fall under Paul's exhortation against building up anew the things that one destroys (Gal. 2:18). But God reveals the cross of Christ as a tree to be thrown into the bitter water of the law. This wisdom of Christ sweetens the water so that it can be drunk. Therefore, the bitterness in the letter of the law becomes palatable through the mystery of Christ's cross (*HomEx* 7.1).

R. P. C. Hanson has pointed out that Origen does not totally reject a literal understanding of individual parts of the law. In his *Commentary on Romans* (2.9) Origen speaks of a "natural law" that is written on the hearts of people. The examples he gives of this natural law parallel the moral commands of the Decalogue. Furthermore, in his *Against Celsus* (2.3) Origen appears to recognize as Christians those Jewish converts who continue to observe the law of their fathers. In addition, Hanson points out, there are various laws in the Old Testament that are not "obvious examples of general moral principle" that Origen believes to be binding on Christians. One such example is the law pertaining to strangers and proselytes.[11] While Origen's overall approach to the law

11. R. P. C. Hanson, *Allegory and Event* (Richmond: John Knox, 1959), 298–303.

is to read it as if it contained an encrypted spiritual message, he does not insist that none of the commands in the law were ever intended to be understood literally.

Origen argued that by reading the law spiritually the Christian was able to preserve it in its entirety. In this way, Christians could keep many laws that the Jews no longer kept literally. Origen was writing in the third century when the Jewish temple in Jerusalem had lain in ruins for more than a century. The Jews, Origen pointed out, could no longer offer sacrifices literally, nor could they keep the law concerning leprosy, for both of these were connected with the temple in Jerusalem (*HomEx* 11.6). In fact, no law related directly to the temple could be kept any longer. In his homilies on Leviticus, Origen notes that when Christ, "God's true temple," had come the former temple of stone ceased to exist. With the appearance of the true high priest, the former high priesthood passed away. And, when the true lamb of God had come there was no longer any place for the altar or the offerings presented on it (*HomLev* 10.1). One might add to Origen's list the laws defining the ministries of the priesthood and the numerous laws regulating the lives of the priests, for the priesthood passed out of existence with the temple. However, Origen asserts that all the laws are kept by the spiritual understanding of the Christians. Consequently, he concludes, the literal interpretation of the law limits the scope of its influence severely, but the Christian interpretation allows it unlimited possibilities (*HomEx* 11.6).

The church continues to wrestle with the issue Origen here addresses head on. How can the church use the material contained in Leviticus and the latter part of Exodus that defines the worship of ancient Israel? Must this material be relegated to the area of historical interest and isolated from contemporary relevance in the understanding of doctrine and life? Or, can it continue to play a role in the theological life of the contemporary church? Origen's answer to the last question is clearly positive. His approach is not so innovative as it may strike us at first. One can find a similar approach to these same topics in Hebrews 9–10 in the New Testament itself. There the law is treated as a "shadow" of the things to come in Christ. The priesthood and the sacrifices come to an end with Christ, but more than this, they are also considered to have been anticipatory offices and activities that pointed to Christ. One need not assume that every interpretation or application that Origen made concerning the laws of Israel that governed temple worship was correct in order to affirm that many of those ancient practices have significant reverberations for the Christian's understanding of the meaning of Christ and the life one is called to live in Christ.

Origen's approach to the law owes more to the tradition of the *Epistle of Barnabas* than to that of Justin. The sophistication of Origen's interpretative skills and his widespread reputation as a biblical scholar gave great prominence to this approach in the early church. As William Horbury has remarked, Barnabas's view that the ritual laws "were never meant to be kept literally was taken in a refined form through Origen into the Alexandrian stream of Christian assessment of the Old Testament" and consequently had "considerable influence on early Christian views of . . . the Jewish scriptures."[12]

Ptolemaeus and the Gnostics on the Law

The Opinions of Various Gnostic Groups concerning the Old Testament

Numerous teachers appeared in the church in the second century who are referred to as Gnostics by church fathers writing in the late second and early third centuries. The Gnostics were, as was noted earlier, a diverse group. In one form or another, however, they seem to have been an extremely pervasive and threatening presence in the early church. Their teachings can be detected from Alexandria to Rome and as far east as Persia. They were attacked in the writings of the fathers because their teachings were thought to undermine many of the basic doctrines of the church. We have treatises containing attacks against Gnostics by Irenaeus, Tertullian, and Hippolytus, and numerous references to Gnostic teachings in the writings of other church fathers. In 1945 several manuscripts were discovered at Nag Hammadi, Egypt, containing Gnostic writings.[13] The summaries of the teachings of the various Gnostic teachers in the church fathers along with the manuscripts found at Nag Hammadi constitute the main sources of our knowledge of these teachings.

One of the features found in many Gnostic teachings is a disparaging attitude toward the God of the Old Testament. Epiphanius, a church father writing against heresies in the fourth century, says that the Gnostics "utilize both the Old and the New Testament, but they reject the one who spoke in the Old Testament."[14] Some Gnostics, such as those represented by the Nag Hammadi treatise titled *The Second Treatise of the Great Seth*, rejected the Old Testament completely: "its heroes of faith, its history of salvation, its legal demands, and its God."[15] Others,

---

12. Horbury, "Jewish-Christian Relations," 316.

13. An English translation of the Gnostic writings was published under the direction of James M. Robinson, *The Nag Hammadi Library in English* (San Francisco: Harper & Row, 1977).

14. Epiphanius, *Against Heresies* 26.5.8, in *The Gnostic Scriptures*, trans. Bentley Layton (London: SCM, 1987), 208.

15. Birger A. Pearson, "Use, Authority, and Exegesis of Mikra in Gnostic Literature," in Mulder and Sysling, *Mikra*, 639–40.

such as the author of *The Tripartite Tractate*, at least had a high regard for the Hebrew prophets. The majority of Gnostics, however, appear to have chosen only those portions of the Old Testament that they could reinterpret and use to express their own viewpoints, such as the early chapters of Genesis, and disregarded or ridiculed the rest.

Moses and the law did not come off well among the Gnostics. In the Nag Hammadi treatise called *The Gospel of Philip*, the law is identified with the tree of the knowledge of good and evil in Genesis 2 and 3. It could give knowledge of good and evil but it could neither empower humanity to do the former nor prevent it from doing the latter. Its only gift to humanity was death (*Gospel of Philip* 74.5–11). The author of the *Apocryphon of John* corrects statements made in Genesis concerning creation and the flood, asserting that Moses's statements are incorrect (*Apocryphon of John* 13.20; 22.22; 23.3; 29.6). In writing against a Gnostic sect called the Archontics, Epiphanius says that they believe the law was given by an inferior deity named Sabaoth and that Sabaoth is the God of the Jews (*Against Heresies* 40.2.8; 5.1). In the same train of thought, Irenaeus relates that the Gnostic Basilides taught that the law was given by the Archon of the Archons, who led the Jews out of Egypt and whom they consider to be God (*Against Heresies* 1.24.4, 5). The God of the Old Testament is often ridiculed for his claims to exclusiveness found in the words of the prophets, such as the statement in Isaiah 45:5, "I am the LORD God, and there is no other God but me" (see *Apocryphon of John* 11.21; 13.9). Such statements, it is claimed, reveal his ignorance of the low position he holds in the hierarchy of the gods. In the Nag Hammadi treatise known as *The Testimony of Truth*, the God of the law is satirized in a contemplation of his words and actions in Genesis and Deuteronomy. He envies Adam because Adam eats from the tree of knowledge (Gen. 3:22–23), he doesn't know where Adam is (Gen. 3:9), and he claims to be a jealous God who visits the sins of the fathers on succeeding generations (Deut. 5:9). The author questions that the God depicted in such passages has the proper qualifications to be God at all (*Testimony of Truth* 47.14–48.8).

The Gnostic Ptolemaeus and the Three Sources of the Law

The one Gnostic, or at least the one we know about, who gave more attention to the law and had a somewhat more positive attitude toward it was a teacher named Ptolemaeus. Around AD 160, Ptolemaeus succeeded the famous Gnostic teacher Valentinus as head of the school of Valentinian Gnostics in Italy. Ptolemaeus wrote a letter to a woman named Flora in answer to questions she had apparently directed to him concerning the

Mosaic law. The fourth-century church father Epiphanius has preserved Ptolemaeus's letter to Flora in his treatise *Against Heresies*.[16]

Ptolemaeus begins by noting that there is much misunderstanding about the law because people lack the proper acquaintance with its source and with the nature of its commands. His discussion falls into two parts, corresponding to these two points. Some, he says, think the law comes from God the Father. While this phrase is the expression commonly used by Christians for God, Ptolemaeus almost certainly does not mean the Judeo-Christian God but the highest Gnostic deity more commonly designated as Bythus or Depth. Others attribute the source of the law to the devil, who they say also created the world. Both views, Ptolemaeus asserts, are wrong. The law could not come from the perfect God because it is imperfect. Neither could it come from the unjust devil, for it is just. At this point Ptolemaeus turns from his analysis of the deity behind the law to a demonstration that many of the laws in the Pentateuch do not come from a divine source.

Some laws come from God, Ptolemaeus claims, others come from Moses, and still others come from the elders of Israel. He bases this claim on words of the Savior found in two passages in Matthew's Gospel. The first passage is Matthew 19:6–8. Here Jesus addresses the topic of divorce, saying that Moses allowed divorce because of the hardness of the Israelites' hearts (Deut. 24:1), even though God did not intend it from the beginning. This shows, Ptolemaeus argues, that there are laws from Moses in the Pentateuch as well as laws from God. He does credit Moses with being forced into his action by the weakness of the people and by his desire to prevent something worse happening to them. Ptolemaeus then turns to Matthew 15:2–8. Here Jesus accuses the Pharisees of breaking the law of God concerning honoring their parents by claiming to give to God the money they would have given to support their parents. Jesus assigns this practice to the tradition of the elders. Ptolemaeus concludes from this that not all the laws in the Pentateuch derive from God.

Ptolemaeus on the Nature of the Commands in the Law

Ptolemaeus is concerned only with the law that comes from God himself. This too, he claims, falls into three divisions. Here he enters the second part of his analysis of the law, which I referred to above as the nature of the commands in the law. He designates the first division as the pure law and identifies it with the Ten Commandments. This is the

---

16. *Against Heresies* 33.3.1–33.7.10. This letter can be found in English translation in Layton, *Gnostic Scriptures*, 306–15; in Robert Grant, *Second Century Christianity: A Collection of Fragments*, 2nd ed. (Louisville: Westminster John Knox, 2003), 63–69; and in abridged form in J. Stevenson, ed., *A New Eusebius* (London: SPCK, 1982), 91–95.

law the Savior came to fulfill. The second division of the law that comes from God is referred to as a law that has inferior, even unjust, elements interwoven into its fabric. This is the law of retaliation: an eye for an eye, a tooth for a tooth. The pure law says, "You shall not kill." This law demands a life in exchange for a life. To prevent murder, a death must be demanded. This contradictory element is what Ptolemaeus means by an inferior element interwoven into the law. The final division of the law that comes from God is the symbolic part that the Savior elevated to its spiritual meaning. These are the ritual laws in the Pentateuch. Once the truth appeared, the referents in all the ritual laws changed. Their literal meaning was abolished. The offerings we are now to offer are those of spiritual praise and thanksgiving. Circumcision applies to our hearts, the Sabbath is kept by being inactive in wicked deeds, and our fasts should involve abstinence from evil.

Having established these three divisions, Ptolemaeus asserts that the first, or pure, division has been fulfilled by the Savior. The demands in the ten commandments have been fulfilled in the Savior's teachings that one should not be angry, as opposed to the demand not to kill; one should not look lustfully, as opposed to the law against adultery; and one should not swear at all, as opposed to the law against swearing falsely. The second division of the law, which contained inferior elements, has been abolished by the Savior. This resulted when he gave a command contrary to it. In contrast to taking an eye for an eye, the Savior taught that one should turn the other cheek. The third, or ritual, division of the law, which contained symbolic images, has been altered. The images were important while the truth to which they pointed was absent. But when the truth appeared, the referent changed for these laws so that now they have only spiritual significance. This is clearly an astute analysis of the law and resembles, in certain points, the position considered above taken by both Justin and Melito. Ptolemaeus has one further point, however. He has not yet identified the God who gave the law.

Who Gave the Law?

After analyzing the law, Ptolemaeus returns to his first question. If the law did not come from God the Father or from the devil, from whom did it come? It came, he says, from the creator and maker of the universe and all that is in it. This creator has a different essence than the other two and is an intermediate deity between them. Since the perfect God is good (Matt. 19:17) and the devil is evil, the intermediate deity must be just. He is inferior to God the Father, for the latter is unbegotten while he is begotten, but he is better and more authoritative than the adversary, whose essence is corruption and material. He is, in fact, the image of the better God. Ptolemaeus, frustratingly for us if not for Flora also, chose to end his instruction at this point, promising Flora that he would teach her about this first principle in a future instruction.

To whom did Ptolemaeus refer by this intermediate deity? Did he intend "the Savior" as the author of the law? There are several things that would suggest he did. Near the beginning of the letter he attributes the creation of the world to the Savior, citing John 1:3 to support this assertion. He also notes there that the creation is the work of a just God. Near the end of the letter, as was noted above, he identifies the God who gave the law as the creator of the world and as just. He also says that the lawgiving God was begotten, in contrast to God the Father who is unbegotten. Christoph Markschies has noted the possibility that Ptolemaeus may have thought that the law came from "the Savior" and suggests that Ptolemaeus's letter to Flora may show him to be not so far removed from the accepted theology of a group of Christian theologians represented by the second-century apologists, especially Justin.[17]

Irenaeus on the Law against Ptolemaeus and Other Gnostics

Irenaeus was the most important Christian theologian of the second century. He had deep roots in the Christian tradition that preceded him, which stretched back to the apostles. His youth was spent in Asia Minor where, in a letter preserved by Eusebius, Irenaeus says that he had known Polycarp (*Ecclesiastical History* 5.20). He claims to have heard Polycarp tell of his conversations with the apostle John and other immediate disciples of Jesus and of what he had learned about the Lord from them. This connection with Polycarp places Irenaeus only two generations removed from the apostles. Similarities between some of Irenaeus's concepts and phraseology and those of Justin have caused some to propose that he may also have been a student of Justin's at one time. This must remain hypothetical, but we do know that he knew at least some of Justin's writings, for he refers to Justin's work against Marcion (*Against Heresies* 4.6.2). He became bishop of Lyons in Gaul (France) in AD 177 after the previous bishop had been killed in a persecution of Christians in that city. Irenaeus's writings were produced in the final two decades of the second century. Only two have been preserved: *Against Heresies* and *Demonstration of the Apostolic Preaching*. Parts of the *Demonstration* will be considered in chapter 4. Only *Against Heresies* has relevance here.

17. Christoph Markschies, "New Research on Ptolemaeus Gnosticus," *ZAC/JAC* (2000): 239–53.

Irenaeus says that *Against Heresies* is aimed primarily at the followers of Valentinus.[18] It embraces, however, numerous other Gnostic sects as well, including that of Marcion. How well Irenaeus knew the teachings of Ptolemaeus, who was discussed in the previous section, is unclear. At the beginning of his treatise Irenaeus says that he is especially concerned with the disciples of Ptolemaeus, whose school was derived from Valentinus. At the end of the eighth chapter of the first book of *Against Heresies*, one finds the words, "And thus Ptolemaeus [taught]." The problem is that these latter words do not stand in the Greek tradition, where much of the first book is preserved, but appear in a Latin translation of the fourth century. Markschies has suggested that the first eight chapters of *Against Heresies* should not be taken as the teachings of the followers of Ptolemaeus, but as the teachings of the followers of Valentinus.[19] This ambiguity in the precise referent of the opponents discussed in the first eight chapters of *Against Heresies* does not significantly affect the discussion in this chapter about Irenaeus's own view of the law. It should warn us, however, about being too confident in precise identifications where Irenaeus's text, as we have it at least, is imprecise.

Irenaeus's Theology of the Divine Economy

Irenaeus developed his understanding of the law in the context of his overall theology. His theology was especially a theology of the divine economy. The church fathers spoke often of God's economy. Our English term was borrowed from the Greek term *oikonomia*. The fathers' use of this word had nothing to do with its modern English connection with markets and financial matters. It is difficult to translate precisely what the fathers meant by the term in a simple and meaningful English expression. It usually refers to God's *plan* for the salvation of humanity. The term "plan," however, is somewhat inadequate for understanding the nuances of the concept because plan may mean to us not much more than an idea about how something should be done. Many plans, as we are well aware, never get beyond the mental stage. When the fathers speak of God's economy or plan, however, they refer not just to the overall idea in the mind of God but also to the way God has worked out that plan in actual history. This economy or plan of salvation has to do primarily with God's work in the incarnation of Christ. This economy, however, involved both preparation and execution. It is this totality that Irenaeus has in mind when he explains the Christian understanding of the law by placing it in the context of the economy of God.

18. Irenaeus, *Against Heresies* is translated into English in *ANF* 1:315–567.
19. Markschies, "Ptolemaeus," 249–52.

The Unity of the Old and New Covenants

Near the center of *Against Heresies*, Irenaeus remarks that he will, in pursuing the plan of his work, discuss the "cause of the difference of the covenants" along with "their unity." The heretics, he asserts, set the Mosaic law in opposition to the gospel because they have not diligently examined the "causes of the difference of each covenant" (*Against Heresies* 3.12.12). The apostles, he says, scrupulously observed those things found in the "economy of the Mosaic law," and this shows that the law came from the same God as the one proclaimed by the Lord. They would not have done so if Christ had revealed to them that the "economy of the law" came from a different God (*Against Heresies* 3.12.15).

Foundational to Irenaeus's theology is his belief that the Word, which he identifies with the Son, has always been present with the Father, as has Wisdom, which he identifies with the Spirit (*Against Heresies* 4.20.3). The Word, or the Son, is the one who speaks in the Bible in both testaments and reveals the will of the one God (*Against Heresies* 4.7.2–4). It was the Word who spoke to Moses at the bush (*Against Heresies* 4.5.2; 4.10.1). Moses's writings can even be referred to as "the words of Christ" (*Against Heresies* 4.2.3). It is the Son who "serves the Father and brings all things to completion from beginning to end, and without him no one can know the Father" (*Against Heresies* 4.6.7). This is the reason for the unity of the covenants: the fact that the covenants come from one and the same God and are executed through the one Son.

Jesus's statement in John 8:56, that Abraham rejoiced to see his day, plays an important role in Irenaeus's development of his concept of the unity of the covenants. The argument attacks Marcion, but branches out to include Gnostics in general and also the Jews. Irenaeus begins by asking what Jesus means by the statement in John 8:56, and juxtaposes this with Paul's statement that "Abraham believed God and it was counted to him for righteousness" (Rom. 4:3). Irenaeus then more or less lists what it was that Abraham did that was counted to him for righteousness. First, Abraham believed that the only God made heaven and earth. Second, he believed that this God would make his (i.e., Abraham's) seed as the stars of heaven. Third, Abraham left his family and followed "the Word." Finally, as a prophet, Abraham saw the day of the Lord's coming and the "economy of his suffering," through which he and those who followed the example of his faith would be saved, and he rejoiced. Abraham, therefore, knew both "the Lord" and the "Lord's Father."

Through the creation, the Word reveals God as creator; he reveals both himself and the Father through the law and the prophets. When the Word came in visible form he revealed the Father. Irenaeus thinks John 8:56 shows that the claim of both the Marcionites and Gnostics, that the true God is other than the God of the Old Testament, is false. It also shows the action of the Jews to be wrong in imagining that they can know the Father apart from the Word (*Against Heresies* 4.5.3–4.7.4). Again, the presence of the Word in both testaments is the key to Irenaeus's understanding of their unity.

The Differences between the Old and New Covenants

The differences between the covenants lie not in the God who ordained them but in the nature of humanity. Irenaeus sets forth this teaching in the context of the parable in Matthew 13:52 in which Jesus compares the kingdom of heaven to a householder who brings both new and old things out of his treasure. There is only one householder, Irenaeus asserts, but he brings forth things both old and new. The old and new refer to the two covenants, one containing the law and the other containing the gospel. Both covenants come from "the Word of God, our Lord Jesus Christ, who spoke with both Abraham and Moses" and set us free by his grace. The law was given because it is suitable for "slaves who are still undisciplined." Those who have been justified by faith and set free likewise receive precepts fitting for them, and those who are sons have access to the Lord's entire inheritance (*Against Heresies* 4.9.1).

The new covenant was known to the prophets and proclaimed by them, as was the one who would carry it out, so that people might at all times "advance by believing in him and attain the perfection of salvation through the covenants." There is only one salvation, Irenaeus claims, and only one God, "but the precepts that form a person are many, and the steps that lead one to God are not few" (*Against Heresies* 4.9.3). Both covenants are, in fact, prefigured in Abraham, who was justified by faith before he was circumcised and consequently is the father of all who follow the Word of God in faith.

Abraham also received the covenant of circumcision, however, "so that both covenants might be prefigured in him." He and all the other righteous people who pleased God prior to circumcision are linked to all Christians who follow Christ on the basis of faith. "Circumcision and the law of works prevailed during the intermediate time" (*Against Heresies* 4.25.1). This shows that Irenaeus perceived the Mosaic covenant to be limited to a narrow period of time that was bounded on both ends by a faith relationship with God.

This understanding in effect marginalizes the significance of the Mosaic covenant while recognizing its limited utility. For Irenaeus, the purpose of the Mosaic covenant was twofold. The first was to cause those who received it to serve God. This was for their benefit. The second was to prefigure aspects of the church that the recipients of the law were not yet capable of understanding (*Against Heresies* 4.32.2). Irenaeus understood the saving work of Christ in the incarnation to have been retroactive. Christ came not only for those who believed on him in the time of Tiberius Caesar, or even in the time of Irenaeus, but for all who in their own times honored and loved God as they were able, lived justly, and desired to see the Christ (*Against Heresies* 4.22.2).

The Law and the "Tradition of the Elders"

When the Son came, Irenaeus asserts, he set free all who lawfully and willingly served him. This assertion is made in reference to the Jews. They followed "outward purifications" and misunderstood the law, which had been intended as a "type of things to come." They also pretended to "observe more than what has been prescribed" (*Against Heresies* 4.11.4). This "more" was the "tradition of the elders," to which Isaiah refers (Isa. 1:22) and which Jesus condemns (Matt. 15:3). The "tradition of the elders," Irenaeus claims, "was contrary to the law given by Moses."

In contrast to Ptolemaeus, whom we considered above, Irenaeus does not find this modified tradition in the Torah itself but identifies it with the oral law, which he refers to as the law of the Pharisees (*Against Heresies* 4.12.1). He is careful to note that Jesus did not "call the law given by Moses commandments of men"; rather, the "invented" tradition of the elders was given this name (*Against Heresies* 4.12.4). In this law of the Pharisees some things are omitted, some added, and others interpreted capriciously.

Irenaeus asserts that the Jews chose the tradition of the elders over the law of God. Had they chosen the latter, he says, they would have been prepared for the advent of Christ (*Against Heresies* 4.12.1). By adhering to the oral law they excused themselves from "keeping the commandment of the law, which is the love of God" and love for one's neighbor (*Against Heresies* 4.12.1–4.12.2). The recognition of these two laws as the greatest commandments in both the law and the gospel shows that both covenants come from the same God. God has given particular laws in each covenant that are appropriate to each, but he has demanded that these two commandments be kept in both because they are essential for salvation (*Against Heresies* 4.12.3).

"Christ Is the End of the Law"

When Paul says, "Christ is the end of the law" (Rom. 10:4), this means that Christ was also its beginning. "For he who introduces the end," Irenaeus says, "has also produced the beginning." It was Christ as the Word of God who said to Moses, "I have seen the mistreatment of my people who are in Egypt, and I have come down to save them" (*Against Heresies* 4.12.4; cf. Exod. 3:7–8). Jesus's statements regarding adultery, swearing, and other matters in Matthew 5:27ff. show that Jesus did not annul the natural precepts of the law, as Marcion taught, but rather fulfilled them and extended their scope (*Against Heresies* 4.13.1). By "natural precepts" Irenaeus means the Decalogue.[20] These natural precepts of the Decalogue were written in the hearts of all the righteous people who preceded Moses and his law (*Against Heresies* 4.16.2–3). There is a continuity between the concept of natural precepts expressed by Irenaeus and that expressed by Justin and Origen, as we noted earlier in this chapter.

Irenaeus next returns to his imagery of slaves and freemen in reference to the law and the gospel (*Against Heresies* 4.13.2). He says that the law was given for slaves and therefore had to have a means of external observance to serve as a fetter to teach people to serve God. The Word, by contrast, freed the soul so that it might serve God without fetters. This new freedom, however, entails "a more complete subjection . . . to the one who set us free" (*Against Heresies* 4.13.3). This is the reason Jesus's teachings "extend and widen" the natural precepts of the law among Christians (*Against Heresies* 4.13.3–4). These "natural precepts," therefore, are common to Jews and Christians (*Against Heresies* 4.13.4).

Common Ground between Irenaeus, Justin, and Ptolemaeus

Like Justin, Irenaeus argues that "certain precepts" were introduced because of the obstinacy of the Jewish people (*Against Heresies* 4.15.2). These are the laws we refer to as the ritual laws. Irenaeus sets the giving of these ritual laws in the context of the overall economy of God, though he does not use the term "economy" in this particular discussion. God did not need humanity when he formed it, Irenaeus asserts. The creation was purely an act of God's gracious generosity. God then chose the patriarchs for their salvation and began to prepare a people for fellowship with himself. God sketched out "the structure of salvation like an architect to those who pleased him." Those who "were dissatisfied in the desert" were given a law "precisely adapted for them"; those "who entered the good land" were granted "a worthy inheritance"; but those "who turned to the Father" were given the best robe and feasted on the fatted calf. So it is, Irenaeus says, "in many ways" that God "prepares the human race for the symphony of salvation" (*Against Heresies* 4.14.2).[21]

---

20. Norbert Brox, trans., *Irenäus von Lyon Adversus Haereses, Gegen die Häresien IV*, Fontes Christiani 8.4 (Freiburg: Herder, 1997), 102.

21. Ibid., 108. "Symphony" is the word Brox uses here to translate *consonantiam*. He points out that Irenaeus has taken the word from the close of the parable of the prodigal son (Luke 15:25), from which he has drawn some of the imagery in this discussion.

According to Irenaeus, the laws concerning the tabernacle, the Levitical order, sacrifices, offerings, and all the other precepts concerning such things were imposed to instruct the people. God needs none of the things demanded in these laws. It was because the people repeatedly turned to idols that God had to use things that were only secondary or types of the realities to recall them to those things that are primary and real. Irenaeus understands God's words instructing Moses to make everything according to the "pattern" he saw on the mountain (Exod. 25:40) to mean that everything Moses delivered to the people, except the Decalogue, was to be understood typologically (*Against Heresies* 4.14.3). "The law, therefore, was both a means of discipline for them and a prophecy of future things" (*Against Heresies* 4.15.1).

Also like Justin, who considered the moral law to be universal and eternal, Irenaeus thinks that keeping the precepts contained in the Decalogue is necessary for salvation at any time and under both covenants. These laws "continue with us," having been written on the hearts of all the righteous people who preceded Moses and extended by the Lord when he came in the flesh (*Against Heresies* 4.16.4; 4.15.1). Irenaeus thinks that Moses's words in Deuteronomy 5:22, stating that God added nothing to the Ten Commandments once he had given them, mean that the law written on the two stone tablets was the only law God had intended to give. The incident concerning the golden calf, however, changed this. The worship of the calf meant that the people had turned back to Egypt in their minds and preferred slavery to freedom. God therefore subjected them to the slavery that they desired by placing them under bondage to the (ritual) law (*Against Heresies* 4.15.1). In contrast to the permanence of the laws contained in the Decalogue, the Lord canceled the "laws of slavery" by the "new covenant of freedom" (*Against Heresies* 4.16.5).

Irenaeus claims, again like Justin, that the laws concerning circumcision and the Sabbath were never intended to have anything to do with righteousness. They were given as signs between God and his people or to make the descendants of Abraham recognizable (*Against Heresies* 4.16.1). As proof of this, Irenaeus cites the fact that Abraham was justified without circumcision and without keeping the Sabbath. He then lists others who were saved without circumcision: Lot, Noah, Enoch, and the whole multitude of righteous people who preceded Moses. These were all righteous because they had "the meaning of the Decalogue written in their hearts." It was only because this innate righteousness and love for God died out among the people in Egypt that God then made the covenant with Moses and wrote the Decalogue on tablets of stone (*Against Heresies* 4.16.3).

Like Ptolemaeus, Irenaeus notes the distinction Jesus makes in Matthew 19:7–8 between the law of divorce given by Moses and the intention of God from the beginning. Unlike Ptolemaeus, however, Irenaeus does not use this to argue that God is not the source for all the laws in the Old Testament. He understands Jesus's statement that the divorce law was given by Moses because of the people's "hardness of heart" to free Moses from blame. He notes, in addition, that the apostles sometimes grant certain indulgences in the New Testament because of human weakness, and cites four examples from Paul in 1 Corinthians 7. If this is so in the New Testament, he argues, then it should not be surprising if God occasionally does the same in the Old Testament for the benefit of his people (*Against Heresies* 4.15.2). It should be noted here that Irenaeus sees the concession as ultimately coming from God, not from Moses as Ptolemaeus had argued, and that it manifests the divine mercy.

The Importance of Irenaeus's Theology of the Divine Economy

Both Justin and Irenaeus argued that there are distinctions within the Mosaic law. The moral law, represented primarily by the Decalogue, and the law to love one's neighbor were considered to stand apart from the rest of the Mosaic legislation and to be universal and timeless. This law was to be read and kept literally by Christians as well as Jews, with some modifications made for the law of the Sabbath.

The remainder of the Mosaic law was considered limited concerning both the people to whom it applied and its time frame. It was a Jewish law and had validity only till the coming of the Christ. This law had no meaning for Christians in its literal sense. It did, however, contain a prophetic, or figurative, element that provided important information for the identification of the Christ. It was this latter aspect of the law, both Justin and Irenaeus claim, that the Jews failed to perceive. Because they thought the ceremonial laws had only a literal significance, they failed to recognize the Christ when he appeared.

Justin's argument was addressed specifically to the Jews. Irenaeus, however, was painting on a larger canvas. He saw the need to discuss the issue of the Mosaic law in a broad theological framework rather than simply to look at it on a law-by-law basis. He was probably pushed in this direction by the Gnostic approach that rarely focused on individual laws but raised the much bigger question of the status of the God of the Old Testament. In this broader context, Irenaeus was especially concerned with what we today refer to as the unity of the two testaments (or two covenants in his vocabulary). We might even say, in an anachronistic way, that he was concerned about the coherence of the Christian Bible. The Gnostic understanding (and that of Marcion in anticipation), had it prevailed, would have ripped the Old and New Testaments apart. Irenaeus worked diligently to show that the same God spoke through Moses and was incarnate in Christ. Both covenants are the work of the one God in the dovetailed design of the divine economy.

Marcion's Rejection of the Law

The issue of the church's use of the Old Testament reached crisis level for Christians in the second century due to a man named Marcion, who was a Christian and a wealthy merchant. Marcion went to Rome around AD 140 and taught in the church there until he was excommunicated for his heretical views in AD 144. His writings, as noted at the beginning of this chapter, have all perished. Nearly every Christian writer in the second half of the second century wrote a book against Marcion.[22] These writings too have all perished except for Tertullian's large treatise *Against Marcion*, written in the first quarter of the third century. This work is our primary source of what Marcion taught.[23]

Marcion seems not to have been a Gnostic, though he does seem to have been influenced by Gnostic teachings. He rejected the Old Testament's use by the church, and did not believe that the creator God of the Old Testament was the same as the Father of Christ. On the basis of Isaiah 45:7, Marcion connected the God of the Old Testament with the evil in the world. He then applied Jesus's words in Luke 6:43–44, which state that a good tree cannot bear bad fruit, to God. He concluded that the God of the Old Testament, who claims in Isaiah 45:7 to create evil things, could not be good. There must be a second God, then, who is good. This good God is the Father revealed by Christ (*Against Marcion* 1.2).[24] He first became known in the fifteenth year of Tiberius Caesar, when Christ, the Marcionites claimed, appeared on earth (*Against Marcion* 1.19.2; 4.6.3). The date is derived from Luke 3:1.

Not only did Marcion reject the Christian use of the Old Testament, he also rejected many writings of the apostles that the church accepted and that later formed the New Testament. Marcion argued that these documents had been adulterated with Jewish ideas by the Jewish disciples of Jesus (*Against Marcion* 1.20.1–1.20.3; 4.3.2–4.3.5). He trusted only Paul, but he thought even Paul's writings had been altered in places. Marcion

22. E. C. Blackman, *Marcion and His Influence* (London: SPCK, 1948), 3.

23. An English translation of Tertullian's *Against Marcion* can be found in *ANF* 3:271–474.

24. Origen, *First Principles* 2.5.4, cites the Marcionite use of this same statement of Jesus about the good and bad trees and indicates that the Marcionites applied it to the law and argued that the law must be judged by its fruits. If its fruits are found to be good then the law is good and comes from a good God, but if its fruits are just rather than good then the one who gave the law must be just.

drew up a list of apostolic writings that he believed represented the teachings of the good God he had discovered. These were the Gospel of Luke, which was believed to have been written by a companion of Paul, and the ten epistles of Paul in the following order: Galatians, 1 and 2 Corinthians, Romans, 1 and 2 Thessalonians, Ephesians (which he called the epistle to the Laodiceans), Colossians, Philemon, and Philippians.

Marcion's Separation of Law and Gospel

Marcion's special achievement, Tertullian says, was "the separation of the law and the gospel." His principal work, a treatise called *Antitheses*, was composed of opposing statements drawn from the law and the gospel to demonstrate "the disagreement of the gospel with the law." The purpose of this work, Tertullian asserts, was to document the diversity of Gods in the two testaments (*Against Marcion* 1.19.4). Tertullian sets out to refute the *Antitheses* in Book 4 of his *Against Marcion*. It is in this book that he takes up Marcion's version of the Gospel of Luke and argues that even Marcion's own Gospel does not support his claims, but shows the Christ of his Gospel to come from the Creator God of the Old Testament (*Against Marcion* 4.1.1–4.1.2; 4.43.9).

Tertullian admits that there are differences in the economy of the Creator and that of Christ. There are different precepts and different laws, but the differences do not indicate opposing deities. He cites several passages from Isaiah and Jeremiah that show, he says, that the first testament was recognized to be temporary even during its own period and that a future eternal testament was anticipated (*Against Marcion* 4.1.3–7). Tertullian's understanding of the law in relation to the gospel follows the approach taken by Justin and Irenaeus. The laws of the Decalogue are cited as "decrees of first rank" (*Against Marcion* 2.17.4), the law of retaliation is defended as a reasonable way to restrain violence, the food laws are given an allegorical interpretation, and the laws concerning sacrifice are understood to have been given to prevent idolatry among the people (*Against Marcion* 2.18). The law in its minute details was given to regulate the obstinacy of the Hebrew people. It also has a prophetic and figurative meaning, Tertullian claims, but he passes over discussing this (*Against Marcion* 2.19.1–2.19.2).

Marcion rejected the Old Testament and the law for two major reasons. First, he believed that Christianity was something totally new. It had no forerunner, no antecedent, and no preparatory stage. For Marcion the gospel began at Luke 3:1 when Jesus came to John the Baptist to be baptized. He believed that the God of Christianity had had no dealings with human history prior to the fifteenth year of Tiberius Caesar (*Against Marcion* 1.19). It was this aspect of Marcion's teaching in particular that

Tertullian attacked. Tertullian's approach was to show the unity between Christ and what is to be found in the Old Testament by using Marcion's own accepted texts.

Marcion's Claim That the Old Testament Teaches Things Unworthy of God

The second factor that led Marcion to reject the Old Testament was his insistence that it must be interpreted literally. This issue was addressed by Origen. Writing in the mid-third century, Origen does not pen a specific work against Marcion but often speaks directly against his teachings, sometimes naming him but more often simply citing his views without mentioning his name. Marcion's teachings are attacked several times in Origen's general theological treatise titled *On First Principles*. Like Tertullian, Origen focuses on the two central tenets of Marcion's doctrine: his denial of the unity of God and his denial of the unity of the two testaments. Origen argues that God is one, that he created all things, that he is the God of all the righteous people of the Old Testament, including Moses and the prophets, and that he is the Father of the Lord Jesus Christ. Furthermore, this one "just and good God" is the source of both the law and the gospel (*First Principles* Pref. 4; cf. 2.4–5; 4.2.1).

Origen notes that Marcion said Scripture must not be interpreted allegorically.[25] One of Marcion's criticisms of the Old Testament was that, read literally, it proclaimed things about God that are "unworthy" of God (*Against Marcion* 2.27.1). God does not know where Adam is, but has to ask; he has to ask Cain where his brother is; he must come down from heaven to see what is going on in Sodom and Gomorrah. Further, God issues contradictory instructions: he forbids labor on the Sabbath but commands that the ark be carried around Jericho seven consecutive days; he forbids the making of likenesses of anything on earth or in heaven but commands Moses to make a brazen serpent. He also repents of some of his actions, as if he had made a mistake (*Against Marcion* 2.21–26). Origen adds that the Marcionites collect all the stories in the Old Testament they can find to support their view that the Old Testament God is just and not good and always repays evil for evil. They point to all those who were drowned in the flood, they cite the devastation of Sodom and Gomorrah, and they note the destruction of an entire generation of Israelites in the wilderness. Origen replies that the Marcionites hold these opinions because they are limited to a literal understanding of the text (*First Principles* 2.5.2).

25. Origen, *Commentary on Matthew* 15.3. See Robert M. Grant, *Heresy and Criticism* (Louisville: Westminster John Knox, 1993), 44.

Platonic Precedents

Marcion's objection that the Old Testament contains statements about God that are unworthy of God was the kind of critique the fourth-century BC philosopher Plato had applied to the poetry of Homer. In Homer's stories the Greek gods lie, cheat, commit adultery, lust, and so forth. Plato considered such activities unworthy of deity. He argued, therefore, that the works of Homer should not be allowed to be used in the education of children, for which they were the traditional, standard works. Later philosophers reclaimed Homer's stories by applying allegorical interpretations to them. The stories, they argued, were never intended to be read literally, but symbolized abstract principles.

Origen was aware of Plato's critique of the Homeric stories and also of how later philosophers had redeemed them by the use of allegory. He took the same approach to the Old Testament. He admitted that many things said about God in the Old Testament were unworthy of God if understood literally. Even statements referring to God's hands, eyes, or limbs were considered unworthy by him. Origen considered God to be a spiritual being. Statements about God's hands or eyes or other such organs could not, therefore, be understood literally. They could only be understood spiritually as pointing to the fact that God sees and acts. God's seeing and acting, however, does not involve any physical parts, such as human eyes or hands. Such statements about God have to be understood spiritually (*First Principles* 4.2.1, 9; 4.3.2). In this way Origen reclaimed the entire Old Testament, including the Law, for the church.

Conclusion

The issue of the Law was of central importance to the church in the second century because it related directly to the question of God. The church believed that God had acted in Christ for the salvation of the world, but it did not believe, as Marcion did, that this was God's first action or his first revelation of himself. Christians believed that the God they worshiped had created the world to which he had most recently sent Christ as Savior. The Old Testament made clear to them that this creator God had also established a special relationship with Abraham and his descendants and that he had given Abraham's descendants the Law through Moses by which they were to regulate their lives. They believed that the Christ whom they followed was a descendant of Abraham and, as we saw in the preceding chapter, that they could find statements about him in the writings of Moses, the prophets, and the psalms. To maintain the continuity of the God they worshiped in Christ with the creator God of the Old Testament, they had to answer the question of the continuity or discontinuity of this one God's demands on his people as expressed in the Law of Moses.

All educated Christians of the second and third centuries recognized the problem that the Mosaic Law posed for their use of the Old Testament, but they did not all take the same approach to solving the problem. The more radical, such as Marcion and the Gnostics, either rejected the Old Testament or attempted to distinguish between laws of divine origin and laws of human origin. Among those Christians who were considered orthodox, some put the emphasis on history and argued that the different covenants were suited to the particular historical situations in which they were given. Others put the emphasis on hermeneutics and argued that the issue was how the Law was intended to be understood. The latter two approaches were not considered to be in tension with each other in the second and third centuries, and those choosing one approach over the other almost always used some aspects of the other approach in dealing with parts of the Law.

We who are heirs of the Reformation cling tenaciously to the slogan "*sola scriptura*," and rightly so, for it is Scripture that provides the foundational stories and teachings of Christian faith. We often act, however, as if nothing significant or positive happened between the age of the apostles and the century in which the first leaders of our own particular traditions arose. Had it not been for the efforts of the fathers of the late second and early third centuries surveyed in this chapter, what we know as Christian Scripture today, if indeed such a concept would even exist, would have a vastly different appearance. Furthermore, we who treasure the Christian Bible and consider the Law to be a part of it still read the law in ways that have direct connections with the lines laid down by the fathers of the second and third centuries.

REIMAGINING THE EXODUS

"These things happened symbolically to them . . ."

1 Corinthians 10:11

A 2001 ISSUE OF the *New York Times* contained a lengthy review of three plays about the Jewish Holocaust that were either running or about to run on and off Broadway. Near the end of the review it was noted that survivors of the Holocaust often insist that precise "historical detail" be maintained when the events of the Holocaust are retold and prefer that re-creations take the form of documentaries. The reviewer remarked that even documentaries, however, are symbolic in their re-creations because they must be selective in what they present. Artists who take the Holocaust as their subject, the reviewer asserts, are "seeking ways to reimagine parts of it—to find forms of expression that are responsible to the event . . . and that explore its wider implications for what we are, or can become, as human beings."[1]

The reviewer's remark about reimagining a historical event in order to explore its wider implications for understanding our own lives is reminiscent of one way the church fathers read the Old Testament. They were by no means, however, the first to take this approach to major events in

1. R. J. Lifton, "The Challenge of Reimagining the Unimaginable" *New York Times*, February 25, 2001, 7–8.

75

the Old Testament. Such a reimagining had already been practiced by various authors in the New Testament and had been done by later writers in the Old Testament itself as they recalled events from the formative period of Israel's history.

The review in the *New York Times* emphasized two aspects in the reimagining process. First, the reimagining must be "responsible to the event." The historical event cannot be ignored or misrepresented to make one's own point. Second, the goal of the process is to explore the implications an earlier event has for our own lives. The reimagining, in other words, must be both responsible and relevant.

One of the principles that guided the church fathers as they read the Bible was what they referred to as the "usefulness" of the biblical text, a principle they had learned in their secular education. Usefulness was one of six standard topics that were normally discussed with a student by a teacher before they began the reading of a text together.[2] The issue of usefulness was quite often associated with that of "obscurity" in the text. This was another point raised by secular teachers in their reading of texts with students.[3] Origen, for example, notes in his twenty-seventh homily on Numbers that many Christians reading Leviticus or Numbers may conclude that there is nothing useful for them in these books because of the numerous obscure things found there. He insists, however, that literature that comes from the Holy Spirit can contain nothing useless no matter how obscure parts of it may appear to some people (*HomNum* 27.1). All Scripture, in the mind of Origen and most church fathers, was useful for the Christian reader. What Origen and the church fathers called "useful," I have referred to above as "relevant" and the review in the *New York Times* referred to as exploring the "wider implications" of a past event in search of what it might mean in our own lives.

This concern for the "usefulness" of Scripture was not something the church fathers learned from their secular lessons alone. They also found it in the way the Old Testament was read by writers of the New Testament. In 1 Corinthians 10:11 Paul refers to some of the things that the Israelites experienced in the wilderness wanderings as happening "symbolically" to them. Paul wants to understand these events in a way that is useful for his Christian readers. The word I have rendered "symbolically" in Paul's text is the Greek adverb *typikōs*. It could be translated "typically," but its meaning, in my opinion, is better represented in English by the adverb "symbolically."

---

2. Ronald E. Heine, "The Prologues of Origen's Pauline Commentaries and *Schemata Isagogica* of Ancient Commentary Literature," in *Studia Patristica* 36, ed. Maurice F. Wiles, Edward Yarnold, and P. M. Parvis (Leuven: Peeters, 2001), 421–39, esp. 422–23.
3. Ibid.

A kind of typology is involved in this reimagining process. The church fathers, however, did not usually distinguish between allegory and what has been called typology. They did not regularly use either of these terms but referred most often to a distinction between a literal and a spiritual understanding of the text. A literal reading understood what was stated in the text to be a description of an event that had occurred at some point in the past. The spiritual understanding was a derivative interpretation that was meaningful for Christian readers based on the description of the past event in the text. The fathers almost always recognized that the Old Testament texts had a literal meaning. They did not think, however, that the events narrated in Scripture had been recorded merely to preserve knowledge of them as history. They had been recorded to instruct later generations of readers in some way.

When Paul said that certain events happened to the Israelites "symbolically," he did not mean that the events did not happen. Symbolic events are real, but they have significance beyond themselves. If the events in Israel's history to which Paul refers happened symbolically, then their larger meanings are missed if one reads them as simple historical reports about the past. The significance of a symbol lies not in the symbol itself but in the reality to which it points. This does not wash out the historical significance of the events related in the Old Testament, but it does imply that there are larger meanings in those events than are to be found in the historical occurrences themselves.

If one recognizes that the great key events in the recorded story of Israel were intended to be understood as symbols, as Paul says, then new vistas of the relevance of the Old Testament for the lives of Christian people open up to be explored. In the previous chapter we considered how the early Christians interpreted the legal sections of the Old Testament. In this chapter we will consider the primary way in which they read its narratives by examining how three readers of the Old Testament in the first four centuries of the church reimagined the major event in the history of Israel as a symbol of various aspects of Christian experience. The three Christian readers are the apostle John, who wrote a Gospel in the late first century, and the church fathers Origen, who wrote in the mid-third century, and Gregory of Nyssa, who wrote in the late fourth century. The event is Israel's exodus from Egypt and journey to the promised land.

The Exodus as Symbol in the Old Testament

The exodus event functions as a paradigm of redemption in the Bible. A reimagining of the exodus in new circumstances can be found in the

Old Testament itself. The book of the prophet Isaiah uses the exodus event symbolically to speak of the return of the exiles from Babylon to their homeland. In Isaiah 52:11–12, for example, the prophet addresses the exiles in exodus language when he urges them to depart from Babylon. But in contrast to the exodus from Egypt, when the Egyptians pressed the Hebrews to depart in haste (Exod. 12:33), the prophet tells the Hebrews in Babylon not to leave in haste. The prophet adds, again in the language of the exodus, that God will both precede the people and guard them from behind. This is reminiscent of the pillar of cloud that led the people in the exodus, but which also took up a position behind them at the Red Sea when pharaoh's army approached (Exod.13:21; 14:19–20). The prophet is speaking of the exiles returning from Babylon to their homeland but he is speaking of the event in terms of the exodus of the Israelites from Egypt. He is reimagining the exodus and its implications for the returning people as a way of thinking about the return from Babylon.

In Isaiah 48:20–21 the prophet again speaks of the return of the exiles as an exodus event. Here the symbolism is drawn from one of the miracles God worked for his people in the wilderness. The people are exhorted to depart from Babylon because God is redeeming his people. Isaiah understands the return of the exiles from Babylon as an action of God symbolized in his earlier redemption of Israel from Egypt. Then the prophet turns to the wilderness journeys that followed the exodus and recalls God's miraculous provision of water for his people in the desert. The miracle at Meribah, where God provided water for the Israelites from a rock (Exod. 17:6), symbolizes God's watchful care over the returning exiles.

When Isaiah relates the return of the exiles from Babylon to the exodus from Egypt, he is exploring what God's actions for his people in this earlier event in Israel's history might mean in the circumstances of the returning exiles. He saw the obvious general similarities between the two events. In both, the people of God are a powerless, stateless group under domination in a foreign land. In both events the people of God leave the foreign land and journey to their homeland. What might the earlier event have to say to or about the later one? For one thing, Isaiah sees that both are the work of God on behalf of his people (cf. Isa. 48:20; Exod. 20:2). A second connection Isaiah makes is that God can be trusted to defend and provide for his people. God is both their forward and their rear guard, and he can provide what they need just as he provided water from the rock. The Israelites could be confident of their future because the God of the exodus was with them.

The story of the exodus and the wilderness journey of the Israelites was already being reimagined in new contexts in the Old Testament in order to explore what meaning these events might have for people of a later generation. This process continues in the New Testament and beyond, and it is to this Christian reimagining of the exodus and wilderness journey of the Israelites that I now want to turn our attention.

The Gospel of John: Reimagining the Exodus in the Life of Jesus

John's Gospel might seem a strange choice to demonstrate this reimagining process. John does not often quote from the Old Testament. In the index of Old Testament quotations in the third edition of the United Bible Society's Greek New Testament, there are only sixteen entries for John's Gospel, and of these sixteen only two are quotations from the books of Law. By contrast, sixty-one Old Testament quotations are listed for Matthew, thirty-one for Mark, and twenty-six for Luke.

John's use of the Old Testament is subtler than explicit quotations. In the index of Old Testament quotations and allusions in the Nestle-Aland Greek New Testament, fifty-six references to the books of Law alone are listed for John's Gospel. But this too does not do justice to John's use of the Old Testament. Brian Capper, in an article discussing possible links between John's Gospel and an Essene community in Jerusalem, refers to John's "intense interweaving of events with symbols drawn from the Old Testament Scriptures."[4] This, in my opinion, reflects the heart of John's use of the Old Testament. There is an "an intense interweaving of events" selected from the life of Jesus "with symbols drawn from the Old Testament Scriptures."

John hints at the beginning of his Gospel that he is going to reimagine some of the major happenings in the Old Testament in relation to the story of Jesus. In the first chapter of his Gospel, John explicitly points to the Old Testament as the place where all the salient features of Jesus's life are to be found. Luke does this at the end of his Gospel, when he relates Jesus's instruction to the two disciples on the road to Emmaus, in which Jesus interprets "the things about himself" in Moses and the prophets (Luke 24:27). John places a similar Old Testament reference to Jesus in the first chapter of his Gospel when he relates Philip's conversation with Nathanael: "We have found him about whom Moses in the Law and also the prophets wrote, Jesus son of Joseph from Nazareth" (John 1:45 NRSV). John repeats this Old Testament reference to Jesus in chapter 5 of his Gospel, where Jesus tells the Jews who were arguing

---

4. Brian Capper, "'With the Oldest Monks . . .': Light from Essene History on the Career of the Beloved Disciple?" *JTS* (1998): 1.

with him that Moses wrote about him (John 5:46; cf. 5:39). Thus, from the beginning of his Gospel, John states that he is going to tell the story of Jesus in the light of the symbolic events that point to him found in the books of Moses.

The Passover and the Passion

How does John reimagine the exodus and wilderness wanderings? The key event of the exodus remembered and celebrated by the Israelites was the slaughter of the Passover lamb and the application of its blood to the doorposts of their houses to save them from the avenging angel. John connects Jesus with the Passover lamb by recording John the Baptist's reference to Jesus as "the lamb of God" (John 1:29, 36), an event that stands at the very beginning of his story of Jesus's ministry. At the crucifixion John alone records that Jesus's legs were not broken on the cross and then quotes the words about the Passover lamb: "You shall not break its bones" (Exod. 12:46; John 19:36). Yet there is another, even subtler connection of Jesus with the Passover lamb in John's Gospel. The Synoptic Gospels place the Last Supper of Jesus with his disciples on the Passover (Matt. 26:18–19). John, however, places the Last Supper on the day before the Passover (John 13:1; 19:31). Joachim Jeremias has argued that John's "dating the events of the Passion twenty-four hours earlier makes the crucifixion of Jesus coincide with the slaughter of the paschal lambs."[5] John sees the significance of Jesus's death symbolized in the slaughter of the Passover lamb at the exodus. The blood of the Passover lamb was the marker of salvation for the people of God.

The Wilderness Wanderings and the Story of Jesus

After the Israelites had crossed the sea and entered the desert of Sinai, the food they had brought from Egypt was soon exhausted. No food could be found in the desert, and the people began to complain that they would die in the wilderness. Because of their complaints, the Lord sent poisonous snakes among them and many Israelites were bitten and died. The people then cried out to Moses for help, and the Lord told Moses to make an image of a serpent and place it on a pole. Everyone who was bitten by a real serpent could look at this bronze image and live (Num. 21:4–9). Jesus applies this image to himself in John's Gospel when he speaks with Nicodemus, who has come to him asking about God. "Just as Moses lifted up the serpent in the wilderness," Jesus says, "so must the Son of Man be lifted up, that whoever believes in him may

---

5. Joachim Jeremias, *The Eucharistic Words of Jesus* (Philadelphia: Fortress, 1977), 82.

have eternal life" (John 3:14–15 NRSV). Here is another aspect of the exodus story that John has brought into the Christian experience by reimagining it in terms of Jesus.

John relates more to Jesus about the Israelites' lack of food in the desert of Sinai, however, than just his reference to the serpent story. He also sets Jesus's miracle of the multiplication of the loaves in the context of the manna miraculously provided for the Israelites in the wilderness. Exodus 16 recounts the story of the Israelites' famine in the wilderness of Sin. The Lord responded to the Israelites' complaint by promising "to rain bread from heaven" (Exod. 16:4 NRSV). In chapter 6 of his Gospel, John relates Jesus's miracle of multiplying five loaves of bread and two fish so that they fed about five thousand people. All four Gospels relate this story, but only John records that Jesus instructed the people in connection with this miracle and proclaimed himself to be "the true bread . . . which comes down from heaven" (John 6:32–33 NRSV).

Not only did the Israelites complain about running out of food in the wilderness, they also ran out of water and complained about that. God instructed Moses to take his staff and strike a rock at Meribah, and when Moses did this, water gushed forth for the people to drink (Exod. 17:6; cf. Num. 20:1–13). A few decades before John wrote his Gospel, the apostle Paul had already related this rock, which provided water for the Israelites, to Christ (1 Cor. 10:4). John, likewise, and perhaps even in this same tradition, sees a connection between the story of Israel at Meribah and Christ.

In chapter 7 of his Gospel, John relates the story of Jesus at the Jewish Festival of Booths, which was held each year in Jerusalem. Each family would build a temporary booth and live in it for the week. This was to remind the people of the life of their ancestors when they were wandering in the wilderness and living in temporary dwellings after the exodus (Lev. 23:42–43). One of the events that had become a regular part of this festival by the time of Jesus was what was called the water libation. Each morning a procession of priests would go to the pool of Siloam and fill a golden pitcher with water. This water would be carried in solemn procession up to the temple. When the procession reached the Water Gate three blasts were sounded on a ram's horn. The pitcher of water was then handed to the officiating priest. The officiating priest took the water up to the altar and poured it in a bowl that had a hole with a spout coming out the bottom so that the water ran out of the bowl in a stream (*m. Sukkah* 4.9). Since this ceremony occurred in the Festival of Booths, which commemorated the wilderness wanderings, it probably was a reminder of the water that God provided from the rock in the wilderness.

In John's story about Jesus at the Festival of Booths, he says that on the last day of the festival Jesus stood up and cried out, "If anyone is thirsty, let him come to me and drink" (John 7:37 NIV). In the setting of the Festival of Booths, which commemorated the wanderings of the Israelites in the wilderness, and perhaps even more narrowly in conjunction with the water libation, which reminded the Israelites that God had miraculously provided water for them in the wilderness, John points to Jesus as the true source of water for everyone who is thirsty. In other words, John has taken another event from the history of the exodus and the journey to the promised land and treated it as a symbol that represents a significant aspect of Jesus's meaning for humanity.

Jesus and the Tabernacle

One other aspect of the exodus and the wilderness experience of Israel is read by John symbolically in relation to Jesus. I have already mentioned the pillar of fire that preceded the Israelites by night and the pillar of cloud by day when they departed from Egypt. The end of the book of Exodus records something very special about this pillar of cloud and fire. When Moses and the Israelites had finished constructing the tabernacle, which was a very elaborate tent where God was to be worshiped and which was to be taken down and carried with the Israelites whenever they moved camp, they consecrated it to the Lord. When the tabernacle was completed and consecrated, Scripture says that "the cloud covered the tent of meeting [i.e., the cloud that had led the Israelites], and the glory of the LORD filled the tabernacle" (Exod. 40:34 NRSV). This pillar of cloud and of fire represented the glory of God present with his people at the tabernacle.

John begins his Gospel in a different way than any of the other Gospel writers. He begins by talking about "the Word," which was present "with God" "in the beginning" and which was divine. Then John adds that this "Word became flesh and *dwelt among us in a tent* and we beheld *his glory* [both italics mine], the glory as of an only begotten from the Father" (John 1:1, 14). The phrase that most Bible translations render as "dwelt among us" or "lived among us" in John 1:14 actually means "dwelt among us in a tent." John's choice of this particular word along with his reference to the glory of Christ that was revealed in this dwelling in the tent of flesh strongly suggests that John wants his readers to look at Christ in light of the tabernacle story in Exodus. It was in the tent of the tabernacle that God chose to make his glory apparent to the Israelites. John is suggesting that it was in the human tent of Christ that God chose to make his glory apparent to all humanity.

John perceives these five major events in the exodus and wilderness experience of the Israelites to have symbolic significance for understanding Jesus: the slaughter of the Passover lamb, the lifting up of the bronze serpent for the healing of the people, the miraculous provision of bread from heaven, the miraculous provision of water from the rock, and the manifestation of the glory of God in the pillar of cloud and fire that settled on the tent of meeting. These were events that the historical Israelites experienced, but they contained the potential of an expanded significance beyond that of their literal meaning. In Paul's words, "These things happened symbolically to them" (1 Cor. 10:6; cf. 10:11). It is precisely to such things that Jesus refers when he says to the Jews in John 5:46, "If you believed Moses, you would believe me, for he wrote about me" (NRSV).

The apostle John has woven these symbolic events from the exodus and wilderness experiences of the Israelites into his telling of the story of the life of Jesus. They function to highlight some of the key aspects of Jesus and his ministry. John's reading of these Old Testament stories expands our understanding of Jesus and who he was. He is the new manifestation of the glory of God among his people; he is the essential food and water that sustains God's people in the wilderness of this world; he is the Passover lamb slaughtered to save God's people from the power of death; and he is the bronze serpent lifted up in the camp in the wilderness to heal those who have fallen into the deadly grip of sin. In a sense one might say that John sees all God's saving works for his people during the exodus and wilderness wanderings summed up in the person of Jesus. John has explored the wider implications of these Old Testament stories to help his readers better understand who Jesus is. We will now examine how two church fathers continued this practice of "reimagining" events of the exodus to explore the implications this story might have for their own times.

Origen: Reimagining the Exodus in the Life of the Followers of Jesus

As I noted above, Paul alerts us to the fact that the story of Israel in the Old Testament is a symbolic story as well as a historical one (1 Cor. 10:11). Origen recognized this Pauline insight and applied it to his own reading of the Old Testament. He begins his fifth homily on Exodus with a programmatic statement about the Christian interpretation of the books of Law. He says that Paul taught the Gentile church how to interpret the Old Testament books of Law. Paul did this because he knew how foreign these books would appear to Gentile converts and how confusing they might be if the proper principle for interpreting them was not understood. Origen asserts that Paul's approach was to give some examples on how to read the Law, and that these examples should then be used as a general pattern for the Christian reading of these books. Paul's desire, Origen says, was to distinguish Christians from Jews by the different ways they understood the Law. The literal understanding of the Jews caused them to reject Christ. The spiritual understanding given to the law by Christians proves that it was intended for the church (*HomEx* 5.1).

After this general statement about the proper way for a Christian to read the Old Testament books of Law, Origen provides a literal reading of the departure of the Israelites from Egypt, the crossing of the sea, and the early encampments in the wilderness, providing only the historical events. He then juxtaposes Paul's restatement of these events to this literal reading. Paul reads the crossing of the sea as baptism, the cloud that led the people as the Holy Spirit, the manna as spiritual food, and the rock from which they received water as Christ (1 Cor. 10:1–4). The Christian, Origen concludes, should follow Paul's lead and apply his approach to other passages in the Old Testament as well (*HomEx* 5.1).

This passage from Origen makes two important points. First, Paul's reading of passages from the Law should serve as models for the Christian exegete. The Pauline methodology seen in these models should be applied to all the texts of the Law, even if Paul himself did not deal with them in his letters. Second, this reading of the Law modeled by Paul is the distinctively Christian approach to the books of the Law. It justifies the Christian use of these books and enables Christ to be seen in them. Origen takes seriously the Pauline example as a pointer to how Christians can appropriate the Old Testament as symbol.

We have already noted how the Gospel of John treats some of the key events of the exodus and wilderness wanderings of the Israelites symbolically in relation to the life of Jesus. Origen took this typology or symbolic reading of the Old Testament stories a step further. Not only might an Old Testament event symbolize something in the life of Jesus but it might also symbolize something in the life of a follower of Jesus. It is this aspect of Origen's reading of the Old Testament that I want to explore briefly as suggestive of how a reimagining of the story of Israel in terms of Christian experience might work.

1 Corinthians 2:13 and the Formation of a Biblical Symbolism

First Corinthians 2:13 was an especially important text in shaping Origen's approach to the Old Testament. In this verse Paul refers to being "taught by the Spirit, comparing spiritual things with spiritual."

These words provided Origen with one of his most used and most important techniques for discerning the meaning of a biblical text. It is the principle that later interpreters would call "interpreting Scripture by Scripture." It was the practice of setting an author's words within the context of his total writings to ascertain the meaning of a particular text. Greek grammarians did this to interpret Homer, philosophers did it to interpret Aristotle and Plato, and some Jews did it to interpret the Old Testament.

Origen used both ideas and specific words to link different texts of the Bible. Because of the repetition of several central images in the Bible, this procedure produced a core of biblical symbolism. Origen may have created some of these symbols himself; he certainly inherited others from earlier interpreters of the Bible, both Jewish and Christian. The symbolism depended on a web of texts woven from common terminology and ideas.[6] Once the symbolism was established, however, it functioned independently of the explicit citation of the texts on which it depended. Persons, places, and events in the Bible became symbols of persons, places, and events in the drama of salvation. For the understanding reader the appearance of these persons, places, or events in an Old Testament text recalled the salvation event symbolized.

One example of how this symbolism functioned involves pharaoh and Egypt in the exodus story. By bringing together a number of biblical texts, it was established that pharaoh symbolizes the devil. If pharaoh symbolizes the devil, then it is obvious that Egypt, over which pharaoh rules, is a symbol of this world, over which the devil rules. Given these two symbols, the exodus from Egypt symbolizes conversion or the departure of people from Satan's realm, and the struggles of Israel in the wilderness represent the struggles of the Christian.[7]

In his *Treatise on the Passover*, Origen argues that 1 Corinthians 5:7–8—which refers to Christ as "our paschal lamb" who has been sacrificed

6. The so-called allegorical interpretation of the early church has been the whipping boy of Protestant hermeneutical studies. Denouncing the allegorical understanding of Scripture has its roots in Luther, though Luther never completely abandoned the use of it himself. It has been depicted as fanciful, like pulling rabbits out of biblical texts. We cannot deny, of course, that allegorical interpretation has often been misused and has produced fanciful interpretations. The approach as used by the fathers, however, was not open ended. An individual biblical symbol did not have multiple meanings. Symbolic meanings were established through comparisons within the biblical text itself, and usually the fathers strictly observed the meaning established for a specific symbol. If on the basis of biblical cross-referencing the fathers established that "Egypt" symbolically refers to this world, they would apply this meaning to "Egypt" every time they read it in a symbolic manner.

7. For the details on the formation of this symbolism, see Ronald E. Heine, "Reading the Bible with Origen," in *The Bible in Greek Christian Antiquity*, ed. P. Blowers (Notre Dame, IN: University of Notre Dame Press, 1997), 136–39.

and urges Christians, consequently, to "celebrate the festival . . . with the unleavened bread of sincerity and truth"—teaches "that the passover still takes place today, that the sheep is sacrificed and the people *come up out of Egypt*" (italics mine). Origen connects God's statement that he has seen his people's affliction in Egypt and has come down to deliver them from their taskmasters and from pharaoh (Exod. 3:7–8)—Origen inserts "pharaoh" into the statement—with the incarnation and crucifixion of Christ. "For he did indeed set us free from Egypt and its leaders whom *he nailed to the cross to make a public example of them, triumphing over them in the cross*." Christ is the "true Lamb," who has "*freed us from the servitude of the world ruler of this present darkness*." The passover lamb slaughtered in Egypt was the type. Egypt means darkness, Origen says, and pharaoh, Egypt's governor, "means dissipater, because he dissipates the works of virtue done in the light by means of his princely power."[8]

The Recorded Events of the Exodus Instruct the Christian

Origen makes frequent use of this exodus imagery to instruct his fellow believers in his *Homilies on Exodus*. Exodus 1:8–11, he asserts, was not written merely to teach us history but to instruct us for living, as Paul says (1 Cor. 10:11). The purpose of these words, Origen claims, is to teach you that if you wish to return to the world after you have been baptized and God has become your king, you "may know that 'another king has arisen in you' . . . and that he is compelling you to his works." This new king who takes control over the Christian is none other than the devil, Origen says, and it is he who says, "The race of Israel is stronger than us" (Exod. 1:9). The devil would say this of Christians if we were stronger than he is. This only happens, Origen continues, if "I . . . repel his 'fiery darts with the shield of faith'" when "he hurls evil thoughts at me." Only by such conscious and repeated rejection of Satan's approaches can we cause him to "say of us also, 'The race of Israel is great and is stronger than us'" (*HomEx* 1.5).[9]

Commenting on God's promise that if they keep his commandments he would not inflict Israel with the sicknesses with which he afflicted the Egyptians (Exod. 15:26), Origen argues that this does not mean that one who keeps God's commandments will not suffer physical illnesses. Job is proof of that. He notes that Egypt is a figure for this world in Scripture and equates the sickness of the Egyptians with loving this world and

8. Origen, *Treatise on the Passover* 3, 47, 49, in *Origen: Treatise on the Passover and Dialogue of Origen with Heraclides and His Fellow Bishops on the Father, the Son, and the Soul*, trans. R. J. Daly, ACW 54 (New York: Paulist Press, 1992), 28, 54, 56.

9. *Origen: Homilies on Genesis and Exodus*, trans. Ronald E. Heine, FC 71 (Washington, DC: Catholic University of America Press, 1982), 234, 236–37.

serving the flesh. If one keeps the commandments, he concludes, one will escape these "sicknesses" (*HomEx* 7.2).[10]

In Exodus 14:11–12, the Israelites complain to Moses when they begin to face the difficulties of life in the wilderness and claim that they would have preferred serving the Egyptians to dying in the barren wilderness. These, Origen says, are the words of a soul weakening in the face of trials. Death in the wilderness, he asserts, is preferable to serving the Egyptians. At least one who dies in the wilderness has broken away from the power of Satan, represented by pharaoh, and has begun to travel on the way of virtue (*HomEx* 5.2).[11]

In the examples cited above, from his *Treatise on the Passover* and his *Homilies on Exodus*, Origen explores the symbolism of three realities in Israel's history—the Old Testament stories involving pharaoh, Egypt, and the exodus—to understand and to interpret the struggle of being a Christian in the hostile environment of his own time. In his *Homilies on Numbers*, Origen takes up the theme of Israel's wilderness wanderings and explores their symbolic significance for understanding Christian existence. The book of Hebrews in the New Testament had already viewed the Christian life through the symbolism of the Israelites' life in the wilderness (Heb. 3:7–4:11; 11:13–16).

Origen focuses especially on the movement of the Israelites from one camping place to another. He notes that in the wilderness the Israelites live in tents, not in houses. This is important because houses rest on foundations and are permanent, whereas tents are used for traveling, when the end of the journey has not yet been reached. The significance of this for Origen is that the Christian is in continual pursuit of the wisdom of God, a wisdom that opens out before one like a road with no end. Each camping place represents an attainment in the pursuit of the divine wisdom, but new vistas inevitably appear and the Christian packs up and moves on toward the next camping place, like Paul, always "pressing forward" on the way (Phil. 3:12–14; Origen, *HomNum* 17.4).

Origen's twenty-seventh homily on Numbers is titled "The Camping Places of the Children of Israel." This long homily follows the course of the Israelites from camping place to camping place and examines the significance of these stops for understanding the progress of the Christian life from baptism (i.e., the crossing of the sea) to entry into the Christian reward at death (i.e., the promised land). Origen notes that Numbers 33:2 states that Moses recorded Israel's departures and camping places "at the command of the Lord." "Why," Origen asks, "did the Lord want these to be recorded?" He answers by appealing to the criterion of usefulness that

10. Ibid., 303–4, modified.
11. Ibid., 281.

I noted above. Would anyone dare, he says, claim "that things recorded at the command of the Lord contain nothing useful, treat nothing regarding salvation, narrate nothing more than the event which, indeed, transpired at that time but whose narration now contains nothing pertinent to us?" Origen dismisses this as an impious suggestion, foreign to the catholic faith, and held only by those who deny that the law and the gospel derive from the same God. We can each, therefore, be said to come out of Egypt spiritually when we forsake the pagan life and accept the divine law (*HomNum* 27.2). Israel's wanderings in the wilderness represent, for Origen, the Christian life in the world. The environment is still hostile, but the tyrannical control of the devil has been left behind.

Origen's reading of Old Testament narrative, as he himself claimed, stood in continuity with that of Paul. Paul claims, for example, that the statement made concerning Abraham's faith—that it "was counted as righteousness to him"—was recorded for our sake as well as for Abraham's (Rom. 4:23–24), and that the trials of the Israelites in the wilderness were recorded to instruct us (1 Cor. 10:11). The spiritual application of Old Testament history to Christian living is rooted in the apostolic age. The fathers took over this approach and expanded it beyond the few examples found in the New Testament itself. Origen read the narrative in the Old Testament books of Law as stories that were alive with meaning for contemporary Christian life in the world. This meaning, however, did not reside in a simple retelling of the history of Israel recorded there. It resided in reimagining these ancient events in new Christian contexts and circumstances. Let us turn now to another influential example of this symbolic reading of Old Testament narratives.

Gregory of Nyssa: Reimagining the Life of Moses as a Model of Christian Virtue

Near the end of the fourth century, Gregory of Nyssa, a bishop of the church in Cappadocia (eastern central Turkey), wrote a treatise titled *On the Life of Moses* in response to a young friend's request for guidance concerning the virtuous life. In this work, Gregory examines the life of Moses as a pattern for one desiring to be perfect in virtue. He realizes that such an examination contains difficulties inherent in both the differences and the distance removing Moses from contemporary life in fourth-century Cappadocia. He asks how one can imitate Abraham or Moses when one is of a different race and does not share any of the particular circumstances that characterized the lives of the ancient heroes.[12]

12. Gregory of Nyssa, *Life of Moses* 1.14.

Gregory realizes that he cannot simply retell the story of Moses and expect his readers to imitate Moses. He has to reimagine the story of Moses in order to explore its "implications" for Christians of his own day.

Gregory approaches his task by first setting forth the literal story of the life of Moses as it is presented in the books of law in the Old Testament. This is essentially a straightforward presentation of the course of Moses's life with few interpretative remarks. After surveying the literal story, Gregory takes up Moses's life, which constitutes the second part of the treatise. Here his interest is not in the literal story but in viewing the events in Moses's life as models of Christian virtue. "Now," he says at the conclusion of the literal section, "we must *adapt* the life which we have called to mind *to the aim we have proposed for our study* so that we might gain some benefit for the virtuous life from the things mentioned" (italics mine).[13] Gregory will, in other words, reimagine the life of Moses to show its *usefulness* for Christian life in his own time. The "identical literal events" can never be repeated in the life of another person. "For how," he asks, "could one again find the people multiplying during their sojourn in Egypt? And how again find the tyrant who enslaves the people and bears hostility to male offspring and allows the feminine and weaker to grow in numbers? And how again find all the other things which Scripture includes?" (*Life of Moses* 2.49).

Gregory recognizes that not everything in the life of his ancient model will fit the goal that he seeks in looking to this model. Some events will be skipped over in his reimagining because they are not relevant to his purpose. The reimagining of Moses's life will, in other words, hold strictly to its goal of presenting a model for perfection in the virtuous life. Gregory will read the literal story of the life of Moses from the perspective of the circumstances of a priest who desires to progress toward perfection in the virtuous life in Cappadocia of the fourth century AD. He will adapt the literal history to the goal of his treatise (*Life of Moses* 2.48–50).

A few examples must suffice to show how Gregory carries out his task. One of the most important events in Moses's early career was his calling. In Exodus 3, God calls Moses to leadership through a miraculous manifestation in a bush that burns without being consumed. Viewed from Gregory's perspective, however, the story of the burning bush points to the truth about God and the world and foreshadows the incarnation. Through this divine manifestation Moses learns the difference between what truly is and what only appears to be. The world confuses what ap-

13. *Life of Moses* 1.77, in *Gregory of Nyssa: The Life of Moses*, trans. A. J. Malherbe and E. Ferguson, Classics of Western Spirituality (New York: Paulist Press, 1978), 51. References to *Life of Moses* are to this translation.

pears to be with true being and, consequently, lives in perpetual error. Moses learns that God alone is true being and therefore truth itself.

One would assume that Gregory's statements about true being would be grounded in the divine name revealed to Moses at this time when God says, "I am he who is." But Gregory never mentions this statement in either the literal presentation of Moses's life or here in his reflection on that story. Gregory grounds all his statements in Moses's visual experience of the bush that burns without being consumed. The revelation of the divine name in this story must have influenced Gregory's thinking but what he actually says seems to be based on the phenomenon of the bush. The senses perceived a bush ablaze. This necessitated that the bush be consumed. But the bush was not consumed. There is, therefore, a higher reality manifest here, something that remains the same through all change, something that Gregory labels the "truly real Being" (*Life of Moses* 2.25).[14]

The bush in which God chose to reveal himself to Moses, however, was a common material thorn bush. In Gregory's mind, this revelation of God, of the truth itself, in a material bush anticipates God's later revelation in which we see the light of God, not in a blazing bush, but in the human person of Jesus Christ, whom Gregory describes as "the thorny flesh" (*Life of Moses* 2.26). In adapting the story of Moses to his goal of presenting the way to perfection in the virtuous life, Gregory has highlighted, at this early stage in Moses's life, that the proper perception of God and his revelation of himself in Christ is foundational to a virtuous life. Virtuous living rests on the correct understanding of God, who is truth.

In the story of the plagues inflicted on the Egyptians, Gregory sees the opportunity to explore the important role that human free choice plays in the virtuous life. The selectivity that Gregory promised to use in treating the story of Moses can be seen at work here. He does not discuss each of the plagues, but selects those that he thinks will enable him to make the point he wants to make in his treatise. The others are passed over in a summary statement in which Gregory suggests that his readers will be able to apply his approach to these plagues themselves (*Life of Moses* 2.85).

When he takes up the plagues, Gregory first notes the devil's deceitfulness in the way the Egyptian magicians were able to imitate Moses's early miracles with tricks of their own so that pharaoh and the Egyptians were able to dismiss Moses's demands. This is in line with what was ob-

14. This phrase is a way by which Gregory refers to God. Everything that exists, or has "being," draws its existence or "being" from the "true being," which is God. It is another way of saying that everything depends on God, but God himself depends on nothing else because he is "being."

served above in Moses's experience at the burning bush. There Gregory noted that the world confuses appearances with truth. Those favorably disposed are enlightened by the truth, but the obstinate remain in the "darkness of ignorance." The former are referred to as "Hebrews" and the latter as "Egyptians." These two terms serve as symbols for a godly life of virtue and truth and an ungodly life of evil and error.

The Hebrew and Egyptian lives are especially contrasted in the plague of frogs—ugly, noisy, foul-smelling amphibians—that "entered the houses, beds, and storerooms of the Egyptians, but . . . did not affect the life of the Hebrews." Gregory uses the frogs, which are associated with "slimy mire," as symbols of "the sordid and licentious life," and says that the person who lives this life is amphibious, being human by nature but becoming "a beast by passion" (*Life of Moses* 2.68).

Gregory explicitly raises the issue of human free will when he treats the statement that God hardened pharaoh's heart (Exod. 9:12). How could pharaoh be held responsible for his obstinacy if God made him obstinate? Gregory finds the answer in Paul's assertion that God gave some up "to shameful passions" because they did not acknowledge God (Rom. 1:26, 28). To attribute pharaoh's actions to God would obliterate the distinction between virtue and evil. It is pharaoh's failure to acknowledge God that lies behind the assertion in Exodus 9:12. Gregory then applies this insight to the plague that brought darkness on all the Egyptians while the Hebrews enjoyed sunlight. The cause of some being in darkness while others are in light is not divine power. On the contrary; the causes of light and darkness for each person lie in that person's own choice. Each of us is the source of our own plagues by how we use our free will (*Life of Moses* 2.73, 80–88).

The death of the firstborn of all the Egyptians prompts Gregory to address the justice of God. If the children are killed for the injustice of the parents, how does this not contradict Ezekiel's assertion that "a son is not to suffer for the sins of his father"? Gregory finds no solution to this problem except to assume that Moses wanted to teach something typologically through this event. What he teaches is this: One who wants to live virtuously must totally destroy the beginnings of evil as soon as they are perceived. This is explained by Jesus's teaching that anger is the beginning of murder and lust the beginning of adultery (Matt. 5:21–22, 28). By destroying anger, lust, and all other evil passions as soon as they appear, their consequences will not be allowed to develop (*Life of Moses* 2.91, 92–94).

The crossing of the sea became a common symbol of Christian baptism after Paul interpreted it as such (1 Cor. 10:2). Gregory follows in this tradition. The Egyptian army that pursues Israel into the sea and is destroyed represents, for Gregory, the passions that enslave humanity. The person who is baptized must be careful to allow none of these passions to survive the water lest the slavery continue. In relation to his assertion above on destroying "the beginnings of evil," Gregory asserts here that "we must put to death in the water both the base movements of the mind and the acts which issue from them" (*Life of Moses* 2.125).

When Gregory comes to the camping places in the wilderness he again exercises selectivity in what he treats, and he leaves the stories of the remaining campsites for the studious among his readers to investigate following his guidelines. His treatment of the first encampment shows how his plan progresses from one event in Moses's life to the next. After crossing the sea the Israelites travel for three days into the wilderness. They find water but cannot drink it because it is bitter. Moses sweetens the water by throwing wood into it at God's command. Gregory understands this experience to represent what many experience after their baptism. After leaving the Egyptian pleasures behind, life seems bitter at first. The wood thrown into the water, Gregory says, is the resurrection, which began with the wood of the cross. Once one "receives the mystery of the resurrection . . . then the virtuous life, being sweetened by the hope of things to come" becomes more pleasant than all the pleasures left behind (*Life of Moses* 2.135, 132c).

The experience of Moses at Mount Sinai forms the centerpiece of Gregory's treatise. This event represents an exceptional rapprochement between Moses and God. Few can attain this experience though all may see it as a kind of ultimate goal of the virtuous life. This is based on the exodus account, where everyone, except Moses, was forbidden to even touch the mountain (Exod. 19:12). As all the people stood back, "Moses drew near to the thick darkness where God was" (Exod. 20:21). Gregory believes this statement holds the key both to the nature of God and to the progress of the human mind in its attempt to know God. According to Gregory, one first experiences religious knowledge as light, in contrast to the darkness in which one has been living. But as the mind progresses and penetrates more deeply into the mystery in its desire to know God, it eventually perceives God in darkness, for God is invisible and incomprehensible. The desired seeing turns out to be a not-seeing, for knowledge of what God is "is unattainable not only by men but also by every intelligent creature. When, therefore, Moses grew in knowledge, he declared that he had seen God in the darkness, that is, that he had then come to know that what is divine is beyond all knowledge and comprehension." What Moses perceives on the mountain is the divine Word, which teaches him (i.e., through the commandments) that the godly life consists of both right belief and right conduct (*Life of Moses* 2.162–66). This is an explicit statement of what was implicit in Gregory's reflection on the theophany at the burning bush: virtuous living depends on the proper understanding of God.

Gregory follows quite closely the sequence of the story of Moses as it is given in the text of Exodus because he believes the sequence has significance in marking the progress of the soul. In Exodus 33 Moses is again on the mountain and requests to see God's glory. Gregory thinks this request is remarkable because of everything Moses had already attained in his relationship with God. It indicates to him that there can be no stopping point in the life of virtue, no plane of attainment where one is satisfied and ceases to move forward. The previous exertions of the soul in virtue strengthen its ability to increase, like exercise strengthens the body. The pursuit of virtue is endless. "Hope always . . . kindles the desire for the hidden through what is constantly perceived." God grants Moses's request, but not precisely as he had requested. Moses is allowed to see God's back. This means, for Gregory, that he is to follow God, for "to follow God wherever he might lead is to behold God." The desire to see or to know God finds its ultimate fulfillment in following God, which in the Bible is a metaphor for obeying God. To see God's face would mean to be in front of God and face him, and this would mean to be in opposition to him. "[A]s the divine voice testifies, *man cannot see* the face of the Lord *and live*" (*Life of Moses* 2.219–55).

Immediately after his account of Moses in Exodus 33, Gregory relates the story of Miriam and Aaron's envy of Moses in Numbers 12. The point of this jump is that the story in Numbers 12 illustrates the significance of the conclusion reached in the discussion of Exodus 33. When Miriam and Aaron envy Moses and speak against him, God confronts them directly and strikes Miriam with leprosy. Moses responds by praying for the healing of Miriam. This, Gregory says, shows the great height Moses had attained in the life of virtue. He does not defend himself, but intercedes for the offenders. "He would not have done this," Gregory observes, "if he had not been behind God, who had shown him his back as a safe guide to virtue" (*Life of Moses* 2.256–63).

The discussion of Moses does not continue much beyond this point. Gregory moves quickly to the account of Moses's death in Deuteronomy 34, where Moses is referred to as the servant of the Lord. Gregory takes the attribution of this title to be Moses's greatest achievement. "What then," he asks, "are we taught through what has been said? To have but one purpose in life: to be called servants of God by virtue of the lives we live" (*Life of Moses* 2.314–15).

Reimagining the Biblical Past: Summing Up

Gregory reimagines the exodus events in a slightly different way than Origen. Both believe the events contain meanings that reach far beyond the events themselves, meanings that reach into their own lives and the lives of their contemporaries. Gregory, however, has fixed a single goal toward which all of his reimagining leads. This guides all of his reimagining. He does not take up incidents in Moses's life that he does not consider to contribute directly to achieving that goal. He fixes his eye on what Greek authors called the *skopos* (goal) of a treatise and does not depart from the path that leads to it.

The way John, Origen, and Gregory of Nyssa read Old Testament narratives rests on the assumption that some historical events are symbols, as Paul says in 1 Corinthians 10:11. When John relates Jesus's use of the story of the manna to show that he is the bread of life, John reimagines a historical event pointing beyond itself to something greater; when Origen reads the difficulties the Israelites experienced in the wilderness after their escape from Egypt as descriptive of the struggle a Christian experiences after baptism, he reads the biblical narrative as symbolic; and when Gregory of Nyssa treats the major events in Moses's life as stages of progress in the development of the character of a true Christian servant, he is reimagining the wider implications of specific historical events.

This symbolic reading of the Old Testament has fallen out of favor in most modern biblical exegesis. It is, nevertheless, a way of reading the Old Testament that pastors often employ, though usually unknowingly, when they make applications from Old Testament texts in their preaching. When I delivered an earlier version of this chapter as a public lecture, a colleague who was a professor of homiletics remarked that I had described the task of the contemporary preacher. The preacher, he said, must not only understand the biblical text and be faithful to it but also reimagine it in the contemporary world. I suspect few preachers are actually taught anything like this in their Old Testament studies at seminary. If they receive this kind of instruction it is more likely to come from homiletic, rather than Bible, departments. There is, however, as this chapter has shown, a continuity between the biblical interpretation of the fathers and the interpretation of biblical stories within the Bible itself. The latter can be found in the prophetic interpretations of earlier biblical events in the Old Testament as well as in interpretations given to Old Testament passages by various authors in the New Testament.

The post-Enlightenment and, to a lesser extent, post-Reformation legacies to academic studies of the Old Testament have dictated that "history" must be the controlling element. Here the question we must answer is what actually happened. This approach negates 1,600 years of Christian exegetical history, and, more important for our present study, it sets aside as irrelevant the work of the earliest interpreters of the Christian Bible. The earliest interpreters, beginning with the apostles, believed the text of the Old Testament suggests things that lay beyond the historical information it conveys. Whether one refers to them as symbols or types, the major events of the Old Testament—such as the exodus, wilderness wanderings, and living in the land of promise—were considered to instruct one about things yet to happen as well as to inform one of what had happened.

This is not to suggest that the Old Testament text should not be mined for history. It is to say, however, that so far as the pastor is concerned the benefits derived from that mining are somewhat limited. The pastor needs to engage also, and perhaps primarily, in the kind of meditative reading of the Old Testament that its earliest Christian interpreters employed. This demands living with the stories in the Old Testament in the manner that I will discuss in chapter 6. It requires pondering the stories in the light of what we know about Christ both from the New Testament and in the light of our own Christian experience. The Victorian poet Gerard Manley Hopkins was once criticized for the many obscurities in his writing style. He defended himself by saying that if his readers applied a reasonable effort they would find that most of the obscurities "explode" into meaning.[15] The works of the Christian interpreters considered in this chapter suggest that the careful, meditative reader of the stories of the Old Testament who attempts to reimagine the implications of those stories for contemporary Christian life might experience something like this.

15. "Editor's Preface to Notes. Hopkins, Gerard Manley. 1918 Poems," http://www.bartleby.com/122/101.html; cf. W. H. Gardner, "Introduction," in *Gerard Manley Hopkins: Poems and Prose*, ed. W. H. Gardner (Middlesex, UK: Penguin, 1983), xiv–xv.

THE GOSPEL IN THE PROPHETS

"Paul, . . . who has been set apart for the gospel of God, which he proclaimed in advance through his prophets in the Holy Scriptures."

Romans 1:1–2

THE PROPHETIC WRITINGS were fundamental for the early Christians' understanding of Christ. His nature, the manner of his life, work, and death, his resurrection, and his glorification were thought to be described in the prophetic writings. While the early Christians wrestled with the law, as we saw in chapter 2, they reveled in the prophets. Isaiah, Jerome said, "seems to me to compose a gospel rather than a prophecy," and David, he added, "makes Christ resound from his lyre" (*Epistle* 53.8).

The fathers considered many texts in the Old Testament to be prophetic that fall outside our present list of prophetic books. They did this because they believed that the authors of these books were recipients of prophetic inspiration. Moses, for example, was thought to have been a prophet as well as the lawgiver. Passages such as Genesis 49:10 and Numbers 24:17 were considered to be prophecies of Christ proclaimed by Moses. This includes the somewhat more obvious prophetic statement Moses makes in Deuteronomy 18:15–19. It was David, however, who was considered preeminently to be a prophet. Christ was often considered to be the true speaker in the Psalms of David. The traditions concerning David and Moses as prophets are present already in the New Testament writings (e.g., Mark 12:36; Luke 24:27, 44; John 1:45; 5:46; Acts 1:16; 2:29–30; 3:22; 4:25). David was also considered to have spoken prophetically by the pre-Christian Jewish community at Qumran (11Q5 27), and they considered God to have spoken through Moses as though he were an angel (4Q377).

The early Christians saw references to Christ in many minor points in the prophets. A number of central passages were, however, consensually recognized from very early times as fundamental to the understanding of Christ. These passages were repeatedly cited by numerous Christian authors in the first four centuries of the church. It is usually assumed that these common passages from the Old Testament were collected in one or more books referred to today as *Testimonies*, and that these *Testimony* books were the sources from which the earlier fathers, at least, drew their quotations.[1] The first reason for the collection of such texts was, no doubt, for use in the debate with the Jews concerning Jesus as the expected Messiah of the Jewish Scriptures. Most of these passages, however, were also cited as messianic prophecies in the Jewish literature of the same period. Per Beskow has pointed out that this setting of conflict between Jews and Christians does not preclude both from having drawn on a common deposit of texts. "On the contrary," he states, "the central Messianic texts of Judaism were taken over by the church, which believed these prophecies to have been fulfilled in Jesus Christ." He cites Numbers 24:17, which, as we will see below, was often applied to Christ by the early Christians, as an example. The passage has also been found in a list of messianic texts drawn up by the Jews at Qumran (4Q175).[2] In this chapter we will discuss how the church fathers understood these core prophetic passages and, where possible, set this in relation to the interpretation given them by the Jews. While Jews and Christians often applied the same passages to the Messiah, they frequently derived dif-

---

1. Rendel Harris, *Testimonies*, Part 1 (Cambridge: Cambridge University Press, 1916) and Part 2 (Cambridge: Cambridge University Press, 1920), presented the strongest argument for this view. Harris argued that there was only one book of *Testimonies* but that it was modified and expanded over the years. He also argued that this work was the earliest actual Christian writing. Per Beskow, *Rex Gloriae: The Kingship of Christ in the Early Church* (Uppsala: Almquist & Wiksells Boktrycheri AB, 1962), 77, points out that Harris's insistence on a single book of *Testimonies* and its extremely early date did not win general acceptance but that many accepted a modified form of his argument. This latter group assumes not one single rather large book of *Testimonies* but several smaller collections of *Testimonies*. No such actual collections of texts by Christians are extant today except the *Testimonia* of Cyprian produced in the third century. Beskow points out, however, that the list of Messianic testimonies found at Qumran (4Q175) has placed "the existence of such texts in Christianity within the bounds of reasonable possibility" (*Rex Gloriae*, 77).

2. Beskow, *Rex Gloriae*, 80–81.

ferent meanings from those passages and, consequently, had different views of the Messiah.

The earliest Christian interpreters of the Old Testament believed that the choice of texts they discussed and their understanding of those texts went back through the apostles to Christ himself. This view is found as early as the Gospel of Luke, where it is attributed to Jesus in the words, "'These are my words that I spoke to you while I was still with you—that everything written about me in the law of Moses, the prophets, and the psalms must be fulfilled.' Then he opened their minds to understand the scriptures" (Luke 24:44–45 NRSV; cf. 24:27). The earliest extant listing and discussion of Old Testament texts understood as prophecies of Christ comes from Justin, who wrote in the mid-second century.[3] He is convinced that his exposition of the prophetic texts stands in continuity with that of the apostles and that they received their understanding of these texts from the risen Christ.[4] Justin's conviction rests on the passages cited above from Luke's Gospel (*Dialogue* 76.6; 53.5; *1 Apology* 50.12).

The "Proof from Prophecy" Argument of the Early Christians

In the early twentieth century a German scholar named A. F. von Ungern-Sternberg made a detailed study of the Christian use of Old Testament prophecy as proof that Jesus was the Messiah and that the gospel of Christ supersedes the law of Moses.[5] Ungern-Sternberg was able to show convincingly that there was a common set of prophetic texts that grounded the fundamental points of the Christian faith from the time of Justin in the middle of the second century to the time of Eusebius in the fourth. He argued, furthermore, that the "elements" of

3. The lost writing of Aristo of Pella, titled *The Dialogue of Jason and Papiscus*, predated the work of Justin and appears to have contained a discussion of the prophetic texts related to Christ and the gospel. See Adolf von Harnack, *Die Überlieferung der griechischen Apologeten des zweiten Jahrhunderts in der alten Kirche und im Mittelalter* 1.1.2, Texte und Untersuchungen 1 (Leipzig: J. C. Hinrichs'sche Buchhandlung, 1883), 115–30; and A. Lukyn Williams, *Adversus Judaeos* (Cambridge: Cambridge University Press, 1935), 28–30.

4. See the excellent discussion in Oscar Skarsaune, *The Proof from Prophecy: A Study in Justin Martyr's Proof-Text Tradition: Text-Type, Provenance, Theological Profile*, Supplements to Novum Testamentum 56 (Leiden: Brill, 1987), 11–13, 256–59; cf. Jack T. Sanders, "The Prophetic Use of the Scriptures in Luke-Acts," in *Early Jewish and Christian Exegesis: Studies in Memory of William Hugh Brownlee*, ed. C. A. Evans and W. F. Stinespring (Atlanta: Scholars Press, 1987), 193–95.

5. A. F. von Ungern-Sternberg, *Der traditionelle alttestamentliche Schriftbeweis "De Christo" und "De Evangelio" in der alten Kirche bis zur Zeit Eusebs von Caesarea* (Halle: Verlag von Max Niemeyer, 1913).

this prophetic proof are already present in the New Testament. From this he concluded that there is a uniformity in the proof from prophecy used by the church in the more than 250 years stretching from approximately AD 50 to AD 315. He noted, further, that Adolf von Harnack, a well-known church historian, had asserted that few things from the time of the apostles passed over so directly into the ancient church as did that which is called the proof from prophecy.[6]

The church fathers used the texts referred to as the "proof from prophecy" in three general settings. The first setting was in the debate with the Jews over the messiahship of Jesus of Nazareth, to which we referred above. The second setting was the struggle of the church against Marcion and his followers, which we discussed in chapter 2. Marcion was anti-Jewish but his view of the applicability of the Old Testament prophetic texts to Jesus of Nazareth was very similar to that of the Jews. He did not believe that the Christ announced in the gospel and proclaimed by Paul was the Messiah promised in the Old Testament. For Marcion, the Christ of the New Testament represented a different God from the one found in the Old Testament. The third context in which the "proof from prophecy" texts were used by the church fathers was in developing and grounding Christian doctrine. Irenaeus's work, titled *Proof of the Apostolic Preaching*, shows that in the last decade of the second century these Old Testament prophetic texts were still being used more extensively than texts found in the New Testament to instruct Christians in the basic Christian doctrines.[7] They continued to be used in this way by many of the later fathers as well. One scholar has noted that in the fourth century, Eusebius considered the proof from prophecy to constitute "the strongest and most definitive proof of the truth of Christianity."[8]

This chapter is structured around the six major points that the "proof from prophecy" texts were used to establish and support: (1) the deity and preexistence of Christ; (2) the incarnation (including the time of Christ's appearance, his birth from a virgin, and the place of his birth); (3) the healing ministry of Christ; (4) the suffering and death of Christ; (5) the resurrection and glorification of Christ; and (6) the calling of the Gentiles.[9] These topics were the foundation stones of Christian

6. Ibid., 295–96.

7. Ibid., 27–28; Harris, *Testimonies*, 1:63.

8. Aryeh Kofsky, *Eusebius of Caesarea against Paganism* (Leiden: Brill, 2002), 75.

9. This outline is drawn from conclusions reached in the studies of Ungern-Sternberg on the proof from prophecy in general (*Schriftbeweis*, 27, 197, 204–5, 221–22) and from Skarsaune's study of Justin's use of the proof from prophecy (*Proof from Prophecy*, 139, 260). Ungern-Sternberg divides his analysis of the texts between those related directly to Christ and those related more generally to the gospel-versus-law controversy. I have taken only those related to Christ, as the question of the law has been treated above in chap. 2. I have added, however, from his second category, that related to the calling of the

doctrine. The early Christians found them addressed in the teachings of the prophets. They believed that the prophetic texts, in fact, interpret the events in the life of Jesus of Nazareth and give them eternal significance in God's plan of salvation for the world.

The Deity and Preexistence of Christ

DID THE CONTEMPORARY JEWISH COMMUNITY ANTICIPATE A DIVINE, PREEXISTENT MESSIAH?

It is difficult to say whether Jews in the time of the church fathers thought the Messiah they awaited to be a divine, preexistent figure. Pre-Christian Judaism appears to have thought of the Messiah as only a human descendent from the house of David.[10] The evidence, which is not extensive, suggests that in the time of Jesus and extending later into the first century the concept of a preexistent, heavenly Messiah was held by some Jews, at least, but that this was later abandoned, perhaps in reaction to the Christian viewpoint.

A Jewish document from the first century AD known as *The Similitudes of Enoch* speaks of a preexistent heavenly Son of Man who is a messianic figure. This Son of Man, it says, was "given a name, . . . even before the creation of the sun and the moon, before the creation of the stars" (*1 Enoch* 48:2–3).[11] It may be that the author of this statement was reflecting on Psalm 72:17, which refers to a "name" and serves as a basis for statements about the heavenly preexistence of the Messiah in later Christian thought.

Scholars have differed strongly on what this passage in *Enoch* suggests about Jewish messianic beliefs. Christian scholars have tended to argue that the term "name" in this passage refers to the actual person of the Messiah and the passage, consequently, proves that at least some Jews thought of the Messiah as preexistent and divine.[12] The Jewish scholar Joseph Klausner argued, however, that among the rabbis of the first two centuries AD "there was still no conception of a . . . 'preexistent

---

Gentiles because that was used by many of the fathers as a proof that Jesus of Nazareth was the Messiah.

10. Emil Schürer, *The History of the Jewish People in the Age of Jesus Christ (175 B.C.–A.D. 135)*, rev. and ed. Geza Vermes, Fergus Millar, and Matthew Black, vol. 2 (Edinburgh: T&T Clark, 1986), 518–19.

11. E. Isaac, "1 (Ethiopic Apocalypse of) Enoch," in *The Old Testament Pseudepigrapha*, vol. 1, ed. James H. Charlesworth (Garden City, NY: Doubleday, 1983), 35.

12. See Wilhelm Bousset and Hugo Gressmann, *Die Religion des Judentums im Späthellenistischen Zeitalter*, 3rd rev. ed. (Tübingen: Mohr Siebeck, 1966), 263; and Schürer, *History*, 2:519–23.

Messiah.'" He argued that the reference to the "name" of the Messiah in this connection can refer only to the *idea* of the Messiah, not to his actual person, so that the *Enoch* passage cannot refer to anything more than a preexistent *concept* of the Messiah.[13]

PROPHETIC TEXTS USED BY THE EARLY CHRISTIANS TO PROVE THE PREEXISTENCE OF CHRIST

The deity and preexistence of the Christ[14] were definitely Christian beliefs from the time of the New Testament (e.g., John 1:1–3; Phil. 2:5–7; Col. 1:15–17). In the late second and third centuries these beliefs were strongly maintained against the views of some Christians who believed that God had adopted the human Jesus for his redemptive work in the world at the time of his baptism. In the third century, Origen argued that the Son had existed eternally with God the Father. This view became accepted orthodoxy and was essentially the point that was used in the argument against Arius and his followers at the Council of Nicaea in AD 325.[15] It was this council that produced the creed that defined the orthodox doctrine of the deity of the Son and the eternal relationship between the Father and the Son.

Prophetic texts from the Old Testament played a significant role both in the debate between Christians and Jews on the subject of the deity and preexistence of the Christ, and in the development of the Christian understanding of Christ. The use of three of these texts will be examined here: Psalm 72:17, Zechariah 6:12, and Psalm 110:1.

JEWISH AND CHRISTIAN UNDERSTANDINGS OF PSALM 72:17

Psalm 72:17 was alluded to above as a possible text that stands behind the mention of an eternal name in the early Jewish writing called *The Similitudes of Enoch*. Later Jewish traditions clearly connect this verse

13. Joseph Klausner, *The Messianic Idea in Israel*, trans. W. F. Stinespring (London: Allen and Unwin, 1956), 459, 461; cf. 465–66. For an opposing view from a Jewish scholar, see Moses Buttenwieser, "Messiah," in *The Jewish Encyclopedia*, vol. 8 (New York: KTAV, n.d.), 511; and Samson H. Levey, *The Messiah: An Aramaic Interpretation. The Messianic Exegesis of the Targum* (Cincinnati: Hebrew Union College-Jewish Institute of Religion, 1974), 98.

14. "Christ" and "Messiah" are interchangeable terms, the first being the Greek term meaning "one who has been anointed" and the second being the Hebrew term for the same. Christians used the Greek terminology and Jews the Hebrew. In this chapter, "Christ" will be used when discussing Christian views and "Messiah" when discussing Jewish.

15. See Ronald E. Heine, "Articulating Identity," in *The Cambridge History of Early Christian Literature*, ed. Frances Young, Lewis Ayres, and Andrew Louth (Cambridge: Cambridge University Press, 2004), 201–6.

with the Messiah. The targum[16] of the Psalms, which cannot be dated precisely but appears not to be earlier than the fourth century AD,[17] treats the entire Psalm as messianic. It translates verse 17 as, "May his name be remembered forever, his name which was made ready even before the sun came into being."[18] Psalm 72:17 is one of seven messianic prophecies cited most often in the Talmud.[19] The verse is also cited in the Babylonian Talmud in a discussion of things that were created before the world, among which was the name of the Messiah: "Seven things were created before the world was created, and these are they: the Torah, repentance, the Garden of Eden, Gehenna, the Throne of Glory, the Temple, and *the name of the Messiah*. . . . The name of the Messiah, as it is written (Ps. 72:17), 'His name shall endure forever, *before the sun his name shall exist*'" (*b. Pesaḥim* 54a).[20]

The verse is cited also in the fourth-century AD midrash on Lamentations in a discussion of names given to the Messiah by various rabbinical schools. "The School of J. Jannai said: His name is '[J]innon'; for it is written, *E'er the sun was, his name is* [J]innon" (Ps. 72:17).[21] There is a wordplay involved in this statement. The Hebrew verb *yinnon* (= Jinnon in pronunciation) in the second clause (translated "continue" in the NRSV) is treated as a name rather than as a verb. This is done to relate the name of the Messiah to the somewhat similar name of the leader of the school.

The earliest documented Christian use of Psalm 72:17 in relation to Christ appears in Justin's *Dialogue with Trypho*, written in the middle of the second century. It is one of the texts that the second- and third-century Christian authors, Justin, Irenaeus, and Tertullian, use in common to prove the preexistence and deity of Christ.[22] Justin indicates that there was a debate between Christians and Jews concerning the

---

16. See "The Text of Scripture Used by the Early Christians" in chap. 1 above. The various translations discussed in that section will be repeatedly referred to in this chapter, as the debate between Jews and Christians sometimes involved what the proper reading or translation of the text itself should be. The latter, however, is not the case with Ps. 72:17.

17. See Philip S. Alexander, "Targum, Targumim," in *ABD* 6, ed. David Noel Freedman, Gary A. Herion, David F. Graf, and John David Pleins (New York: Doubleday, 1992), 326.

18. Levey, *Targum*, 117.

19. Jean-Joseph Brierre-Narbonne, *Exégèse Talmudique des prophéties messianiques I* (Paris: Librairie Orientaliste Paul Geuthner, 1934), 34–35.

20. Klausner, *Messianic Idea*, 460; cf. the third- or fourth-century AD midrash *Genesis Rabbah* 1.4, in H. Freedman, trans., *Genesis*, vol. 1 of *Midrash Rabbah*, ed. H. Freedman and Maurice Simon (London: Soncino Press, 1961), 6.

21. A. Cohen, trans., *Lamentations*, in vol. 7 of *Midrash Rabbah*, ed. H. Freedman and Maurice Simon (London: Soncino Press, 1961), 138. The comment in the midrash is quoted from the *b. Sanhedrin* 98b.

22. Ungern-Sternberg, *Schriftbeweis*, 141.

proper referent in Psalm 72. The Jews, he says, referred the psalm to Solomon because the title of the psalm relates it to Solomon. Justin, expressing the Christian viewpoint, says the psalm refers to Christ; he is the one who "existed before the sun" (Ps. 72:17; *Dialogue* 64.5–7). In a second citation of Psalm 72:17, Justin says it predicts that Christ would "be born from the womb before the sun and moon" (*Dialogue* 76.7). This citation conflates Psalm 72:17 with Psalm 110:3, as the latter is translated in the Septuagint.

Irenaeus begins his proof of the preexistence of Christ with a peculiar interpretation of the Hebrew text of Genesis 1:1. Irenaeus did not know the Hebrew language, so he must be dependent on some other source for his remarks. He treats the Hebrew verb "created" (*bara*) as if it were the Aramaic noun meaning "the son" (*bara*) and understands it to mean, "The Son was in the beginning; later God created the heavens and the earth."[23] This interpretation probably grew out of reflection on John 1:1–3, which Irenaeus subsequently cites. We should compare this methodology with that of the rabbinical school of Jannai noted above, which said that the Messiah's name would be Jinnon on the basis of Psalm 72:17. Irenaeus finds additional support for the preexistence of Christ in a conflation, like that noted above by Justin, of Psalms 110:3 and 72:17: "'I brought you forth before the morning star,' and 'your name exists before the sun.' That means," Irenaeus comments, "before the creation of the world, for the stars came to exist at the same time as the world" (*Proof of the Apostolic Preaching* 43).

Tertullian attacks the Marcionite/Jewish view that Psalm 72 refers to Solomon. There are statements in the psalm, he argues, that can apply only to Christ, and these should prove that the entirety refers to him and not to Solomon. Psalm 72:17 is one of those statements. Tertullian understands the statement "before the sun" to mean, "The Word of God, that is Christ, was before the sun" (*Against Marcion* 5.9.9–11). We noted above that both Justin and Irenaeus conflate Psalm 110:3 with Psalm

23. This is the suggestion of Norbert Brox in *Irenäus von Lyon*, vol. 1, Fontes Christiani 8.1, trans. and intro. Norbert Brox (New York: Herder, 1993), 62n22. Skarsaune (*Proof from Prophecy*, 235–36) cites a different reconstruction of Irenaeus's words, proposed by J. P. Smith ("Hebrew Christian Midrash in Iren. *Epid*. 43," *Biblia* 38 [1957]), that would mean "'In the beginning God (blessed be his name!) created a Son, afterwards the heaven and the earth.'" Jerome knew of an understanding of Gen. 1:1 that, as he relates it at least, was based on the Hebrew word meaning "in the beginning" (*bereshith*) and was understood to mean, "In the Son, God made heaven and earth." He says this interpretation appeared in the *Dispute of Jason and Papiscus* by Aristo of Pella, which has been lost but which was earlier than Justin's *Dialogue with Trypho*. He says the interpretation is also found in Tertullian's work *Against Praxeas* (5.1) and in Hilary's *Commentary on the Psalms* (2.2) (*Saint Jerome's Hebrew Questions on Genesis*, trans. with intro. and commentary by C. T. R. Hayward, OECS [Oxford: Clarendon, 1995], 30, 100–101).

72:17. Tertullian does not conflate these verses in this section, but he does discuss Psalm 72 immediately after his discussion of Psalm 110, which suggests, at least, that he knew of a connection between the two psalms in Christian tradition.

Christian discussion of Psalm 72 as late as the fourth century indicates that the debate about the proper referent in the psalm had still not been settled. Theodoret of Cyrus indicates that the Jews continued to hold that the psalm was about Solomon and suggests that some Christians also held this view. He argues, much like Tertullian above, that because so much of the psalm can apply only to Christ, so too must the whole (*ComPs* 72).[24] Theodoret gives Psalm 72:17 the standard Christian interpretation, which understood "name" to refer to Christ and which placed the existence of Christ prior to that of the sun. Psalm 72:17 is also used in the fourth century to defend the eternity of Christ in Christian doctrinal debates. Hilary of Poitiers cites this verse in an argument directed against the Arian Christians, who denied the eternality of the Son. The verse proves, he says, that Christ precedes all time measured by the sun and moon (*On the Trinity* 12.34).

THE DIFFERENT WORDING OF ZECHARIAH 6:12 AMONG JEWS AND CHRISTIANS

Justin joins Zechariah 6:12 with Psalm 72:17 in an interesting discussion that demonstrates how divergent passages in the Old Testament could be brought together on the basis of a common word in both texts. Both Jews and Christians made these connections in their interpretation of Scripture. "His name will rise above the sun" (Ps. 72:17), Justin says. "And again," he adds, "His name is 'Rising' Zechariah says" (Zech. 6:12; *Dialogue* 121.2). Justin, or his source, has made two major adjustments to the text of Psalm 72:17 as it appears in the Septuagint. First, he has substituted the preposition "above" for the preposition "before," which stands in the Septuagint text. Second, he has used the verb "to rise," which appears in the Septuagint text of Zechariah 6:12, rather than the verb "to continue," which appears in the Septuagint text of Psalm 72:17. Both adjustments appear to have been made to bring the verse into closer alignment with the name "Rising," which stands in the text of Zechariah 6:12 in the Septuagint. The verb and noun in Zechariah 6:12 both come from the same root in Greek, and the preposition "above" was thought, perhaps, more appropriate to the concept of "rising."

There is a similar relationship between the key noun and verb in the Hebrew text of Zechariah 6:12, but here the Hebrew words present

---

24. *Theodoret of Cyrus: Commentary on the Psalms, Psalms 1–72*, trans. Robert C. Hill, FC 101 (Washington, DC: Catholic University of America Press, 2000), 413.

an agricultural image. The Hebrew text refers to the man's name as "Sprout" (translated "Branch" in the NRSV) and says he will "sprout up." The Greek verb and noun (rising) used in the Septuagint can also be used of plant growth, but they are much more commonly used to refer to heavenly bodies, which are seen to rise in the sky. Greek readers of the text, such as Justin, who had no knowledge of the Hebrew text, naturally understood the term in an astronomical rather than an agricultural sense. The first-century AD Jewish philosopher, Philo of Alexandria, who wrote in Greek and read the biblical text in the Septuagint, also understood the term in its astronomical sense. Because of his dependence on the Septuagint, he noted, much like the Christians, that the text could not refer to someone of bodily nature but must refer to the bodiless one who is an exact reflection of the divine image (*Confusion of Tongues* 4.45). The rabbis, of course, understood the term in its agricultural sense.

The messianic understanding of the name "Shoot" ("Branch") appears in Jewish literature as early as the Qumran texts, which predate the Christian era. The immediate connection of the term there, however, appears to be with Jeremiah 23:5, "the righteous shoot of David," rather than with Zechariah 6:12 (4Q174 1.1.11; 4Q252 5.3–4). The later rabbis joined Zechariah 6:12 with Jeremiah 23:5 and understood both to refer to the Messiah. *"Behold, a man whose name is the shoot, and who shall shoot up. . . . This refers to the Messiah, of whom it also says I will raise unto David a righteous shoot and he shall reign as king and prosper, and he shall execute justice and righteousness in the land"* (Korach 18.21).[25]

Rabbinic interpretations of Zechariah 6:12, while messianic, did not relate the verse to the concepts of preexistence or of deity, as Justin did in his association of the verse with Psalm 72:17 cited above. The difference may have lain in the versions of the Scriptures used: the astronomical association of the key terms in Zechariah 6:12 was understood by Justin, who was reading the Greek of the Septuagint, while the earthy, plant-related understanding of those terms was highlighted by the rabbis, who were reading the Hebrew text. Justin's astronomical understanding of the verse is made clear in a later citation in which he joins the verse in Zechariah with Numbers 24:17. Here Justin says, "Moses insinuated that he would rise like a star when he said, 'A star shall rise from Jacob and a leader from Israel.' And another Scripture also says, 'Behold a man, his name is Rising'" (*Dialogue* 106.4; cf. 126.1).

The astronomical understanding of the term "rising" continued in the Greek- and Latin-speaking churches of the third and fourth centuries as

---

25. Judah J. Slotki, trans., *Numbers*, vol. 6 of *Midrash Rabbah*, ed. Freedman and Simon, 734.

they applied Zechariah 6:12 to Jesus.[26] While both Jews and Christians understood Zechariah to refer to the Messiah, the kind of Messiah they understood the verse to suggest differed significantly. Readers of the Hebrew Bible read of a man who was to come whose name would be "Sprout" or "Branch," and they expected a human descendant of David. Readers of the Septuagint, who saw the astronomical term "Rising" applied to the one who was to come, could not understand this person to be merely human and concluded that he was divine and preexistent. These divergent understandings of the Messiah rested on the different images conveyed by the vocabulary in the two biblical texts being read. The differing views of the Messiah derived from the same biblical passage underline how important it is for us, as we look back at these early exegetical debates, to know what the biblical text that an ancient interpreter was reading actually said.

PSALM 110

Psalm 110 was another significant prophetic text used by the early Christians to prove the preexistence and deity of the Christ. The first and fourth verses were often cited in the New Testament; the third verse began to be applied to Christ, so far as the extant literature reveals, in Justin in the middle of the second century.

Psalm 110 is the most frequently cited Old Testament passage in the New Testament.[27] The Synoptic Gospels show Jesus himself confounding the Pharisees concerning the Messiah by using Psalm 110:1 (Matt. 22:41–46 and par.). It would appear from this passage in Matthew that the psalm was a text commonly considered to be messianic by the Jews. No pre-Christian messianic interpretation of this psalm can be found in Jewish literature, however. It has been suggested that the rabbis may have censored the messianic use of Psalm 110 among the Jews after the Christians began to use it so extensively of the Messiah.[28] The Jews took offense at the concept of the Messiah seated at God's right hand in heaven. This fit very well with the Christian understanding of a divine Messiah but ran counter to the Jewish understanding of the Messiah as merely a descendant of David, as Jesus's debate with the Pharisees noted above shows.

26. See Origen, *HomJud* 8.1, *HomLev* 9.10; Gregory of Nyssa, *On the Inscriptions of the Psalms* 2.5; Eusebius, *Preparation for the Gospel* 11.15.5; Ambrose, *ExpPs118* 12.2.3, *The Mysteries* 2.7.

27. Hermann L. Strack and Paul Billerbeck, *Kommentar zum Neuen Testament aus Talmud und Midrasch* 4.1, 2nd ed. (Munich: C. H. Beck'sche Verlagsbuchhandlung, 1956), 452; David M. Hay, *Glory at the Right Hand: Psalm 110 in Early Christianity*, Society of Biblical Literature Monograph Series 18 (Nashville: Abingdon, 1973), 15.

28. Beskow, *Rex Gloriae*, 133, following Billerbeck.

Rabbi Akiba was involved in an early-second-century debate with other rabbis concerning the Messiah "sitting" in heaven, which is what Psalm 110:1 would imply if it refers to the Messiah. Rabbi Akiba cited the reference to the use of the plural term "thrones" in heaven mentioned in Daniel 7:9 and said that this refers to a throne for God and one for the Messiah. His opponents thought this profaned the deity (*b. Sanhedrin* 38b). This debate shows that the rabbis were opposed to the idea of the Messiah exalted beside God in heaven, but it also shows that some rabbis of the second century did consider the idea.[29] The normal Jewish understanding of this psalm applied it to David. Some, on the basis of verse 4, understood it to apply to Abraham[30] and, according to Justin (*Dialogue* 33, 83) and Tertullian (*Against Marcion* 5.9.7–9), some also understood it to be about Hezekiah. Nothing is known in Jewish literature of the application to Hezekiah.

Justin argues that the psalm cannot refer to Hezekiah because verse 4 cannot be applied to Hezekiah in any way (*Dialogue* 33). Later, Justin carries this argument further, arguing that in addition to not being a priest after the order of Melchizedek, Hezekiah also was not the redeemer of Jerusalem, did not send a rod of power into Jerusalem, and did not rule in the midst of his enemies, all things asserted of the referent in Psalm 110. These assertions, Justin says, can all be made of Jesus. Furthermore, he asserts, the statement made in Psalm 110:3 (as it stands in the Septuagint), "I have begotten you from the womb before the morning star," refers to Christ (*Dialogue* 83).

At the end of the second century, Irenaeus uses Psalm 110:3 to prove that the Son of God was born before the creation of the world (*Proof of the Apostolic Preaching* 43, 48). This understanding of the verse is simply assumed by Origen in the early third century. He argues that the saints of the Old Testament had already been instructed by Christ because prior to the incarnation he had "existed before the morning star" (*ComJn* 6.18). In the fourth century, Cyril of Jerusalem cites Psalm 110:1 as proof that Christ was Lord with the Father even before the incarnation (*Catechetical Lectures* 10.9) and Psalm 110:3 as proof that he has existed "before all ages" (*Catechetical Lectures* 11.5).

Psalm 110 became an important text in the third- and fourth-century controversies between Christians concerning Christ and his relationship to the Father. Tertullian, in his argument against Praxeas, who denied that there was any distinction between the Father and the Son, argues that the term "Lord" is applied to two divine beings in Psalm 110:1: the Father and the Son (*Against Praxeas* 13.3). Novatian uses the same verse

29. Beskow, *Rex Gloriae*, 134.
30. Levey, *Targum*, 122; cf. Hay, *Glory*, 27–30.

against the followers of Sabellius, who held a view of the Father and Son like that of Praxeas, to argue that the Son is a second being after the Father (*On the Trinity* 26.6). In the fourth century, Basil of Caesarea uses Psalm 110:1 to show the error of the Arian view that the Son is inferior to the Father. "'On the right hand' does not indicate a lower position, as they think," Basil argues, "but an equal relationship" (*On the Holy Spirit* 6.15).

Rowan Greer has pointed out that Psalm 110:1 is used in two ways in the New Testament. In the Synoptic Gospels it is used by Jesus, as I noted above, to prove that the Messiah is David's Lord. This application of the verse supports the argument that the Christ is divine and preexistent, an argument we have discussed in this section. Acts and Hebrews use this verse as proof of Jesus's resurrection,[31] as do the church fathers. We will return, therefore, to Psalm 110:1 when we discuss the resurrection of Jesus.

The Incarnation of Christ

Several subjects were connected with the incarnation of Christ in the early Christian mind. Each of these subjects was based on one or more prophetic passages in the Old Testament. The time of Christ's appearance was discussed in relation to Genesis 49:10 and connected with a star on the basis of Numbers 24:17. The place of his birth was proved from Micah 5:2, his Davidic ancestry from Isaiah 11:1, and his birth from a virgin from Isaiah 7:14. Genesis 49:10, Numbers 24:17, Micah 5:2, and Isaiah 11:1 are all texts used in common by Justin, Irenaeus, and Tertullian to speak of the incarnation.[32] Genesis 49:10f., Micah 5:1–4, and Isaiah 11:1–4 are also three of the seven messianic prophecies cited most frequently in the Talmud.[33]

GENESIS 49:10, NUMBERS 24:17, AND ISAIAH 11:1

The Old Testament texts applied to Christ are often discussed in clusters rather than in isolation. Genesis 49:10, Numbers 24:17, and Isaiah 11:1 compose one such cluster. None of these texts, however, is important in the New Testament. They are never quoted, and they are rarely alluded to.[34] In contrast to this relative neglect in the New Testament,

31. Rowan Greer, "The Christian Bible and Its Interpretation," in James L. Kugel and Rowan A. Greer, *Early Biblical Interpretation* (Philadelphia: Westminster, 1986), 131–32.

32. Ungern-Sternberg, *Schriftbeweis*, 142.

33. Brierre-Narbonne, *Exégèse Talmudique I*, 34–35.

34. Gen. 49:10 is alluded to in Heb. 7:14 and Rev. 5:5. In the latter text an allusion to Isa. 11:1 is joined with it. A similar allusion to Isa. 11:1 appears in Rev. 22:16 along with a loose allusion to Num. 24:17. The latter passage also probably stands behind the statement

two of these texts are frequently cited as messianic texts by the Jews, and all three are major messianic texts to which the church fathers appeal.[35] We will note the use of these texts in conjunction with one another later in this section. We must begin, however, by discussing a significant difference in the wording of Genesis 49:10 in the ancient texts read by the Christians and the Jews.

The wording of the text of Genesis 49:10 differs as reported by various church fathers, all of whom were reading the Septuagint. This difference is rooted in a variation in the wording of the Hebrew text of Genesis 49:10 itself. The majority of the ancient copies of the Hebrew text have the word *shiloh* in the third clause of the verse. This was treated as the name "Shiloh" by later Jewish interpreters. Some copies of the Hebrew text, however, have *shelō*, which can mean either "he to whom it belongs" or "that which belongs to him."[36] The first stresses the person and the second stresses the "belongings." In my translations of Genesis 49:10 from the Hebrew text and the Septuagint that follow, I have italicized the clause in question. The Hebrew text, as we have it today, reads: "A scepter shall not depart from Judah nor a commander from between his feet *until Shiloh comes and the obedience of the peoples is his.*" What "Shiloh" means puzzled the ancient interpreters and translators as much as it does us today. The Septuagint text that we have reads: "A ruler shall not depart from Judah and a leader from his thighs *until the things which have been stored up come to him and he is the expectation of the nations*" (i.e., the Gentiles).[37] It would appear that the translators of the Septua-

---

about the "star" in Matt. 2:2. The Hebrew word for a "shoot" (*nēzer*) in Isa. 11:1 is probably the basis for the statement in Matt. 2:23 that Jesus would be called "a Nazarene."

35. Skarsaune notes that there is a minimal correspondence between Brierre-Narbonne's list of the seven messianic texts cited most frequently in the Talmud and the most important messianic texts used in the New Testament. He suggests that this disparity can be explained by assuming that the first Christians had to explain those things about the Messiah that were not part of the normal Jewish messianic expectations, such as his death, resurrection, and ascension, and that they called on Old Testament texts that would support these explanations. Later Christians, he surmises, who were still in contact with Jewish messianic views, attempted to fill out their dossier of proof texts by including the traditional Jewish messianic texts (*Proof from Prophecy*, 260–61).

36. These are the two meanings given for the construction by F. Brown, S. R. Driver, and C. A. Briggs, *A Hebrew and English Lexicon of the Old Testament* (Oxford: Clarendon, 1959), 1010.

37. Jerome, in his fourth-century Latin translation of Genesis in the Vulgate, claims in his "Preface to the Pentateuch" that his translation is based on the Hebrew rather than the Septuagint text, though he notes that he has carefully studied Origen's *Hexapla*, which contained a critical text of the Septuagint. Jerome's rendering of Gen. 49:10 reads: "A scepter shall not depart from Judah nor a leader from his thighs *until he who is to be sent comes, and he will be the expectation of the nations.*" The Syriac Peshitta, which was perhaps translated in the third century AD, renders the clause in question to mean "'until the one to whom it . . . belongs'" comes (as cited in Ludwig Köhler and Walter

gint had a Hebrew text that contained *shelō* and that they understood the expression to mean "the things which belong to him."

The *Targum Onqelos*, a Jewish interpretative translation of the Pentateuch into Aramaic made in Palestine in the late first or early second century AD, renders the phrase, "until the Messiah comes, to whom the Kingdom belongs, and whom nations shall obey."[38] This rendering of the phrase as "the Messiah" suggests that the targum, like the Septuagint, depended on a Hebrew text containing the word *shelō* understood to refer to the *person* who was to come. This way of understanding Genesis 49:10 is very close to the way Justin claims the correct text of the Septuagint reads, as we will see in the following paragraphs.[39] Justin was born in Samaria in the early second century and must have spent some of his early life there. We can only wonder if this was the common way of understanding Genesis 49:10 in Palestine at that time.

Justin reports two different readings of the Greek text of Genesis 49:10. One, which he says the Jew Trypho relates, means, "until the things which have been stored up come to him." This is the reading of the Septuagint text that we possess (see above). But Justin asserts that this is not the true text of the Septuagint. He claims that the correct text of the Septuagint reads, "until he comes for whom it has been stored up" (*Dialogue* 120.4), and this is the way he understands the verse. Origen, who was the greatest scholar in the early Christian centuries and who worked intensely on the text of the Septuagint, has the text both ways in different writings.[40]

It does make a difference which way the text is read, and Justin was aware of this. The reading Trypho accepts puts the emphasis on "the things which have been stored up," and, as Justin points out, on the tribe of Judah as the recipient of these things; the reading Justin accepts puts the emphasis on the person who is to come (*Dialogue* 120.4–5). The reading that Justin claims is the correct one makes the verse more easily understandable as a prophecy of the Christ than the reading that stands in the Septuagint today. Justin's reading was widely accepted in the early church.[41] Some think, however, that the text Justin claims is correct was never the text of the Septuagint but originated as a way of interpreting Genesis 49:10 by a Christian in a collection of prophetic texts belonging to the testimony

Baumgartner, *The Hebrew and Aramaic Lexicon of the Old Testament*, vol. 4 [Leiden: Brill, 1999], 1478–79).

38. Levey, *Targum*, 7.

39. See Skarsaune, *Proof from Prophecy*, 27.

40. See *La Bible d'Alexandrie LXX 1: La Genèse*, trans., intro., and notes by M. Harl (Paris: Éditions du Cerf, 1986), 308–9.

41. List in Skarsaune, *Proof from Prophecy*, 29, compiled by Smit Sibinga.

tradition I discussed at the beginning of this chapter.[42] I am inclined to leave the question open given the limited nature of our knowledge of the text of the Septuagint in the first and second centuries AD.

The church fathers believed that Genesis 49:10 proved that Jesus was the one anticipated in the prophecy because there were no Jewish rulers from the tribe of Judah after the time of Jesus.[43] The problem with this interpretation was that rulers descending from Judah had ceased before the coming of Jesus. Herod the Great was an Idumean. He had received his crown to rule over Judea from the Romans. The Jews also felt this tension between history and the words of Genesis 49:10 because they too, though not regarding Jesus of Nazareth to have been its fulfillment, believed the verse to be messianic.[44] The Dead Sea Scrolls have shown that the Jewish messianic understanding of the verse was pre-Christian.[45] They believed that the Messiah promised in Genesis 49:10 had not yet come but they were faced with the historical fact that rulers from Judah had ceased. They solved the problem by a creative exegesis of the second clause in the verse that is usually rendered, "nor a leader from his thighs." Since the Hebrew word translated "leader" here is related to the word that means "law" or "statute," the *Targum Onqelos* understood the word to refer to a teacher of the law and rendered the clause in Genesis 49:10 as "nor the *scribe* from his children's children, forever, until the Messiah comes" (italics mine).[46] This interpretation, which transferred the idea of rule from the political to the spiritual leadership of Israel, was frequently used in later Jewish interpretations of the verse.[47] The midrash Genesis Rabbah, parts of which at least date from the third century AD, interprets the "scepter" of the first clause of Genesis 49:10 as an allusion to the "Exilarchs in Babylon who chastise the people of Israel with the staff," and takes the "lawgiver" of the second clause to refer to "the Patriarchs of the House of Rabbi" who teach the Torah in the land of Israel.[48]

42. Skarsaune, *Proof from Prophecy*, 29.

43. See Irenaeus, *Proof of the Apostolic Preaching* 57; cf. *Against Heresies* 4.10.2; Justin, *1 Apology* 32.1–3.

44. Skarsaune (*Proof from Prophecy*, 264) asserts that there was "an unanimous exegetical tradition in Jewish sources" that regarded the verse as messianic.

45. Text in Joseph L. Trafton, "Commentary on Genesis A (4Q252 = 4QCommGen A = 4QBless)," in *The Dead Sea Scrolls. Hebrew, Aramaic, and Greek Texts with English Translations*, vol. 6B, *Pesharim, Other Commentaries, and Related Documents*, ed. James H. Charlesworth et al. (Tübingen: Mohr Siebeck, 2002), 217.

46. See Moses Aberbach and Bernard Grossfeld, *Targum Onqelos on Genesis 49: Translation and Analytical Commentary*, Society of Biblical Literature Aramaic Studies 1 (Missoula, MT: Scholars Press, 1976), 13.

47. See Skarsaune, *Proof from Prophecy*, 262–63.

48. H. Freedman, trans., *Genesis*, vol. 2 of *Midrash Rabbah*, ed. Freedman and Simon 906–7.

Origen is familiar with a Jewish interpretation similar to that described above concerning the exilarchs and patriarchs continuing the line of rulers from Judah. He refers to those who attempt to solve the difficulty in Genesis 49:10 by arguing that "the ethnarch, who is from the tribe of Judah, rules the people, and that his descendants will not cease until the advent of the Christ they imagine." Origen annuls this interpretation with two arguments. First, he appeals to Hosea 3:4, which speaks of the cessation of kings, sacrifices, priesthood, and oracles in Israel, and says that if this has been fulfilled, which he asserts is true, then "a ruler has ceased from Israel." Second, he appeals to the final clause in Genesis 49:10 about the coming of one who will be "the expectation of the Gentiles" and says it is clear that he has come because of the large number of Gentiles who have turned to God through Christ (*First Principles* 4.1.3).

It is the fourth-century historian Eusebius, however, who goes into great detail trying to reconcile Genesis 49:10 with actual history. He argues that because people who were not directly descended from the man Judah ruled over the Jews both before the Davidic dynasty and after the return from exile, the reference in Genesis 49:10 cannot be to Judah, the individual, or to his descendants. The tribe of Judah, he argues, enjoyed perpetual prominence so long as the nation existed. This prominence ended, Eusebius says, in the time of Augustus Caesar, when Christ appeared on earth and "the whole nation became subject to Rome." "And then," he continues, "instead of their ancestral and constitutional rulers they were ruled first by Herod, a foreigner, and next by the Emperor Augustus" (*Proof of the Gospel* 8.1; *Ecclesiastical History* 1.6.1–8).[49] Eusebius solves the disparity concerning the cessation of rulers from Judah and the beginning of the reign of Herod by noting that Christ was born during the reign of the first non-Jewish ruler of the people and, therefore, fulfilled the prophecy of appearing at the time that the hegemony of Judah ceased. Although Genesis 49:10 is not a significant prophecy applied to Christ in the New Testament, it clearly became such in the debates about Jesus the Christ in the succeeding centuries of early Christian history.

Numbers 24:17 and Isaiah 11:1, which the early Christians often joined with Genesis 49:10, are the oldest Jewish proof texts we know that Christians borrowed to prove Jesus was the Messiah.[50] Numbers 24:17 appears in a collection of Jewish messianic proof texts found at Qumran (4Q175).[51] The Qumran documents known as *The Damascus Document* (4Q265–73

49. Eusebius, *The Proof of the Gospel*, vol. 2, ed. and trans. W. J. Ferrar (Grand Rapids: Baker Academic, 1981), 102.

50. Beskow, *Rex Gloriae*, 94.

51. For the text, see Frank Moore Cross, "Testimonia (4Q175 = 4QTestimonia = 4QTestim)," in Charlesworth et al., *Dead Sea Scrolls*, vol. 6B, 308–27.

7.18–21), *The War Scroll* (1QM 11.6–7), and *The Book of Blessings* (1Q28b 5.27–28) also apply Numbers 24:17 to the Messiah.[52] The latter text blends Isaiah 11:4 and Numbers 24:17 with words from the blessing of Judah in Genesis 49:9. The *Targum Onqelos*, which we noted above as originating in Palestine in the late first or early second century, makes an explicit identification of Numbers 24:17 with the Messiah when it translates, "[A] king shall arise out of Jacob and be anointed the Messiah out of Israel."[53]

In the early second century AD, Bar Kozeva, the leader of the Jewish revolt against Rome, changed his name to Bar Kokhba, "Son of the Star," surely intending a connection with the prophecy in Numbers 24:17. The Palestinian Talmud relates that the early second-century Rabbi Akiba identified Bar Kokhba with the star of Numbers 24:17 and that when he saw Bar Kokhba he cried out, "That is the King, the Messiah" (*y. Ta'anith* 4:5).[54] The midrash on Lamentations reports, however, that Akiba was rebuked by Rabbi Johanan ben Tortha for identifying the Messiah with Bar Kokhba. Rabbi ben Tortha replied, "Akiba, grass will grow in your cheeks and he will still not have come."[55] The messianic usage of Numbers 24:17 is not found, however, in the Babylonian Talmud. This may have been the result of the association of the prophecy with Bar Kokhba, whose revolt against Rome had catastrophic results for the Jews.[56]

A portion of Jewish commentary on Isaiah 11:1–6 found at Qumran, while fragmentary, clearly suggests that the Qumran community understood Isaiah 11:1 to speak of the coming Messiah.[57] The fragments of *The Book of Blessings* found at Qumran also contain a messianic interpretation of the early verses of Isaiah 11 (1Q28b 5.21ff.). The *Targum Jonathan* makes explicit in its translation the understanding that the shoot from Jesse's roots is the Messiah.[58]

The church fathers often bring Numbers 24:17 and Isaiah 11:1 into close connection with Genesis 49:10. Justin blends Numbers 24:17 with Isaiah 11:1 and 11:10 and attributes the whole to Isaiah: "a star will arise from Jacob, and a blossom will come up from the root of Jesse, and the Gentiles will put their hope in his arm" (*1 Apology* 32.12).[59] This cita-

---

52. *La Bible d'Alexandrie LXX 4: Les Nombres*, trans., intro., and notes by Gilles Dorival (Paris: Les Éditions du Cerf, 1994), 451–53. The same texts are cited by Skarsaune, *Proof from Prophecy*, 265.

53. Levey, *Targum*, 21.

54. As quoted in Strack and Billerbeck, *Kommentar*, 1:76.

55. Cohen, *Lamentations*, vol. 7 of *Midrash Rabbah*, 157.

56. Skarsaune, *Proof from Prophecy*, 265.

57. Maurya P. Horgan, "Isaiah Pesher 4 (4Q161 = 4QpIsaᵃ)," in Charlesworth et al., *Dead Sea Scrolls*, vol. 6B, 95–97; cf. 4Q285 fr. 5.

58. Levey, *Targum*, 49.

59. Skarsaune, *Proof from Prophecy*, 143, thinks the third clause comes from Isa. 51:5. Harris (*Testimonies*, 1:8) considers erroneous ascriptions of authorship to be an indica-

tion follows immediately on Justin's interpretation of Genesis 49:10–11, which he used to establish the cessation of Jewish rule at the time of the appearance of Jesus.

Hippolytus sees a reference to the virgin birth in a combination of Isaiah 11 and Genesis 49. He thinks the statement in Genesis 49:9 that Judah will "go up from a shoot as the Septuagint reads," suggests that the one who descended from Judah and David according to the flesh was conceived by the Holy Spirit and came forth as "a holy shoot from the earth." He then quotes Isaiah 11:1 and says, "what Isaiah called a blossom Jacob called a shoot" (*Christ and the Antichrist* 1.7–8).

Irenaeus also treats Isaiah 11:1 as a testimony to the virgin birth of Christ, connecting Mary, rather than Joseph, with the lineage of Jesse. He follows Hippolytus in believing that Genesis 49 both identifies the time of Christ's appearing and suggests his virgin birth. Numbers 24 shows that Christ descended from the race of Jacob and that he came down from heaven. The star of Numbers 24:17 is linked with the star of Matthew 2, which guided the magi to Jesus (*Proof of the Apostolic Preaching* 57–59). Tertullian also sees the connection between Jesus and David to be through Mary rather than Joseph. He asserts that Isaiah 11:1 shows that the virgin from whom Christ was to be born must descend from David's seed (*Answer to the Jews* 9.26; cf. *Resurrection of the Flesh* 21.5). In the fourth century, Hilary blends Genesis 49:9 with Isaiah 11:1 and also identifies Mary with the tribe of Judah, saying that she "was the mother of our Lord according to the flesh."[60]

The fathers usually applied the "rod" in Isaiah 11:1 to Christ himself, however. Origen uses the verse to prove that the gifts promised in Isaiah 11:2–3 cannot be applied to just anyone but are specifically to rest on the "rod which proceeds from the root of Jesse" (*HomNum* 6.3). Eusebius says that even the Jews agree that Isaiah 11:1 can refer to none other than the Christ (*ComIs* 1.62–65).

In the mid-third century AD, Cyprian, who was bishop of Carthage, used Isaiah 11:1, 2 Samuel 7:12–16, and Psalm 132:11 to prove the Davidic ancestry of Christ (*Testimonies against the Jews* 2.11), and Isaiah 11:1 and Numbers 24:17 to prove that his nature was composed of both humanity and deity. The "star" of Numbers 24:17, it was thought, pointed to the divine nature. The proof of humanity in the prophecy depended on the reading of the Septuagint; where the Septuagint says "a *man* will arise from Israel," the Hebrew text states "a scepter will arise" (my

---

tion that such texts were drawn from a Testimony book rather than directly from the Old Testament itself.

60. *Tractates on the Psalms* 131.8, in *S. Hilarii Episcopi Pictaviensis Tractatus super Psalmos*, Corpus Scriptorum Ecclesiasticorum Latinorum 22, ed. A. Zingerle (Leipzig: G. Freytag, 1891), 668.

italics; *Testimonies against the Jews* 2.11, 10). Origen applies the same two parts of the prophecy to the two natures of Christ in his *Homilies on Numbers* (18.4; cf. *Against Celsus* 1.59–60), which appeared around the same time as Cyprian's treatise. In the fourth century, Eusebius continues this interpretation of the "star" and the "man" (*Proof of the Gospel* 9.1). Ambrose identifies the star seen by the magi with the star of Numbers 24:17 and says that they "recognized that this was the star which makes known the man and God" (*ComLk* 2.48).

ISAIAH 7:14 AND THE VIRGIN BIRTH OF CHRIST

The virgin birth of Christ and his death on the cross were the two things the Jews found most offensive in the Christian message.[61] Justin devotes a lengthy section of his *Dialogue with Trypho the Jew* to each of these questions. He introduces the discussion of the virgin birth by noting the two points on which the Jews disagreed with the Christians on the interpretation of Isaiah 7:14. First, he says, the Jews argue that Isaiah 7:14 does not say "the *virgin* will conceive, but the *young woman* will conceive and bear a son." Second, he says, the Jews understand the prophecy to refer to Hezekiah, who was king in the time of Isaiah (*Dialogue* 43.7). The first argument involves the language of the text and the second its referent.

The Hebrew text of Isaiah 7:14 uses the word *almah* of the woman who will conceive. The Septuagint translated this Hebrew word with the Greek word that means virgin. The later translations of the Hebrew Old Testament into Greek by the Jews Aquila, Symmachus, and Theodotion all translated the Hebrew word *almah* with the Greek word that means young woman.[62] The Jews of Justin's time and later insisted that this was the proper understanding of Isaiah 7:14 and that the verse said nothing about a birth from a virgin. Later church fathers develop arguments, which we will consider below, against this Jewish interpretation based on the use of language. Justin argues against the Jewish interpretation but does not employ any significant arguments involving the language itself.

The application of Isaiah 7:14 to Hezekiah is widely attested in Jewish literature. Some thought Hezekiah had been the Messiah and that the messianic times were past, while others thought he would return as the Messiah. In the fourth century, Rabbi Hillel said, "There is no

---

61. Ungern-Sternberg, *Schriftbeweis*, 23.

62. Symmachus was a Jewish Christian who belonged to a group known as the Ebionites. The Ebionites did not consider Christ divine by birth, but a normal man who was given divine power at his baptism. See Hans-Joachim Schoeps, *Jewish Christianity*, trans. D. R. A. Hare (Philadelphia: Fortress, 1969), 61–62.

more Messiah for Israel, for they have already enjoyed him in the days of Hezekiah."[63] In contrast, the important late-first-century AD Rabbi of Jamnia, Johanan ben Zakkai, believed that Hezekiah was about to come and rule over Judah.[64]

Justin advances two arguments against Trypho's insistence that the text of Isaiah 7:14 does not refer to a virgin but only to a young woman. His first argument stresses that the term "virgin" was the word chosen by the authoritative Jewish translators of the Old Testament who produced the Septuagint in the pre-Christian period when Ptolemy was king of Egypt. When Trypho and the Jewish teachers say that Isaiah 7:14 does not refer to a virgin conceiving, they are asserting that the conclusion of their own seventy Jewish elders who produced the Septuagint was wrong (*Dialogue* 68.8; 84.3; 71.1). The point of this aspect of Justin's argument is to emphasize that the term "virgin" stands in that Jewish translation of the Hebrew Scriptures that might be referred to in our terminology as "the authorized version of the Bible."

Justin's other argument that Isaiah 7:14 must refer to a virgin and not to a young woman lies in the logic of the birth being a sign. How, he asks, could the conception and birth of a child be a sign if the conception were the result of natural sexual reproduction? All women who give birth conceive in this way (*Dialogue* 84; cf. Tertullian, *Against Marcion* 3.13.4–5). He then suggests that a virgin birth should not be thought impossible, for God had caused the barren mothers of Samuel, Isaac, and John the Baptist to give birth.

Justin's argument against Isaiah 7:14 referring to Hezekiah depends on Isaiah 8:4, which in the text that Justin claims to be quoting from the Septuagint stands between Isaiah 7:16a and 7:16b. Justin quotes the text as follows, beginning at Isaiah 7:14:

> Behold the virgin will conceive and bear a son, and they will call his name Emmanuel. He will eat butter and honey. Before he either knows or prefers evil he will choose the good. For before the child knows evil or good he rejects evil to choose the good. *For before the child knows how to say father or mother he will receive the power of Damascus and the spoils of Samaria before the king of Assyria.* And the land will be deserted. (*Dialogue* 66.2–3; the italicized words are Isa. 8:4)

Justin quoted this passage with the same addition of Isaiah 8:4 earlier when he first introduced the issue of Isaiah 7:14 and the virgin birth (*Dialogue* 43.5–6). He never indicates that the text he quotes does not stand in the Septuagint exactly as he quotes it. It may be that Justin

---

63. *B. Sanhedrin* 99a, cited in Strack and Billerbeck, *Kommentar*, 1:31.
64. *B. Berakhot* 28b, quoted in Klausner, *Messianic Idea*, 396.

knew the quoted words from a testimony book and that Isaiah 8:4 had been added to the text by a Christian.[65]

Justin argues from the above text that Trypho cannot prove that Hezekiah or any other Jew ever waged war against Damascus and Samaria in the presence of the king of Assyria and overcame them while he was still a child too young to call out "father" or "mother." But, he asserts, this can be said of Christ. Magi came from Arabia to worship him when he was born, and this took place in the time of Herod. Scripture here refers to Herod as the king of Assyria, Justin claims, because of his wicked character. The power of Damascus and the spoils of Samaria refer to the power of the evil demon who lived there. That the magi from Arabia came to worship Christ at his birth shows that Christ overcame the demonic power when he was born. The magi, who had previously been under the power of the demon, were set free from its control and demonstrated this by their pilgrimage to Bethlehem to worship the Christ child. Trypho, however, did not think Justin's exposition any more convincing than we probably do (*Dialogue* 77–79).

Origen does not make the same argument that Justin does, but he is familiar with a similar understanding of the connection of the magi with the demonic powers and the affect that the birth of Christ had on them. His purpose is to explain why the magi of Matthew's Gospel followed the star to Bethlehem. Origen notes that magi in general depended on communion with demons for the power to perform their works. He proposes that at the birth of Jesus the divine power that visited the earth, both in the persons of the angelic host Luke reports and in the person of the infant Jesus himself, overthrew the power of the demons. The magi then found that their sorcery no longer worked. Seeking to discover why, they noticed the sign in the heavens. Origen thinks they probably knew Balaam's prophecies.[66] They must have surmised that the person connected with the star in Balaam's prophecy in Numbers 24:17 had arrived and that he was superior to the demonic powers. Therefore, they set out to find and worship him (*Against Celsus* 1.60). While Origen's account does not vindicate Justin's arguments, it does show that Justin is working within the framework of generally accepted assumptions of the contemporary worldview.

Eusebius attempts to set Justin's general argument on a historical basis. Emmanuel, he argues, can refer only to God, whom Abraham had seen earlier in human form. The name cannot be given to Hezekiah because he was not "God with us," and there was no indication of a divine nature in him. Furthermore, Hezekiah had already been born prior to the giving

---

65. Skarsaune, *Proof from Prophecy*, 32–34.
66. See the discussion of Num. 24:17 above.

of this prophecy, so Isaiah's reference to a future birth could not refer to Hezekiah's birth.[67] Eusebius then turns to the histories of Damascus and Judah and argues that Emmanuel should be born at the time when these two kingdoms were deprived of their kings. Both countries continued to have kings, he argues, until the appearance of Jesus. He bases his argument concerning Damascus on Paul's reference to Aretas, king of Damascus (2 Cor. 11:32), and says that the Jews also continued to have kings, though "irregular" and not of David's line, through Herod and his successors in the time of Jesus. But after the appearance of Jesus, Roman rule removed all local authorities from all states. This marked the literal fulfillment of Isaiah's prophecy (*Proof of the Gospel* 7.1).

It has been pointed out that the fathers of the fourth and fifth centuries use a new argument based on the language of Isaiah 7:14. They argue that the Greek word meaning young woman, which the other translations of the Hebrew Scriptures into Greek used to render the Hebrew word *almah* in Isaiah 7:14, can mean the same as the word "virgin," which the translators of the Septuagint had used. Consequently, the use of the word "young woman" to translate Isaiah 7:14 does not mean that the young woman is not a virgin. The fathers based this argument on Deuteronomy 22:23–29, which discusses the rape of betrothed and unbetrothed virgins. There, they argue, the words "young woman" and "virgin" are used interchangeably. The fathers then apply this evidence to Isaiah 7:14 to show that the use of "young woman" does not cancel the understanding that the sign involved a virgin birth. This argument is based on the Greek translations of the Hebrew Scriptures and takes no account of the Hebrew text.[68]

Jerome, who knew Hebrew better than any other church father, advances the argument concerning the language of Isaiah 7:14 on the basis of the Hebrew text. He agrees with the Jews that the Hebrew word *almah* is not the normal word used of a virgin but, he insists, it is also not the normal word used of a young woman as they wish to understand it.[69] He uses an etymological approach to argue that while the Hebrew word *almah* does not explicitly mean virgin, it does mean a young woman who is protected from the public eye by her family so that by necessity

---

67. Cyril of Jerusalem, *Catechetical Lectures* 12.22, offers the same argument against the prophecy referring to Hezekiah.

68. Adam Kamesar, "The Virgin of Isaiah 7:14. The Philological Argument from the Second to the Fifth Century," *JTS* (1990): 52–57. Kamesar notes that Origen seems to have known this same argument in the third century. He was one of the few church fathers who had some knowledge of the Hebrew language. Origen transfers the argument to the Hebrew text and asserts that the Hebrew word *almah*, which appears in Isa. 7:14, is used of a virgin in Deut. 22:23–26 (*Against Celsus* 1.34). This is not, however, the case. The Hebrew word for virgin in these verses is the word *bethula* (Kamesar, "Virgin," 58–60).

69. Kamesar, "Virgin," 62–63.

the term implies that the young woman is a virgin. He also asserts that *almah* is never used in Scripture of any woman other than a virgin, and he challenges the Jews to show him one place in the Hebrew Scriptures where the word is used of "a young woman already married" (*Quaestiones hebraicae in Genesim* 24.43).[70]

MICAH 5:2 AND THE TOWN OF CHRIST'S BIRTH

Micah 5:2 (5:1 LXX) is a verse used in common by Justin, Irenaeus, and Tertullian in their proof from prophecy arguments.[71] It was an important Christian messianic proof text as early as the New Testament evangelist Matthew (2:5–6). The evangelist John (7:41–42) indicates that the Jews already understood it to indicate the birthplace of the Messiah, and later Jewish literature bears this out. In the *Targum Jonathan*, Micah 5:1 (5:2 NRSV) is translated, "And you, O Bethlehem Ephrath, you who were too small to be numbered among the thousands of the house of Judah, from you shall come forth before Me the Messiah, to exercise dominion over Israel, he whose name was mentioned before, from the days of creation."[72]

The Palestinian Talmud relates a story, repeated and expanded in the midrash on Lamentations, that claims that a son of Hezekiah named Menahem, or "the Comforter," was the Messiah. When the question of the place of his birth is posed, the response is that he is from "the royal village of Bethlehem in Judea" (*y. Berakhot* 5a).[73] This is a clear reference to Micah 5:2 and indicates that it was commonly understood in the Jewish community that the Messiah would come from Bethlehem.

The Micah prophecy was important to the church fathers because of its geographic specificity. Tertullian begins the argument he bases on Micah 5:2 by assuming the Jewish understanding of it. He states that the Christ had to be born in Bethlehem because of the prophecy in Micah. He then assumes the Jewish denial that Jesus of Nazareth was the expected Messiah and asks what the fulfillment of this prophecy might be, then, since Bethlehem had been bereft of Jewish people since the Roman edict forbidding Jews to live in the district.[74] How can the

70. *Saint Jerome's Hebrew Questions on Genesis*, trans. with intro. and commentary by C. T. R. Hayward, OECS (Oxford: Clarendon, 1995), 58.

71. Ungern-Sternberg, *Schriftbeweis*, 142. See Justin, *1 Apology* 34.1, *Dialogue with Trypho* 78; Irenaeus, *Proof of the Apostolic Preaching* 63; Irenaeus, *Against Heresies* 4.33.11; Tertullian, *Answer to the Jews* 13.2.

72. Levey, *Targum*, 93.

73. Brierre-Narbonne, *Exégèse Talmudique I*, 41; Cohen, *Lamentations*, vol. 7 of *Midrash Rabbah*, 137.

74. Tertullian is here referring to the Roman edict that prohibited Jews from living in the entire neighborhood of Jerusalem after the Jewish rebellion led by Bar Kochba, which was put down in AD 135.

Christ come from Bethlehem now, Tertullian asks, when there is no one of the house of Israel there from whose stock he could be born? This, he argues, is a proof that the Christ promised in Micah 5:2 has already come in Jesus of Nazareth (*Answer to the Jews* 13.1–8).

Origen uses the Micah passage to refute Celsus's assertion that the Old Testament prophecies used by Christians could fit any number of people who wander about living off others and claiming to have descended to earth from God. Micah 5:2, Origen insists, would not fit just any claimant of divinity, for the person mentioned in this prophecy must have been born in Bethlehem. To strengthen the Christian claim that Jesus fulfilled this prophecy, Origen calls attention to what appears to have already become a sort of tourist attraction at Bethlehem. He says that in Bethlehem there is a cave containing a manger that is pointed out as the place where Jesus was born, adding that this site was famous in the locality even among non-Christians (*Against Celsus* 1.50–51).

Eusebius, in the fourth century, also stresses the specificity of the Micah passage and argues that only two famous men had been born in Bethlehem, David and Jesus. David, however, lived and died before this prophecy had been uttered. Furthermore, the latter part of the prophecy could not refer to David for it speaks of the person born in Bethlehem being from eternity. Micah 5:2, therefore, can refer only to Jesus. Like Origen, Eusebius also notes that the local inhabitants of Bethlehem "to this day" show visitors the cave where the virgin lay her infant (*Proof of the Gospel* 7.2.2). In another passage in the same work, Eusebius says that in his day Bethlehem was so famous for being the place of Jesus's birth that people came from the ends of the earth to see it (*Proof of the Gospel* 1.1.2).

The Healing Ministry of Christ

Jesus's ministry of healing the sick and raising the dead appears to be considered an important messianic indicator by the earliest Christians. Two passages from Isaiah (35:5–6 and 61:1–2), which sometimes were not carefully distinguished, were seen as prophetic proof texts pointing to this messianic ministry. Luke uses Isaiah 61:1–2 to introduce Jesus's ministry (Luke 4:18–21) and, again, to answer the question of John the Baptist concerning Jesus's messiahship (Luke 7:22; cf. Matt. 11:5). Mark appears to have Isaiah 35:5–6 in mind when he records the multitude's response to Jesus causing a deaf mute to hear and speak (7:37). Isaiah 35:6 also appears to lie behind Luke's narrative in Acts 3:8, in which the lame man healed by Peter enters the temple "walking and *leaping*" (italics mine). In the fourth century, Cyril of Jerusalem also viewed Peter's healing of the lame man as a fulfillment of Isaiah 35:6 (*Catechetical Lectures* 17.21). Luke also suggests that an argument for understanding Jesus as the Messiah based on these prophecies of healing was part of the earliest Christian preaching. In Acts 2:22, he records Peter referring to Jesus's "mighty works, wonders, and signs" in his address at Pentecost, and in Acts 10:38, he records Peter's conversation with Cornelius in which Peter again refers to Jesus's ministry of healing.

While there was a Jewish belief in a general resurrection of Israelites in the time of the Messiah (*2 Bar.* 30:1–5), ancient Jewish literature does not suggest the anticipation of a Messiah who would heal the infirm and raise the dead. The time of the Messiah was identified with the age to come. The Mishnah relates that the sages said the phrase "all the days of thy life" includes "the Days of the Messiah" and does not refer to "this world only" (*m. Berakhot* 1:5).[75] Rabbi Phineas ben Jair, of the last half of the second century AD, also appears to locate the resurrection in the messianic era. The resurrection, he says, "shall come through Elijah of blessed memory" (*m. Sotah* 9:15).[76]

There is, however, a fragment found at Qumran (4Q521) that describes the Messiah as one "who liberates the captives, restores sight to the blind," and "straightens the b[ent]." He is further praised as one who "will heal the wounded, and revive the dead and bring good news to the poor."[77] The last statement clearly echoes Isaiah 61:1, which, as we noted above, was an important messianic text for the earliest Christians, and may allude also to Isaiah 26:19.[78] The previous statement about the Messiah appears to be drawn from Psalm 146:7–8.

It was Isaiah 35:3–6—which speaks of God coming to save with the consequent actions of healing the blind, the deaf, the lame, and the dumb—to which the church fathers turned especially in their search for Christ in the prophets. Isaiah 35:3–6 heads the list of a number of prophetic passages that Cyprian cites in his *Book of Testimonies* to show that the promised Savior of humanity had come (*Testimonies against the Jews* 2.7). Irenaeus joins Isaiah 35:3–6 with Isaiah 53:4, 29:18, and 26:19 to show that Christ's healings and raising of the dead substantiate that he is the Son of God (*Proof of the Apostolic Preaching* 67). He brings the same constellation of passages together again, but without Isaiah 29:18,

75. *The Mishnah*, trans. Herbert Danby (London: Oxford University Press, 1958), 3.
76. Ibid., 307.
77. Geza Vermes, *The Complete Dead Sea Scrolls in English* (New York: Penguin, 1997), 391–92.
78. Suggested by Craig A. Evans, "Qumran's Messiah: How Important Is He?" in *Religion in the Dead Sea Scrolls*, ed. John J. Collins and Robert A. Kugler (Grand Rapids: Eerdmans, 2000), 139.

as passages that proclaim the works of healing done by Christ (*Against Heresies* 4.33.11).

Justin cites Isaiah 35:5–6 as proof that it had been prophesied that Christ would "heal all diseases and raise the dead" (*1 Apology* 48.1–2). He also suggests that the pagan mythmakers read the Old Testament prophecies about the coming Christ and invented the various mythological gods to correspond to the things they learned there, specifically about who Christ was or what Christ was to do. They created the healing god Asclepius after they read the prophecy in Isaiah 35 that the Christ would "heal every disease and raise the dead" (*1 Apology* 54.10; cf. 22.6–23.3). Justin incorporates the Asclepius argument into his *Dialogue with Trypho the Jew* but gives it a new twist. He quotes the entirety of Isaiah 35:1–7 and refers to it as "one" Scripture that prophesies that Christ would raise the dead and heal all diseases. He understands the "thirsty wilderness" of Isaiah 35:1 to be the Gentiles, who had been destitute of knowledge of God but had now received it through Christ.[79] This Christ, Justin says, appeared among the Jews, where he performed the healings and restorations to life referred to in the Isaiah passage. The response of the Jews to his mighty works, however, was to label him a magician and a deceiver. Nevertheless, there were some among the Jews who believed because of his works. And now, Justin continues, anyone with a physical infirmity who holds to the teachings given by Christ will be raised with a sound body at the second advent (*Dialogue* 69.3–7).

Tertullian considers the Rule of Faith to be the touchstone for testing all interpretation of Scripture. In the Rule of Faith, the ministry of Christ is summed up in two activities: preaching the new law and performing mighty works (*Prescription against Heretics* 13.4). Tertullian alludes to these two points of the Rule in his treatise *Against the Jews* and turns to the prophecy of Isaiah to confirm that it had been predicted that the Christ would perform each of these activities. Isaiah 58:1–2 confirms the Christ's preaching ministry and Isaiah 35:4–6 shows that he was to do miraculous works. Tertullian adds that the Jews cannot deny that Christ performed miraculous works, for they attacked him not for the works but for doing them on the Sabbath (*Answer to the Jews* 9.29–31; cf. Jn. 5:1–18). In his treatise *On the Resurrection of the Flesh*, Tertullian argues that Isaiah 35:5–6 speaks of Christ in direct, nonfigurative language. "Were not the eyes of the blind opened?" he asks. "Did not the tongues of the speechless speak distinctly? Did not shriveled hands and weak knees regain their strength? Did not the lame leap like the hart?" (*Resurrection of the Flesh* 20.6).

---

79. Eusebius also identifies this wilderness with the church of the Gentiles (*Proof of the Gospel* 6.21).

Origen gave Isaiah 35:5–6 both a literal and a figurative meaning. The philosopher Celsus attacks Christians, saying that they considered Jesus to be Son of God because he healed the lame and the blind. Origen replies that this is true and that this belief is grounded in the prophecy of Isaiah 35:5–6. In other words, it is the prophecy that interprets the meaning of the miracles and shows Jesus to be the Son of God because he performs them. Origen concludes his argument by asserting that Jesus's disciples have outdone even his physical miracles by healing those blind and deaf in their souls and lame in the inner person so that they now see and hear about God and tread on the powers of evil in their new walk (*Against Celsus* 2.48).[80]

In the mid-third century AD, Novatian of Rome employs Isaiah 35:3–6 to prove the deity of Jesus Christ. Isaiah 35:4 speaks of God himself coming to save. This is followed immediately by a list of healings that will take place at that time. Novatian argues that since these healing miracles are to be the sign of God's coming, and since such healings were performed by Christ, one must either acknowledge that he is the Son of God or, in agreement with the heretical group known as the Monarchians, who denied any distinction between God the Father and the Son, say that Jesus Christ is God the Father himself. One or the other of these conclusions is necessary, Novatian asserts, because the signs Christ performed fulfill the prophecy of Isaiah 35:3–6, which announces the advent of deity (*On the Trinity* 12).

In the fourth century, Eusebius of Caesarea also uses Isaiah 35:3–6 to argue for the deity of Christ. He understands the passage to state that these healing activities were the work of God and, because Christ performed them, it shows that he is divine (*Proof of the Gospel* 9.13). Athanasius quotes Isaiah 35:3–6 and takes it to mean that God will come when these signs of his advent appear. There is no time in Israel's history, he argues, when these signs were manifest "except when the Word of God himself came in the body" (*On the Incarnation* 38).[81]

The Suffering and Death of Christ

The apostle Paul declared that the Christian message of Christ crucified was "a stumbling block to Jews" (1 Cor. 1:23 NRSV). Justin's dialogue partner Trypho tells him that all Jews expect the Messiah but they do not think that expectation was fulfilled in Jesus of Nazareth because they cannot believe that "the Christ should be so dishonorably crucified, for the

---

80. Origen makes a similar double application of Isa. 35:5–6 in his discussion of Jesus's healings recorded in Matt. 15:29–31 (*ComMt* 11.18).

81. Athanasius, *"Contra Gentes" and "De Incarnatione,"* ed. and trans. R. W. Thomson, Oxford Early Christian Texts (Oxford: Clarendon, 1971), 229.

law says that one who has been crucified is accursed" (*Dialogue* 89.1–2; Deut. 21:23). A graffito discovered in 1856 in the servants' quarters of the Imperial Palace on the Palatine hill in Rome depicts someone named Alexamenos gesturing with his right hand toward a cross on which a man with a donkey's head is crucified. The graffito reads, "Alexamenos, worship God." It is an ancient graffito, but a fixed date cannot be given for it. It shows, nevertheless, the derogatory nature of the mocking heaped on the Christian message of the crucified one.

PSALM 22 AND ISAIAH 53

Because the crucifixion was so central to early Christian preaching it was absolutely essential that the early church be able to show that it was part of the divine plan. Justin's response to Trypho's objection, that a crucified man could not be the Messiah, makes this clear:

> The statement in the law that everyone hanged on a tree is accursed accentuates our hope which depends on the crucified Christ. This hope does not rest in the fact that the crucified one has been accursed by God, but in the fact that God announced in advance the things which you and all those like you were to do because you did not understand that he is the one who exists before all things, even the eternal priest of God, the king, and Christ. (*Dialogue* 96.1)

The early Christians turned especially to Isaiah 53 and Psalm 22 to support what Justin asserts. After quoting a large portion of Isaiah 53 in connection with the passion of the Messiah, Irenaeus comments that clearly it was the Father's will that these things should happen to the Christ (*Proof of the Apostolic Preaching* 68–69).

There is a long and unsettled debate among scholars whether pre-Christian Judaism ever entertained the idea of a Messiah who would suffer. There are a few references to the Messiah suffering in one way or another in later rabbinic Judaism but none, it appears, to him dying so shameful a death as crucifixion.[82] The late *Targum Jonathan*, for example, understands the servant referred to in Isaiah 52:13 to be the Messiah. The translation of Isaiah 53, however, reworks the text in such a way that the resulting picture is not that of a suffering servant but a triumphant Messiah who overpowers the enemies of Israel.[83]

In *Against Celsus*, which was Origen's last written work, Origen says that he remembers having a discussion once with some rabbis in which he appealed to the prophecy of Isaiah 53. The rabbinic response to his

82. Schürer, *History*, rev., 2:547–48.
83. Levey, *Targum*, 63–67.

argument, he says, was to assert that Isaiah 53 speaks of the Jewish people as a whole and refers to their suffering in the dispersion (*Against Celsus* 1.55). The much later *Midrash Rabbah* on Numbers continues this Jewish understanding when it applies Isaiah 53:12 to the people of Israel, whose souls, it says, were "exposed . . . to death in exile."[84] Origen claims that the most effective argument he advanced against this Jewish view in his discussion with the rabbis was based on the statement in Isaiah 53:8: "He was led to death because of the lawless deeds of my people." "For if, as they took it," Origen argued, "the prophecy had reference to the people, how were the people said to be led 'to death because of the lawless deeds of the people' of God if these same people were the people of God?" (*Against Celsus* 1.55).

It also appears that Psalm 22 was never associated with the Messiah in Jewish tradition. Justin says to the Jews he was addressing concerning Psalm 22, "You say that this Psalm does not refer to the Christ. You are blind in all respects and do not understand that no one of your race called 'king' or 'Christ' was ever pierced in feet or hands while alive and died in this mysterious way, that is by crucifixion, except this Jesus" (*Dialogue* 97.4). In the fourth century, Theodoret of Cyrus says that the Jews refer Psalm 22 to David.[85] The fourth-century Syrian father Aphraat indicates that some Jews also referred Psalm 22 to Saul (*Demonstrations* 17.10).

Isaiah 53 was a crucial passage for the early-Christian understanding of the passion of Christ, probably going back to traditions associated with Jesus himself in the Gospels. It is most likely that Isaiah 53 should be understood as a major part of the teaching Jesus is said to have given the disciples about his passion. Each of the synoptic Gospels relates that immediately after Peter's confession identifying Jesus as the Messiah, Jesus began to teach the disciples that he must suffer and be killed (Matt. 16:21; Mark 8:31; Luke 9:22). In the final chapter of his Gospel, Luke narrates two occasions on which the risen Jesus instructed his disciples about the prophetic texts that predicted the messianic sufferings. The first occasion refers to the instruction being from "Moses and the prophets," and the second adds "the psalms" to the list of texts (Luke 24:25–27, 44–46). Luke further shows that Isaiah 53 was a central text for the earliest Christians' understanding of what happened to Jesus when he relates that Philip "preached Jesus" to the Ethiopian treasurer from the text of Isaiah 53:7–8 (Acts 8:32–35).

Psalm 22 was so much a part of the earliest Christian understanding of the passion that statements, phrases, and terminology drawn from the psalm are woven into the texture of the story of the crucifixion related

---

84. Slotki, *Numbers*, vol. 6 of *Midrash Rabbah*, 501.
85. On Ps. 22:30–31, in Hill, *Theodoret of Cyrus: Commentary on the Psalms*, 154.

by the Synoptic Gospels without any explicit indication that Scripture is being cited. The division of Jesus's garments and the casting of lots for them, for example, are related in the words of Psalm 22:18, but no indication is given that the words come from Scripture (Matt. 27:35; Mark 15:24; Luke 23:34).[86] The same is true of the use of Psalm 22:7–8 to relate the actions and words of the bystanders at the cross (Matt. 27:39, 43; Mark 15:29; Luke 23:35), and of Jesus's cry of dereliction, which quotes Psalm 22:1 (Matt. 27:46; Mark 15:34).

Justin assumed that the Christian understanding of the prophetic texts that related to Christ's passion was derived from Christ himself. He asserts that Christ "revealed to us everything which we, through his grace, have discerned from the Scriptures" (*Dialogue* 100.2). In this statement, which appears in his application of Psalm 22 to Christ, Justin is not claiming a supernatural intervention that gives himself and others special powers of discernment. He is claiming that Christ taught the apostles how to understand the Old Testament texts that prove his messiahship and that the apostles passed this understanding on to the Christian community.[87] In another context, Justin clearly associates Isaiah 53 with the teaching about messianic sufferings that Luke 24 says Christ gave his disciples after the resurrection (*1 Apology* 50). Even earlier than Justin, Clement of Rome, who wrote in the last decade of the first century AD, understands both Isaiah 53 and Psalm 22 to be written about Christ. He cites both to demonstrate the humility in which Christ visited the earth (*1 Clement* 16).

Marcion, a heretical Christian but a Christian nonetheless, had argued that Jesus of Nazareth could not have been the expected Messiah because the Jews had rejected and killed him. Tertullian replies that this happened because two advents of the Christ are prophesied. The first, which was to take place in humility, was prophesied figuratively in parables. Because of this, Tertullian argues, the Jews failed to recognize Jesus as the Messiah. The second advent, which is to be in power and majesty, was clearly prophesied in passages such as Daniel 7:13–14 and Psalm 45:2–9. These were the prophecies, he asserts, on which the Jews had based their messianic expectations. Tertullian's description of the first advent of the Messiah is saturated with the language of Isaiah 53. He also draws on a few other Old Testament texts, including Psalm 22:6 (*Against Marcion* 3.6.9–7.2). Justin, using the same language of parable,[88]

---

86. John 19:24, in contrast, states that the soldiers cast lots for Jesus's tunic, and then it quotes Ps. 22:18 as the "Scripture" that this action fulfilled.

87. Skarsaune, *Proof from Prophecy*, 12.

88. Tertullian may have borrowed this concept from Justin, as he may have borrowed the whole idea of the two advents of the Messiah, for Justin uses this argument against Trypho much as Tertullian uses it against Marcion.

asserts that Psalm 22 is a "mysterious parable" of the passion and the cross of Christ (*Dialogue* 97.3). He then quotes nearly the entire psalm and provides a lengthy christological commentary on it showing how it was fulfilled in the sufferings of Christ (*Dialogue* 98–106). Eusebius, likewise, shows how Psalm 22 was written about Christ by providing a commentary on the whole of the psalm. He begins by noting Jesus quoted the first verse of this psalm on the cross (Matt. 27:46) and argues that this shows that "the Psalm refers to Him and no one else" (*Proof of the Gospel* 10.8).[89]

Lactantius, writing in the early fourth century, shows that the crucifixion of Jesus was still a scandal in his lifetime. He asserts that Christians are often reproached for the passion and charged with worshiping a man who experienced a terrible punishment. Lactantius responds to this reproach by appealing to the prophecies of the Old Testament to show that the passion was part of the "divine plan." Like Tertullian and Justin, Lactantius claims that the Jews had based their messianic expectations on those prophecies that spoke of the Messiah coming in power and glory. They were ignorant, he says, of the fact that two advents of the Messiah are actually proclaimed by the prophets and that the first was to occur in humility. Isaiah 53:1–6 is quoted as the primary testimony for the advent of the Messiah in humility (*Divine Institutes* 4.16).

ISAIAH 53 AND THE REDEMPTIVE WORK OF CHRIST

In addition to functioning as proof that the sufferings of the Christ were part of the divine plan, Isaiah 53 also serves to substantiate the redemptive significance of Christ's death on the cross. *The Epistle of Barnabas*, written probably in the first third of the second century, uses Isaiah 53:5 and 7 as proof that the Lord "delivered his flesh to corruption" to sanctify us by the forgiveness of sins (5.1–2). In *Dialogue* 13 Justin states that the death of Christ occurred to effect the removal of sins through faith in his blood. He then quotes Isaiah 52:10–54:6 as proof of this assertion. He also understands Isaiah 53:7 to link Jesus with the paschal lamb. In a statement that recalls Paul's words in 1 Corinthians 5:7, Justin says, "The paschal lamb was Christ, who was later sacrificed, even as Isaiah said, 'He was led like a sheep to the slaughter.'" Justin then compares the delivery from death that the blood of Christ offers to those who believe with the deliverance of the Israelites in Egypt provided by the blood of the paschal lamb (*Dialogue* 111.3). Melito of Sardis, in

---

89. *The Proof of the Gospel: Eusebius*, vol. 1, ed. and trans. W. J. Ferrar (Grand Rapids: Baker Academic, 1981), 216. Unless otherwise noted, subsequent references appear in the text and are to this translation.

his paschal homily delivered near the end of the second century, reads the story of the Passover lamb and the crucifixion of Jesus as type and reality via Isaiah 53:7. He begins with the story of the Passover, "how the sheep was sacrificed, and how the people was saved." Isaiah's simile about a person who suffers like a sheep being slaughtered then enters Melito's account and guides the Passover story to the story of Jesus, who, "though led to the slaughter like a sheep, . . . was no sheep," and "though speechless as a lamb," was not "a lamb."

> For instead of the lamb there was a son,
> and instead of the sheep a man. . . .
> For he was born a son,
> and led as a lamb,
> and slaughtered as a sheep,
> and buried as a man,
> and rose from the dead as God. (*On Pascha* 1–8)[90]

Eusebius refers to the Jewish sacrificial system, in which animals were offered as the ransom for individual lives, as the imperfect precursor to the sacrifice that Christ offered when he was "sacrificed like a sheep for the whole human race" (*Proof of the Gospel* 1.10). Isaiah 53:7 is then cited, followed by verses 4–9, as prophetic proof for the sacrificial nature of Christ's death. It is Origen, however, who makes the most forceful statement about Christ's sacrificial death for humanity on the basis of Isaiah 53. He notes that there were numerous stories circulating among the Greeks about heroes who ended plagues or famines by offering themselves as sacrifices to the offended deities. But it has never been related, he says, that someone took up the burden of purifying the whole universe. "Jesus alone has been able to take up into himself on the cross the burden of the sin of all on behalf of the whole universe." Origen then makes his way through numerous verses from Isaiah 53, but verse 7 is central: "The Father delivered this Jesus for our sins, and because of them, 'he was led as a sheep to slaughter, and was dumb, as a lamb before its shearer'" (*ComJn* 28.160–170).[91] Athanasius adds, on the same note, that by Jesus's "death salvation was effected for all and all creation was saved." The basis for the assertion is an echo of Isaiah 53:7. Jesus, "like a sheep[,] delivered his own body to death as a ransom for the salvation of all" (*On the Incarnation* 37).[92]

90. *Melito of Sardis: On Pascha*, trans. Alistair Stewart-Sykes (Crestwood, NY: St. Vladimir's Seminary Press, 2001), 37–39.

91. *Origen: Commentary on the Gospel according to John, Books 13–32*, trans. Ronald E. Heine, FC 89 (Washington, DC: Catholic University of America Press, 1993), 325–27.

92. Athanasius, *"Contra Gentes" and "De Incarnatione,"* trans. Thomson, 227.

The Resurrection and Glorification of Christ

The apostle Paul's statement to the Corinthians that his gospel contained the assertion that Christ had been raised on the third day in fulfillment of the Scriptures is our earliest reference to the application of Old Testament prophecies to the resurrection of Christ. Paul does not indicate, however, what those Scriptures were that he used to prove this (1 Cor. 15:1–4). Matthew appears to relate Jesus's citation of the "sign of Jonah" to his resurrection (Matt. 12:39–40). John suggests that there was Scripture that, as the disciples later learned, proved the necessity of the resurrection, but he does not specify any (20:9). It is Luke who gives the most detailed example of the earliest Christian appeal to prophecy in regard to the resurrection. At the conclusion of his Gospel he indicates that Christ included Old Testament prophecies about the resurrection in his postresurrection instructions to his disciples, but no specific prophecies are mentioned (Luke 24:46). Then, in his report of Peter's Pentecost sermon, Luke cites Psalm 16:8–11 as central to Peter's argument about the resurrection. The crucial verse is verse 10, which says that the Lord did not abandon "my soul to Hades" or let his "Holy One see corruption." Peter argues that David could not have been speaking of himself because his tomb was still in Jerusalem. But both statements can apply to Jesus, he continues, because "God raised him up" (Acts 2:25–32). Luke cites the same verse with the same general argument later in Acts in a sermon by Paul (13:35–37).[93] In this same context Luke also cites Psalm 2:7 and Isaiah 55:3 in relation to the resurrection (Acts 13:33–34).

PSALM 16

Of these prophetic texts cited in the New Testament concerning the resurrection, only Psalm 16 plays a role in the church fathers' discussions of the resurrection and glorification of Jesus, and its role is rather checkered. Psalm 16:10 does not appear as a prophecy of the resurrection in the Christian literature of the second century. Its only appearance in this literature is not a direct citation but as part of Irenaeus's quotation of Peter's address in Acts 2 (*Against Heresies* 3.12.2). Tertullian, in the early third century, makes a loose allusion to Psalm 16:10 but not in a context concerning the resurrection (*Against Marcion* 4.7.11). The verse appears once in Cyprian's writings as a text proving that the Christ would not be overcome by death (*Testimonies against the Jews* 2.24), and once in a treatise falsely attributed to Cyprian where it forms part of a prayer that Christ prays (*Against the Jews* 3).

---

93. In the early fourth century, Lactantius cites Ps. 16:10 as prophetic proof that the Christ was to rise on the third day (*Epitome of the Divine Institutes* 47).

Only Origen, it appears, makes rather extensive use of Psalm 16:10, in the third century. He cites it twice in his apology against Celsus as one of what he implies were numerous prophecies of the resurrection (*Against Celsus* 2.62; 3.32). The majority of his uses of the verse, however, are doctrinal rather than apologetic. In his *Dialogue with Heraclides* he uses the first clause of the verse as proof that Christ's soul was in Hades (*Heraclides* 7). He uses the same clause in a similar way in his *Commentary on John*, where he uses John the Baptist's reference to the "sandals" of Jesus to point to two sojourns of the Son of God: the first being the taking of flesh and the second the descent into Hades (*ComJn* 6.175; cf. 1.220, *ComRom* 1.5). In the *Commentary on Matthew* it is also used to support the view that after his death Christ descended to Hades and preached to the spirits who were imprisoned there. It also shows that Christ did not remain in Hades, but ascended on high to his rightful Father where he says to death, "Where, O death, is your sting?" (*ComMt* ser. 132: cf. 138). In another passage in the *Commentary on Matthew*, the first clause of Psalm 16:10 is used in conjunction with Origen's emphasis that it was the soul of Jesus, not his spirit or body, that was given as "a ransom for many" (Matt. 20:28). Jesus's soul did not remain, however, with the one to whom it was given as a ransom, Origen continues, as Psalm 16:10 demonstrates (*ComMt* 16.8). Origen takes the final clause of Psalm 16:9, "my flesh will rest in hope," to show that Christ ascended to heaven with his body of flesh. He says that these words of the psalm are spoken by Christ for his was the first flesh to rest in hope. After the resurrection, Christ "ascended to heaven and lifted up his earthly body along with himself." Origen then adds Isaiah 63:1 to his interpretation of the ascension of the risen Christ. It is the sight of flesh ascending to heaven that causes the heavenly powers to call out the words of Isaiah, "'Who is this that comes from Edom,' that is from the earth? 'His garments are red from Bozrah.' For they saw in his body the vestiges of the wounds from Bozrah, that is, the wounds received in his flesh."[94] Origen clearly understands Psalm 16:9–10 to speak of the resurrection and glorification of Jesus.

In the early fourth century, Lactantius and Eusebius again take up the apologetic use of the verse as proof of the resurrection, as does the Syrian father Aphraat. Lactantius twice uses Psalm 16:10 as proof that the Christ was to rise from the dead (*Divine Institutes* 4.19; *Epitome of the Divine Institutes* 47), and Eusebius understands this verse to be David prophesying about Christ's resurrection as if Christ himself were speaking (*Proof of the Gospel* 3.2). Aphraat cites Psalm 16:10 as words

---

94. These comments of Origen on Ps. 16:9 are preserved in *The Apology of Pamphilus the Martyr for Origen* 7 (*PG* 17:599D–600B).

that could be appropriately used only of Christ (*Demonstrations* 17.10). Athanasius uses the verse in relation to the resurrection (*On the Incarnation* 21) and says in his commentary on this psalm that it is as though Christ were singing the words. Interestingly, he adds that Peter, in Acts 2, taught us to think this way about the psalm.[95]

PSALM 110:1

Psalm 110:1 is the one text that is important both in the New Testament and in the church fathers in speaking of the glorification of Jesus. In the discussion of Psalm 110:1 in the section on the preexistence of the Christ above, I noted Rowan Greer's observation that this verse is used in two ways in the New Testament. One is in reference to Christ's preexistence with God and the other relates to his glorification after his death. Luke cites it in the latter sense in Peter's Pentecost sermon in conjunction with his argument from Psalm 16 (Acts 2:33–35), and alludes to it in a later speech by Peter (Acts 5:31), and again in Stephen's speech (Acts 7:55–56). In the book of Hebrews, this verse is an important testimony to Christ's exaltation (Heb. 1:3, 13; 8:1; 10:12–13; 12:2). The Pauline epistles employ Psalm 110:1 in conjunction with Christ's resurrection, ascension, and sitting at the right hand of God (Rom. 8:34; 1 Cor. 15:25–27; Eph. 1:20; Col. 3:1), and in 1 Peter it is used in reference to Christ's exaltation and the subordination of the heavenly powers to him (3:22).

The earliest application of Psalm 110:1 to the exalted Christ after the New Testament appears in *1 Clement* 36.5–6, where it is quoted in a context reminiscent of Hebrews 1. Polycarp, who wrote sometime in the first half of the second century, alludes to Psalm 110:1 in connection with the resurrection and ascension of Christ, who, he says, has been given "glory and a throne at" God's "right hand" (*Epistle to the Philippians* 2.1). Justin uses Psalm 110:1 to show that God took Christ to heaven after raising him from the dead (*1 Apology* 45.1). Tertullian understands Psalm 110:1 to refer to the exalted state of the Son after his resurrection (*Against Praxeas* 30.4–5). Irenaeus believes the statement that Jesus "was taken up into heaven and was seated at the right hand of God" in Mark 16:19 confirms the prophetic word in Psalm 110:1 (*Against Heresies* 3.10.6). He also identifies the "enemies" of Psalm 110:1, who are to be subjected to the glorified Christ, as rebellious heavenly beings (*Proof of the Apostolic Preaching* 85).[96] Hippolytus joins Psalm 110:1 with the statement about the child caught up to the throne of God in Revelation 12:5 and uses the two together to show that Christ was a heavenly, rather than

---

95. *PG* 27:100.
96. Irenaeus, *Proof of the Apostolic Preaching*, trans. and annotated by Joseph P. Smith, ACW 16 (New York: Newman Press, 1952), 100.

an earthly, king (*Christ and the Antichrist* 61.2). Lactantius quotes Psalm 110:1 as proof that Christ would ascend to the Father after his passion and resurrection (*Divine Institutes* 4.12.17). Both Cyprian (*Testimonies against the Jews* 2.26) and Novatian (*On the Trinity* 9.8) cite the verse to show the exaltation of Christ.

It is obvious that Psalm 110:1 had a tremendous influence on the Christian doctrine of the exalted Christ. Its language became a part of all the creeds of the church that speak of "Christ's 'sitting at the right hand' of the Father."[97] These include the Apostles' Creed and the creeds of Nicaea and Constantinople, the most widely used creeds of the church today.

PSALM 24

Although not used in the New Testament in relation to the glorification of the Christ, Psalm 24:7–10 vies with Psalm 110:1 in the importance given it in this respect by the fathers. This psalm was also important to the Jews. The Mishnah indicates that it had been sung in the temple by the Levites every first day of the week (*m. Tamid* 7:4). The inscription of the psalm in the Septuagint, "A psalm for David on the first day of the week," reflects this.[98]

PSALM 24:7–10 APPLIED TO SOLOMON AND JESUS

Justin says that the Jews applied these verses to Solomon when he took the ark into the temple (*Dialogue* 36.2).[99] The application to Solomon was rather common in later Jewish literature. The Babylonian Talmud says that when Solomon had built the temple and wished to take the ark of the covenant into the Holy of Holies, the gates of the temple refused to open. After Solomon prayed and repeated the words of Psalm 24:7, "Lift up your heads, O gates . . . ," the gates rushed at him in a threatening manner, demanding, "Who is the King of glory?" Solomon then repeated the words of Psalm 24:9–10. Still the gates would not open. It was only after he added the words of 2 Chronicles 6:42, "Lord God, turn not away the face of your anointed one [i.e., Messiah]," that the gates opened (*b. Shabbat* 33a). This story is repeated several times in the *Midrash Rabbah* in slightly modified versions.[100]

---

97. Jean Daniélou, *The Theology of Jewish Christianity*, vol. 1 of *The Development of Christian Doctrine before the Council of Nicaea*, trans. John A. Baker (London: Darton, Longman & Todd, 1964), 258.

98. Skarsaune, *Proof from Prophecy*, 267.

99. In *Dialogue with Trypho* 85.1 Justin says that some Jews applied the verses to Hezekiah and others to Solomon. I have not found the application to Hezekiah in later Jewish literature.

100. Slotki, *Numbers*, vol. 6 of *Midrash Rabbah*, 570–71, 654; Cohen, *Lamentations*, vol. 7 of *Midrash Rabbah*, 176.

The early Christians seem to have known the Jewish interpretation that connected the words of this psalm with Solomon approaching the gates of the temple. They, however, adapted it to the risen Christ approaching the gates of heaven. Justin, for example, in a blend of Psalm 24:7–9 with Psalm 110:1, says the words of the psalm are addressed to the heavenly rulers who are commanded to open the gates of heaven to the risen Christ when he ascends to sit at the Father's right hand until his enemies are made his footstool. The rulers of heaven, however, did not recognize the ascending Christ because his form still lacked glory. They ask, therefore, "Who is this King of glory?" The Holy Spirit answers, "The Lord of hosts, he is the king of glory." Justin concludes that no one who had charge of the gates of the temple in Jerusalem would have dared refer to Solomon as "King of glory" (*Dialogue* 36.3–6).

PSALM 24 AND THE ASCENSION OF CHRIST IN THE FLESH

These verses were used by the early Christians to show that it was Christ in the flesh who ascended into heaven. This was due partly, no doubt, to confirm that he had been raised from the dead in the flesh. Tertullian, however, knows Psalm 24 as a psalm that speaks of the ascension of Christ but says nothing about the heavenly powers not recognizing Christ as he ascends (*Flight in Persecution* 12.2; *Scorpiace* 10.7; *Against Marcion* 5.17.5). Consequently, he says nothing of the ascent of the body of Christ, though he certainly believed that Christ arose from the dead in the flesh.

The dialogue in Psalm 24:7–10 is understood by the majority of the fathers as follows: Those commanded to open the gates are the heavenly powers. They respond by questioning the identity of the one approaching because they do not recognize the body of flesh. The one approaching is then identified as "the King of glory" to whom the gates should be opened. This theme is repeated by several of the fathers with minor modifications.[101]

Irenaeus sets the dialogue in the context of resurrection, ascension, and the sitting at the father's right hand announced in Psalm 110:1. Christ had escaped the notice of the heavenly powers, he says, when he descended from heaven to earth because he had been invisible. Now, however, after his incarnation, he is visible and the powers do not recognize him. This occasioned the dialogue between the angels in the higher heavens, who had charge of the gates, and the angels below, who had already seen and recognized the ascending Christ and who demanded that the gates be opened. Irenaeus closes out this entire sequence with the words of Psalm 110:1. The Christ who has risen and has ascended now waits at the Father's right hand until the judgment, when all his

---

101. See Daniélou, *Jewish Christianity*, 259–63.

enemies will be made subject to him (*Proof of the Apostolic Preaching* 83–85; cf. *Against Heresies* 3.16.8).

THE BLENDING OF PSALM 24:7–10 WITH ISAIAH 63:1–3 TO DESCRIBE CHRIST'S ASCENSION

Origen makes the ascension scene more complex by blending Isaiah 63:1–3 with Psalm 24:7–10.[102] After Christ destroyed his enemies by his passion and took up our infirmities, diseases, and sins, his garments were stained with the blood of battle. He must therefore ascend to the Father and be cleansed in a kind of baptism, Origen argues, before he can descend and distribute gifts to humanity (cf. Eph. 4:8–11). As Christ, with his escort, approaches heaven, the powers ask in the words of Isaiah 63:1, "'Who is this that is coming from Edom, with scarlet garments from Bosra, so beautiful?' And those escorting him say to those stationed at the gates of heaven, 'Lift up your gates, and the king of glory will come in.'" The gatekeepers, however, hesitate because of the visible blood and ask further, in the words of Isaiah 62:2, "Why is your apparel red and your garments like the residue of a full wine-vat which has been trampled down?" Christ answers in a paraphrase of Isaiah 63:3, "I have crushed them in pieces" (*ComJn* 6.287–292; cf. *ComMt* 16.19).[103] In this dialogue it is the bloody wounds of the passion in the body of the ascending one that raise questions among the powers in heaven. This implies, of course, that it is the body of flesh that is ascending, as in the accounts of Irenaeus and Justin, which we noted above.

Origen was admired and read by many fathers in both East and West in the fourth century, and like him these fathers use Psalm 24:7–10 in either explicit or implicit conjunction with Isaiah 63:1–3 to emphasize the ascension of the body to heaven. Jerome, who is certainly dependent on Origen, uses these passages to interpret Ephesians 3:10–11 in his *Commentary on Ephesians*. He states Origen's doctrine that Christ's passion was for the angels and heavenly powers as well as for humans. The passion, he thinks, was that part of God's wisdom the heavenly beings had not known. "Accordingly," Jerome says, "they are amazed at God returning to heaven with a body and say, 'Who is this who comes from Edom with scarlet garments from Bosra, so beautiful in his bright robe?' (Isa. 63:1). And in another passage, 'Who is this king of glory? The Lord of the powers, he is the king of glory' (Ps. 23[24]:8)."[104]

---

102. We have already seen Origen blend Isa. 63:1 with Ps. 16:10 concerning the ascension. See n. 94 above.

103. *Origen: Commentary on the Gospel according to John, Books 1–10*, trans. Ronald E. Heine, FC 80 (Washington, DC: Catholic University of America Press, 1989), 246–47.

104. Ronald E. Heine, *The Commentaries of Origen and Jerome on St. Paul's Epistle to the Ephesians*, OECS (Oxford: Oxford University Press, 2002), 150.

Ambrose, another fourth-century Latin-speaking admirer of Origen, blends Isaiah 63 and Psalm 24 in his presentation of the ascension in his treatise *On the Mystery*. The sight of flesh ascending into heaven causes the powers to have doubts about Christ's identity, so they ask, "Who is this king of glory?" When some wanted to admit him and said, "Lift up your gates," others responded with the question of Isaiah 63:1: "Who is this that comes up from Edom, in garments red from Bosor?" (*On the Mystery* 7.36). In his treatise *On the Faith*, in which he argues against the Arians, who considered Christ less than God, Ambrose places a somewhat different emphasis on Psalm 24. In this context it is the glory of the ascending one and the numerous trophies he brings with him as conqueror of death that, Ambrose says, causes astonishment among the heavenly powers. Consequently, the angelic host seeks a more lofty entrance for Christ on his return than the gates through which he had departed. They cry out, therefore, that the gates be "lifted up." Some among the heavenly host, however, are still so overcome with amazement at the sight that they ask, "Who is the King of glory?" Other angels, who had been present at the resurrection and know who he is, reply, "It is the Lord, strong and mighty, the Lord mighty in battle." The cry goes out again to "lift up the gates," but the objectors repeat their question, "Who is the king of glory?" They ask, Ambrose explains, because they had seen him in his humiliation and cannot associate that with the glorious being they see before them. The first group replies to their question, "The Lord of hosts, he is the king of glory." The Son, Ambrose then remarks, is the Lord of Hosts of Psalm 24:7–10. But "Lord of Hosts" is an appellation of the Father in the Old Testament. How, then, he concludes, can the Arians say the Son is less than the Father (*On the Faith* 4.1.5–14)? Isaiah 63 is not cited in this treatment of Psalm 24, because the use made of it in the Origenist tradition to highlight the ascension of the wounded flesh of Jesus would have detracted from the point Ambrose wants to make. Ambrose needs to emphasize the glorious nature of the Christ, not his humiliation, against the Arians.

Gregory of Nyssa, an ardent admirer of Origen in the East, repeats Origen's blend of Isaiah 63:1–2 with Psalm 24:7–10. Gregory emphasizes that the ascending Christ was unrecognized by the heavenly powers because he was wearing "the dirty robe of our life" and his garments were red "from the wine-vat of human evil."[105] Gregory of Nyssa's friend, Gregory of Nazianzus, uses this same Origenist blend to discuss the ascension in his "Second Oration on Easter." He joins the emphasis on the ascension of the body to that on the exalted nature of the ascending

105. "In Ascensionem Christi," in *Sermones Pars I*, Gregorii Nysseni Opera 9, ed. G. Heil, A. van Heck, E. Gebhardt, and A. Spira (Leiden: Brill, 1967), 326.

one, which we noted above in Ambrose. On the one hand, Gregory of Nazianzus says that the gates should be "lifted up" or "made higher" to "receive him, exalted after his passion." This implies, as it did in Ambrose, that the gates are not adequate to receive the one approaching them. On the other hand, some of the heavenly beings doubt his identity because he "brings his body up with him along with the tokens of his passion," neither of which he had when he descended. These doubters who ask, "Who is this King of glory?" are to be answered with the words of Psalm 24:8. If they also ask in Isaiah's words, "Who is this that comes from Edom?" they are to be told of the "beauty" of "the body that suffered, adorned by the passion, and made splendid by the Godhead" (*Oration* 45.25).[106] According to the fathers, Isaiah's questions apply more explicitly to the suffering of the passion and the ascension of the flesh than do those of Psalm 24.

Psalm 24:7 and the Opening of Heaven for Humanity

Athanasius, another fourth-century Eastern father, uses Psalm 24:7 to speak of the ascension of the body of the Lord, but with a rather different emphasis. He argues that the Lord said, "Lift up your gates, you rulers, and be lifted up eternal gates" to open the gates of heaven for humanity. He did not need the gates to be opened for himself, Athanasius says, for he is "Lord of all" and "nothing of creation has been closed to the creator." Just as his body was delivered to death for humanity, so he now "paved the way of the ascent into heaven with it" (*On the Incarnation* 25).

The Calling of the Gentiles

The conversion of non-Jews to Christ was seen as an important validation of the early Christian claim that Jesus of Nazareth was the Messiah God had promised. This followed logically from the claim of his exaltation to the "right hand of God," where he sits until his enemies are made his subjects.[107] Psalm 2:7–8 is the most important Old Testament testimony the fathers use to prove Christ's universal kingship.[108] It is sometimes used in conjunction with either Isaiah 42:6–7 or Isaiah 49:6–7, both of which refer to the addressed person as "a light to the Gentiles."[109] Psalm 2:7–8 was especially important because it combines a statement understood to refer to the exaltation of Jesus, "The Lord said

---

106. *NPNF* 2 7, Sage Digital Library (Albany, OR: Sage Software, 1996), 833, modified.

107. See *1 Clement* 36.4–6, where Ps. 2:7–8 and Ps. 110:1 are cited in conjunction.

108. Beskow, *Rex Gloriae*, 97.

109. These latter two texts appear together in a messianic argument in *Epistle of Barnabas* 14.7–8 without the addition of Ps. 2:7–8.

to me, 'You are my son; today I have begotten you'" (see Acts 13:33), with a statement that makes the calling of the Gentiles the consequence of this exaltation, "Ask from me, and I will give you the nations (Gentiles) as your inheritance, and the ends of the earth as your possession." That the Gentiles, who were scattered to the ends of the earth, were turning to faith in Christ confirmed the Christian belief that Jesus of Nazareth had been the one indicated in Psalm 2:7–8.

Justin: The Messiah Will Inherit the Nations

Justin begins his examination of the conversion of the Gentiles with the promise made to Abraham in Genesis 12:1–3 that "all the tribes of the earth" would be blessed in him. He focuses on the promise, however, as it is repeated to Isaac (Gen. 26:4) and to Jacob (Gen. 28:14). In the latter two passages the promise is made that "all the nations (Gentiles) of the earth" (26:4) or "tribes of the earth" (28:14) would be blessed "in your seed." In this context, Justin also cites Genesis 49:10, specifically the statement about the coming of a descendant of Judah who will "be the expectation of the nations." These words must be understood of Christ, he argues, for we who are Gentiles expect Jesus. A citation of Psalm 72:17, "All the nations (Gentiles)[110] will be blessed in him," brings Justin back to the discussion of Abraham's seed with which he began. Here his point is that David no longer speaks of "seed" as the source of blessing for all the nations, but rather he speaks of a person, "him." "Now if," Justin argues, "all the nations are blessed in the Christ, and we, who come from all the nations, believe on him, then it follows that he is the Christ and we are those who are blessed through him."

"We are the ones," Justin continues, "who have received the gift of hearing, understanding, and being saved through this Christ." Justin's argument proceeds by linking key phrases repeated in the prophecies he cites: "a light for the nations," "a covenant for the race," and an "inheritance." Isaiah 49:6 points to the salvation of the Gentiles, Justin claims, because God says to Christ, "I have made you a light for the nations (Gentiles), that you might be their salvation to the farthest part of the earth." Justin insists to his Jewish opponents that these words refer to those Gentiles "who have been enlightened through Jesus." The words of Isaiah 42:6, which refer to one who has been appointed as "a covenant for the race" and who will be "a light for the Gentiles," are then cited and applied to Christ and the nations, who have been enlightened by him. This citation is followed closely by Isaiah 49:8, which also refers to the person addressed by God as a "covenant for the race" and which

---

110. Justin's text has "nations"; the text of the Septuagint (Ps. 71:17), as we have it today, has "tribes." The text of the Hebrew Bible has "nations."

says that this person will be given "the deserted as" his "inheritance." This provides the introduction for the testimony of Psalm 2:7–8, which serves as the lynchpin of Justin's argument. "What is Christ's inheritance?" Justin asks. "Is it not the nations? What is the covenant of God? Is it not the Christ? He says as much elsewhere: 'You are my son, I have begotten you today. Ask from me and I will give you the nations (Gentiles) as your inheritance, and the ends of the earth as your possession" (*Dialogue* 119.4–122.6).[111]

TERTULLIAN: HAS THE MESSIAH WHO INHERITS THE NATIONS COME?

While Tertullian follows the main lines of Justin's argument, he provides a more vivid and forceful form of it. The argument appears most fully in his treatise *Against the Jews*, where it shapes a large portion of the work, with a briefer version also appearing in *Against Marcion* 3.20. That the Christ was to come, Tertullian argues, is not at issue. Both Jews and Christians agree that the Christ is promised in the Old Testament. The point at issue is whether the Christ who was promised to come has actually come. Tertullian begins his argument by appealing to the evidence of the conversion of the Gentiles. Unfortunately, the first text to which he appeals is faulty in the version he uses. He cites Isaiah 45:1 from a text based on a Greek reading that has "Lord" (*kyriō*) instead of Cyrus (*kyrō*) in the opening clause and thus translates this verse, "Thus says the LORD God to Christ my Lord."[112] For Tertullian, this establishes that the verse is about the Christ. He concludes that the remaining words of the verse, which speak of nations hearing the Christ and cities being opened to him, refer to the acceptance of the gospel by the Gentiles. He then applies Psalm 19:4 to the preaching of the apostles as they go forth to the ends of the earth. A similar application of Psalm 19:4 was made by the apostle Paul in an argument that draws on several Old Testament texts to explain the Jewish rejection of the gospel (Rom. 10:18).

Tertullian next provides a list of nations into which the gospel has penetrated to prove that the Gentiles have turned to Christ in great

---

111. Irenaeus has a much briefer argument than Justin for the testimonial power of the conversion of the Gentiles. He does argue, however, that Ps. 2:8 must be understood of Christ and not of David, for only the former has dominion over the nations (*Proof of the Apostolic Preaching* 49; cf. *Against Heresies* 4.21.3). Eusebius devotes book 2 of his *Demonstration of the Gospel* to the subject of the conversion of the Gentiles and ransacks the Old Testament for texts that can be applied to the subject. He finds far more texts than have been included in our discussion. All the key texts used by Justin, however, make their appearance in Eusebius's argument (*Proof of the Gospel* 2.2).

112. Isa. 45:1 is cited in the same way in the earlier Greek text of *Epistle of Barnabas* 12.11.

numbers. He begins with a list that depends on Acts 2:9–10 but supplements this with people from the North African regions of Gaetulia and Mauretania, western Europeans from the regions of Spain and Gaul (France), inhabitants of Great Britain, Slavic people of Sarmatia (modern Russia), Dacians from the regions around Transylvania, Germans of central Europe, and nomadic tribes of northern Europe and Asia known as Scythians. There are people bearing the name of Christ in all these places, Tertullian asserts, and therefore it can be said that Christ is reigning over all nations. This could be said of no previous king in human history, whether a Hebrew or a pagan king (*Answer to the Jews* 7.1–8). "The name of Christ," Tertullian claims, "is spread everywhere, is believed everywhere, is revered in all the nations previously listed, rules everywhere, is worshiped everywhere" (*Answer to the Jews* 7.9).

At this point in his argument Tertullian runs through a series of prophetic texts concerning the Christ, many of which we have considered earlier in this chapter (*Answer to the Jews* 8–14). In the middle of this discussion, Tertullian returns to the argument of the conversion of the Gentiles and anchors it in Psalm 2:7–8: "You are my son; I have begotten you today. Ask of me and I will give you the nations as your inheritance and the ends of the earth as your possession." The "son" mentioned here, he argues, cannot refer to David because of the promise of ruling the "ends of the earth." David ruled only Judea. This must be understood of the Christ, who has "now taken the entire world as his possession by faith in his gospel." Tertullian then cites Isaiah 42:6–7 with a midrashic explanation of its phrases to confirm this understanding.

> "Behold, I have given you as a covenant for my race, a light for the Gentiles, to open the eyes of the blind," that is of the erring, "to release the bonds of those bound," that is to free them from transgressions, "and those held in prison," meaning death, "who sit in darkness," referring, of course, to ignorance.

If, Tertullian argues, all these things have been accomplished through Christ, then no other should be expected as the referent of these prophecies (*Answer to the Jews* 12).

Tertullian then returns to further prophecies of the Christ concerning topics that I have discussed already in this chapter—his birth, his passion, and his glorification. At the conclusion of this treatise, Tertullian returns once more to Psalm 2:7–8 and the topic of the conversion of the Gentiles. Whole nations, Tertullian argues, are rising up from the depth of human error to the creator and his Christ. The words of Psalm 2:7–8 prevent anyone from denying that such action by the nations had been prophesied. Nor can anyone argue that the words of these verses apply to anyone other than Christ, "who has illuminated the entire world with the rays of his gospel" (*Answer to the Jews* 14.12–13). While Tertullian mines most of the proof from prophecy in this treatise, his overall argument is unique in the stress he puts on the proof related to the conversion of the Gentiles. This is clearly the argument that he believes carries the most weight. He begins with it, as noted above, inserts it again in the middle of the treatise, and concludes with it. It is this argument on which he hangs the burden of his claim that the Christ who has come is the Christ who was to come. "You cannot maintain that to be future" he says, "which you see occurring" (*Answer to the Jews* 14.13).

Mortar and Bricks

The prophetic texts that have been considered in this chapter, and others like them, shaped the early Christians' understanding of Jesus. They identified him as the promised one sent by God for the salvation of humanity. It was the understanding of Jesus derived from these texts that caused the early Christians to spread the message that the promised one had come and that salvation was now available through his name. It was the image of Jesus shaped by these texts that was expressed in the later doctrines known as Christology and soteriology.

It might be said that the prophetic texts of the Old Testament served as the mortar for the church's construction of its understanding of Christ. Mortar is not the primary material in the edifice. Bricks are the primary material. The primary material in the church's understanding of Christ is the life, death, and resurrection of Jesus of Nazareth. Mortar, however, is essential to the edifice, enabling it to take form and hold together. Without the prophetic texts of the Old Testament, the early Christians would not have drawn the conclusions that they did concerning Jesus. The ancient Jewish prophetic texts that the early Christians read and wrestled with in their attempt to understand who Jesus of Nazareth had been and what his life meant for their lives lie close at hand in the Christian Bible. The early Christians were the first to make their way through these texts from a specifically Christian viewpoint. This gives them the right to a voice in all subsequent discussions of how Christians read these texts.

Praying the Psalms

"When you assemble, each one has a psalm . . ."

1 Corinthians 14:26

I N H E R F A S C I N A T I N G book *The Cloister Walk*, Kathleen Norris describes and reflects on her experiences as an oblate (a kind of associate member) in a Benedictine monastery in South Dakota. One of the things about monastic life that she, a Protestant who had left the church behind for a number of years, found most appealing was the communal praying of the psalms, which occurred several times a day. "You come to the Bible's great 'book of praises' through all the moods and conditions of life," Norris says, and "to your surprise, you find that the psalms do not deny your true feelings but allow you to reflect on them, right in front of God and everyone."[1]

It was the honesty with God in the prayers of the psalms that gradually drew me into the practice of praying them regularly. I have notes in sporadically kept journals that inform me that more than thirty years ago I had begun to notice this in the psalms. The journal notes were written a few years after I had become fully aware that, in spite of numerous medical attempts and the prayers of many people, nothing was going to reverse the brain damage that my son had suffered in some unknown

1. Kathleen Norris, *The Cloister Walk* (New York: Riverhead, 1997), 92.

way either during his birth or shortly thereafter. I was then serving as minister for a small congregation in central Illinois. Prayer became a very difficult exercise for me. I knew how to pray, or at least I thought I did. Prayer consisted of praise, thanksgiving, and petition. But I did not feel like praising or giving thanks, and what I considered the most important petitions I had ever presented to God had been ignored so far as I could tell.

It was in the following years when, as a young theologian, I was teaching at a Christian college and struggling to understand my own faith that the language of the psalms first began really to penetrate my understanding. My journal notes from those days refer to the impression the psalms made on me as I read them reflectively. In addition to the praise and thanksgiving in the psalms, I detected signs of an occasional fist raised to heaven in prayer. I heard the psalmist cry out in frustration and anger, "How long, O LORD? Will you be angry forever?" (Ps. 79:5; NRSV). I heard him express self-pity when he compared his own sorry state with the prosperous conditions of the wicked (Psalm 73). I heard him doubt whether God would ever look favorably on him again (Psalm 77). And all this was said directly to God in prayer! I cannot say that I immediately began praying the psalms or that my prayer life was instantly transformed. But my attention was drawn to the full range of emotions they expressed to God. Dietrich Bonhoeffer once observed that we only gradually grow into the meaning of the psalms as prayer.[2]

The early Christian mind was soaked with psalms. Jesus used Psalm 22 as a prayer to express his anguish on the cross (Matt. 27:46). There are more quotations from the book of Psalms in the New Testament than from any other book of the Old Testament. The church fathers composed numerous commentaries and homilies on the book of Psalms. Many psalms provided prophetic proof that Jesus was the Messiah and also suggested points of doctrine concerning his nature and work. The psalms were sung in the worship services of the early church and later in the monasteries. They were used for spiritual formation, celebration, and prayer. The early Christians carried the psalms in their minds and in their hearts.

Near the end of the patristic period in the mid-fifth century AD, Pope Leo the Great affirmed that the church everywhere sang and revered the psalms (*Sermon* 9.4). Later, at the end of the sixth century, Pope Gregory the Great gave a presbyter's ignorance of the psalms as the reason he refused to ordain him. Ignorance of the psalms, Gregory said, indicated that the man was not serious enough about himself (*Epistle* 48). Jerome,

2. Dietrich Bonhoeffer, *Life Together*, trans. J. W. Doberstein (New York: Harper & Row, 1954), 48.

the fourth-century monk and scholar, has numerous references to the use of the psalms in Christian piety in his *Epistles*. The majority of his references are to the practices in monasteries. He gives as an example the cenobite monks of Egypt, who assemble after the ninth hour to sing psalms and read Scripture (*Epistle* 22.35). In another letter Jerome describes the prayer life of the women in the monastery that his friend Paula founded and presided over in Bethlehem: "At dawn, at the third, sixth, and ninth hours, at evening, and at midnight they recited the psalter each in turn. No sister was allowed to be ignorant of the psalms, and all had every day to learn a certain portion of the holy scriptures" (*Epistle* 108.20).[3] The prominence of the psalms in monastic life comes out again when Jerome contrasts his rural monastic life in Bethlehem with city life in Rome. In visits to the city, he says, he is confronted with magnificent architecture along with the loud noise of the crowded markets. At home in his monastery, the architecture "is simple and rustic" and all is silence "except for the chanting of psalms," which the laborers sing as they go about their work. The psalms, Jerome adds, "are the songs of the country" (*Epistle* 46.12).[4]

In the early fifth century, the Spanish nun Egeria recorded her observations as she traveled about the Holy Land visiting famous churches and shrines of Old and New Testament saints. She refers repeatedly to the singing and reading of psalms in the worship she participated in at these holy places.[5] Gregory of Nyssa, on a pilgrimage to Jerusalem in the late fourth century, commented that the wagon accompanying the group of pilgrims was like a church, for the entire group continually sang psalms and fasted during the whole journey (*On Pilgrimages*).[6] Basil, the fourth-century bishop of Caesarea in Cappadocia, was criticized by some clergy in a neighboring province for practices they considered to deviate from earlier practices in the church. One point of attack concerned the singing of psalms. He responded that the custom he followed was in accord with that in all churches. "The people rise early at night," Basil says, "to go to the house of prayer, and in labour and affliction and continuous tears confessing to God, finally rise from their prayers and enter upon the singing of psalms." Then, he says, they divide into two groups and sing antiphonally, with one leading the chant and the others singing the response. In this way they pass the night singing psalms and praying. At dawn, Basil adds, "all in common . . . intone the psalm of confession to the Lord, each one forming his own expressions of repentance." If one

3. *NPNF* 2 6:206.
4. Ibid., 64–65; cf. *Epistle* 53.8.
5. See *Egeria: Diary of a Pilgrimage*, trans. and annotated by George E. Gingras, ACW 38 (New York: Newman, 1970).
6. *NPNF* 2 5:383.

objects to this, Basil concludes, then one will object to the practices of the Egyptians, Libyans, Thebans, Palestinians, Arabians, Phoenicians, Syrians, and those who live near the Euphrates, for all practice vigils, prayers, and the common singing of psalms (*Epistle* 207).[7]

There is a long tradition of using the psalms in Christian worship. The words of Paul in 1 Corinthians 14:26 are our earliest description of a Christian worship service. They were written in the mid-first century AD. The first thing Paul mentions there about the assembly is that each worshiper came with a psalm to be shared. This use of the psalms in worship was probably a practice brought to the church by the early Jewish Christians when they were converted to Christianity. The late second-century AD Jewish work called the Mishnah relates that there was a psalm for each day of the week sung by the Levites in the temple (*m. Tamid* 7:4). Athanasius, the Christian bishop of Alexandria in the mid-fourth century AD, appears still to have known this Jewish practice of singing a particular psalm each day of the week. In his *Letter to Marcellinus* he recommends a psalm to be recited on the first, second, fourth, and sixth days of the week.[8] He does not take the assignment of psalms to particular days any further than this, but the psalms he recommends for these four days are the same as the psalms previously sung by the Levites in the temple on the same four days (*Letter to Marcellinus* 23). There was a continuity with Judaism in the church's use of the psalms in worship.

The Psalms as the Prayers of the Christian: Athanasius, Diodore of Tarsus, John Chrysostom, and John Cassian

Athanasius

In his *Letter to Marcellinus*, Athanasius says that he had learned that Marcellinus, while diligent in studying all of Scripture, had a special preference for the book of Psalms and wanted to learn the meaning of each psalm. Athanasius confesses that he too, while highly regarding all Scripture, has a special liking for the psalms. All Scripture is inspired, he says, "but the book of Psalms has a certain persuasive precision of expression for those who devote themselves to it" (*Letter to Marcellinus*

---

7. *Saint Basil: The Letters*, trans. Roy J. Deferrari, Loeb Classical Library 3 (Cambridge, MA: Harvard University Press, 1962), 187–89.

8. The letter is available in English translation in *Athanasius: "The Life of Antony" and "The Letter to Marcellinus,"* trans. Robert C. Gregg, Classics of Western Spirituality (Mahwah, NJ: Paulist Press, 1980), 101–29. On the use of specific psalms for set days in the early Christian liturgy, see E. Ferguson, "Athanasius' 'Epistola ad Marcellinum in interpretationem Psalmorum,'" in *Studia Patristica* 16.2, ed. E. A. Livingstone (Berlin: Akademie Verlag, 1985), 300.

1–2). Furthermore, one gets a kind of synopsis of all the Old Testament Scriptures in the book of Psalms. It is like a garden, he says, containing things from the law, the histories, and the prophets set to music. Various psalms sing of creation or themes found in Exodus, Numbers, and Deuteronomy. The times of Joshua, the judges, the kings, and the return from exile are also alluded to in the music of the psalms. Moreover, prophetic themes about Christ are abundant (*Letter to Marcellinus* 3–8). In addition to providing a brief summary of the contents of the entire Old Testament, the book of Psalms also contains its own elements that are sung along with what it repeats from the other books (*Letter to Marcellinus* 2).

The unique element in the book of Psalms is that it allows the reader to get inside the personalities and events of the Old Testament as a participant; or, perhaps better said, it allows these personalities and events to get inside the reader as an emotive factor in shaping his or her life in accordance with the teachings found there. "In addition to the other matters in which the book of Psalms is related to the other books," Athanasius says, "it also possesses the unique and marvelous feature that the emotions of each soul have been recorded there. The changes and corrections of these emotions are described and portrayed in the book. Consequently, someone who desires to receive and learn from it without limit, as it were, shapes himself in this way" (*Letter to Marcellinus* 10). What Athanasius means, as he proceeds to explain, is that in the book of Psalms we are not only told what we should do, as we are in the law, for example, but we are actually helped to do it. We are not only instructed to repent, we are also given the emotions and the words of repentance. We are not only told we should praise or petition God, we are also led into the emotions of praise and petition and given the words to use in expressing them (*Letter to Marcellinus* 10). We are invited, as it were, to make the words of the psalms our own. We could never do this with the words of Moses or the prophets. But, except for the prophecies in the book of Psalms that concern the Messiah and the calling of the Gentiles, when we recite the psalms we treat them as if they were written about ourselves and as if the words they address to God were our own prayer (*Letter to Marcellinus* 11). The psalms, Athanasius says, are "like a mirror" in which one beholds "oneself and the emotions of one's own soul." When we sing the third psalm, cognizant of our own afflictions, we consider the words of the psalm to be our own. In a similar manner, Psalm 51[9] expresses "the words of one's own repentance." The Spirit has so composed the psalms

9. I cite the psalms according to their numbering in the English Bible. This means that the number of the psalm is one higher than in the LXX after Ps. 9. The verse numbers also differ by one because the LXX numbers the title of the psalm as the first verse.

that they comprehend our emotions and may be spoken as our own words (*Letter to Marcellinus* 12).

Diodore of Tarsus

Diodore, bishop of Tarsus, was a younger contemporary of Athanasius. He was originally from Antioch and shared the approach to understanding Scripture that was common to the teachers in that vicinity. These teachers believed that the Bible should be understood literally. They were especially opposed to the figurative kind of interpretation known as allegory that was associated with the teachers in Alexandria. The latter believed that Scripture contained a hidden meaning that did not lie on the surface of the literal text.[10] Diodore rejected this understanding of Scripture and insisted that the reader of Scripture must take it in its literal sense.

One must not, however, draw too sharp a line between these two approaches to understanding Scripture. John Chrysostom, who had been a student of Diodore, is a major representative of the approach to Scripture taken by the school of Antioch. Certainly Chrysostom's overall reading of Scripture is literal, but he can occasionally take the approach associated with the school of Alexandria in his exegesis of the Old Testament. In his homily on Psalm 7, he is struck by the language of weaponry that is used of God in verses 12 and 13. He cannot bring himself to assert that there are bows and arrows in heaven, nor that there are whetstones and swords there. One must, he says, take from these words "ideas appropriate to God." And if this is true of these, he goes on to say, one must do the same with the concepts of "anger and wrath" (*Exp. Ps* 7:11).[11] This great Antiochene exegete follows in the footsteps of Origen, the father and greatest representative of the Alexandrian understanding of Scripture,[12] when he insists that one must derive "ideas appropriate to God" from the literal text of Scripture. This is the key that controls Origen's entire approach to Scripture.[13] We will see below that Diodore too can move beyond the literal sense of the text of the psalms in his interpretation.

Diodore shares the common concern of most ancient Christian interpreters of the psalms, whether they agree with the teachers of Antioch

10. See, for example, the interpretations of Origen and Gregory of Nyssa discussed in chap. 3.

11. *St. John Chrysostom: Commentary on the Psalms*, 2 vols., trans. with intro. by Robert Charles Hill (Brookline, MA: Holy Cross Orthodox Press, 1998), 1:134–35.

12. On Origen's exegesis and its influence, see chap. 2 above, pp. 55–58.

13. See Ronald E. Heine, "God," in *The Westminster Handbook to Origen*, ed. John Anthony McGuckin (Louisville: Westminster John Knox, 2004), 107.

or those of Alexandria, that it is of primary importance to identify the speaker of each psalm.[14] "The first thing to be understood in the psalms," Hilary, the fourth-century Western bishop of Poitiers, says, "is to discern who the speaker is or to whom the words are addressed" (*On the First Psalm* 1).[15] This provides the clue to the psalm's meaning, for one understands the psalm in the context of the historical situation of the speaker and his audience. It is for this reason that in the prologue to his commentary on the psalms Diodore identifies a number of psalms he believes treat the subject of the Babylonian captivity. "Some of these psalms," he says, "seem to be spoken by people facing deportation, others by people already in captivity, others by people hoping to return, still others by people who have returned." These four separate situations of people in relation to the captivity provide the key to interpreting each psalm. There are other situations, of course, in which the speakers of the psalms were located. Some of the psalms reach back into the early days of Israel's history and describe "what happened in Egypt and in the desert." Others come from the much later Maccabean period of Israel's history and are "spoken in the person of specific individuals such as Onias and leaders like him; others in the collective person of all Israelites enduring the sufferings of that time." Finally, there are psalms whose speakers must be "Jeremiah and Ezekiel specifically."[16]

Although Diodore believes firmly that the secret of the meaning of Scripture lies in its literal sense, he does not limit the meaning of Scripture necessarily to its historical occasion. He believes, for example, that Psalm 30 contains the words of King Hezekiah when he was healed from his illness and delivered from the threat of the Assyrians (see 2 Kings 19–20). Yet Diodore is willing to admit that once this meaning is recognized, the psalm can also be seen to apply to humanity in general. For Hezekiah, the "foes" of Psalm 30:1 were the Assyrians and his own physical illness. The "foes" of humanity are "the whole range of experiences connected with mortality." All the words of the saints in Scripture, Diodore says, "are made to fit the events of their own time but are also adapted to the events of the future."

Diodore's remarks remind us of how untidy the classification of forms of ancient exegesis could be. The difference between the schools of Antioch

14. On this subject, see the important study by Marie-Josèphe Rondeau, *Les commentaires patristiques du Psautier*, 2 vols., Orientalia Christiana Analecta 219, 220 (Rome: Pont. Institutum Studiorum Orientalium, 1982, 1985). The relevant material is in vol. 2.

15. *S. Hilarii Episcopi Pictaviensis Tractatus super Psalmos*, Corpus Scriptorum Ecclesiasticorum Latinorum 22, ed. A. Zingerle (Leipzig: G. Freytag, 1891), 19.

16. Karlfried Froehlich, trans. and ed., *Biblical Interpretation in the Early Church* (Philadelphia: Fortress, 1984), 84.

and Alexandria were often not much more than a difference in emphasis. The Alexandrian school also believed that the words of Scripture spoke to the literal situations to which they were addressed but thought what they called the "hidden" or "higher" meaning to be more important. The Antiochene school, however, put more emphasis on the literal meaning but also thought the meaning of the words could be "adapted" to a more general meaning relevant to people outside the original biblical context. Diodore discusses this principle of adaptation in the preface to his commentary on Psalm 119, which he understands to have been in the first instance the prayer of the exiles in Babylon longing to return to Jerusalem. He believes that this prayer could be lifted from its historical setting and understood as the prayer of all saints for the resurrection. While the psalm expresses the prayer of the exiles, "it adapts itself even more precisely," he says, "to those who fervently long for the general resurrection."[17]

In the prologue to his commentary on the psalms, Diodore indicates that the psalms were regularly sung by Christians. He notes, however, that the full impact of the message of the psalms does not usually register with us in the regular singing of them but that we understand them "when we find ourselves in those very same situations which suggest to us our need for the psalms." Those are few, he says, "who need only the psalms of thanksgiving." The difficulties and necessities arising in our human condition force the psalms expressing other sentiments upon our attention. "Thus, when our souls find in the psalms the most ready formulation of the concerns they wish to bring before God, they recognize them as a wonderfully appropriate remedy." This is the work of the Holy Spirit, Diodore says, who anticipated the variety of our problems and provided "through the most blessed David the proper words for our sufferings." We do not usually recognize this aspect of the psalms as we sing them. It is as we face affliction that "we come to understand and own" the psalms as the "wound in us attracts the proper remedy, and the remedy adapts itself in turn, expressing the corresponding sentiment."[18] This understanding of the ability of the psalms to recognize our emotions and provide the wording for our prayers is very similar to that of Athanasius, which we considered above.

John Chrysostom

John Chrysostom was probably the greatest preacher among the church fathers. He spent his early years preaching in Antioch and later was made bishop of Constantinople. Throughout his life, however, he was attracted to the disciplines of the monastic life. Before he began

17. Ibid., 87–94, quotations 91–93.
18. Ibid., 82–83.

preaching, he spent time under the guidance of an elderly monk. He was certainly aware of the practice of praying the psalms in monastic life. In his fourteenth homily on 1 Timothy he praises the spiritual discipline of the monks who divide the hours of the day and night by singing hymns from the prophets and the psalms of David at set times. In another homily, he praises the monks who end their evening meal by reciting hymns of thanksgiving to God and turn the nights into days with their thanksgiving and singing of psalms (*HomMt* 55.6, 8). Chrysostom must have practiced something like this himself, though we are granted few personal glimpses into his own life in his writings. In his instructions to people preparing for baptism at Antioch, he suggests that the craftsman sing psalms as he works. If he prefers not to do this audibly he should do it in his heart. In this way he will make his workshop a kind of monastery (*Instructions to Catechumens* 2.4).

In his ninth homily on Colossians, Chrysostom again praises the value of singing the psalms. There he scolds his audience, saying that their children sing the songs of Satan and do not know the psalms. They are even ashamed of the psalms, he says, and treat them as a joke. Parents should, on the contrary, instruct their children through the singing of psalms. He then quotes a string of individual verses from the psalms to show both the variety and the importance of the subjects that can be taught in this manner. When he comments on Paul's words that one should "put on the Lord Jesus Christ and make no provision for the lusts of the flesh" (Rom. 13:14), he clarifies what it means to make "provision for the lusts of the flesh" by referring to those who drink excessively, eat excessively, overdress, are effeminate, and live a soft life. These, he says, do what they do, not for the sake of health, but to kindle desire. This indulgent party life, he charges, lulls the soul into a drunken slumber. Rather than living in this manner, Christians should "rejoice in the Lord with trembling," as Psalm 2:11 exhorts. This is done by singing hymns, offering prayers, and replacing the songs of the street with psalms (*Homily 24 on Paul* on Rom. 13:11).

The psalms were regularly chanted in the worship services of the church in Chrysostom's time. Christians assembled and sang psalms just as the Christians of old did. The difference between the two, Chrysostom observes, is that in the earlier period Christians assembled with a united heart but now there is division among them (*Hom1Cor 37.[8]* on v. 33). Not everyone, it seems, was well versed in the singing of psalms. Commenting on Ephesians 5:18–19 Chrysostom urges his hearers to *learn* to sing psalms because those who sing psalms are filled with the Holy Spirit (*HomEph* 19). Further, not everyone in his congregation was caught up in the spirit of prayer when they did sing psalms. He warns his congregation of the uselessness of singing psalms without giving attention to what is being said. He says that some who come to worship think that by chanting two or three psalms and offering random prayers they have satisfied the requirements for salvation. He likens this to those whom God accuses through the prophet Isaiah of honoring him with their lips while their heart is far from him (Isa. 29:13; *HomMt* 11.9). On the positive side, he praises the widows who come to the church day and night to sing psalms (*Hom1Cor 30.[7]* on v. 20). He also views the singing of psalms at Christian funerals to be a comfort to those who mourn, for he urges those overcome with grief to think about the meaning of the psalms they have sung at the funeral (*HomHeb* 4).

Chrysostom also wrote a rather lengthy commentary on the book of Psalms.[19] One finds him giving instructions on how to pray but never referring to the use of the psalms themselves as prayer. R. C. Hill, the translator of this commentary into English, refers to Chrysostom's approach to prayer in the work as rather "pedestrian" and thinks that he "reels off the qualities of prayer to God like a physician writing a prescription."[20] The medical image, as Hill points out, comes from Chrysostom himself. "Prayer, you see, is a medicine; but if we do not know how to apply the medicine, neither will we gain the benefit from it."[21] Chrysostom here lays out a six-step formula for success in having one's prayers heard by God: (1) The person offering the prayer must be worthy to receive something from God. (2) The prayer must be in compliance with God's laws. (3) The person praying must be persistent in offering the prayer, (4) must ask for nothing earthly, but (5) must want truly beneficial things, and (6) must personally contribute everything he or she possibly can to the realization of the prayer.[22]

There are other passages in Chrysostom's commentary on the Psalms, however, where his comments on prayer suggest a deeper spirituality than this list of laws for successful praying might indicate. The psalmist's words in Psalm 130:1–2—for example, "Out of the depths I have cried to you, LORD. Lord, hear my voice"—cause him to remark that prayer must rise up from the bottom of one's heart to be effective and cannot simply be words tossed off by the tongue as the mind wanders. Prayers that arise from the depths of our being are like the roots of a great tree that reach deep into the earth and hold the tree firm in the stormy blasts of wind. Such prayers "remain intense and unyielding," never failing even if "the devil's whole battle array" attempts to distract them. This is the way the saints pray, Chrysostom says. He points to Elijah and Hannah

19. Hill, *St. John Chrysostom: Commentary on the Psalms*.

20. Robert C. Hill, "The Spirituality of Chrysostom's *Commentary on the Psalms*," *JECS* (1997): 569, 572.

21. Hill, *Chrysostom*, 1:118.

22. Ibid., 117.

in the Bible and to holy women whom he has seen praying with a flood of tears for "an itinerant husband or sick child." People who pray in this manner profit in their souls even before their requests are granted. This kind of prayer represses the passions, assuages anger, repels envy, quells desire, extinguishes earthly lusts, reduces the soul to tranquility, and raises the soul to heaven. "When, therefore, you practice prayer," he adds, "do not look only to get what you ask but also to make the soul better from prayer itself; for this too is a result of prayer."[23]

When he comes to discuss Psalm 141:2, "Let my prayer be directed as incense before you, the lifting up of my hands as the evening sacrifice," Chrysostom turns to the morning and evening sacrifices in the temple to explain these words to his audience. These were obligatory daily sacrifices of a lamb in the temple and had to be offered whether or not anyone came throughout the day to offer sacrifice. They indicated that God must be worshiped continually "at the beginning and end of the day." The offerings that were made for the sins of an individual might or might not be acceptable, depending on the disposition of the offerer. The morning and evening sacrifices, by contrast, were always acceptable for they were not tied to the sins of the offerer but were a requirement of law. In light of this Chrysostom says, "The psalmist therefore asks for his prayer to become like that sacrifice defiled by no blemish of the offerer, like that pure and holy incense."[24] Here Chrysostom recognizes prayer as an act of worship offered to God rather than a request for something to be granted to the petitioner.

John Cassian

John Cassian, a monk of the early fifth century and an acquaintance of John Chrysostom, describes how the psalms could be incorporated into a kind of mystical prayer. Cassian, while writing at a monastery he had established at Marseilles, had spent ten years in Bethlehem and from there had often visited monasteries in Egypt. In his treatise known as *The Conferences* he relates the teachings of various Egyptian abbots. *The Second Conference of Abbot Isaac* treats the subject of prayer.

Abbot Isaac suggests that Christians who have advanced in the virtues and who feed continually on the words of the apostles and prophets will assimilate the thoughts of the psalms and begin to sing them, not as the compositions of the psalmist but as our own words expressing the deepest emotions of our own souls in prayer. We will perceive that the psalms were fulfilled not only in the life of their ancient authors but that they

23. Hill, *Chrysostom*, 2:180–81, modified.
24. Ibid., 268–69.

also find fulfillment in our own lives as well. When this happens, Isaac says, we no longer depend on an exposition of a psalm to understand its meaning. We enter into the state of mind in which the psalm was written and "anticipate the meaning rather than follow it."

In language reminiscent of Athanasius (noted above), Abbot Isaac refers to the psalms as a "clear mirror" of our own feelings. As our emotions and those expressed in a psalm come into line with one another our feelings become our teacher and we understand the psalm, not by reading it, but by anticipating it through our own experience. When this happens, Isaac says, our mind will attain "incorruptible prayer." This is prayer without words and images. It arises from a mind aflame and an ecstatic heart and, in Paul's words, is expressed in "wordless groanings" (Rom. 8:26).[25]

The Psalms as Prayers of Christ: Origen, Jerome, and Augustine

Origen as a Man of Prayer

Origen is known as the first systematic theologian and the greatest biblical scholar of the early church. More than both of these, however, he should be known as a man of prayer. Both his theology and his technical studies of the Bible are infused with his piety and prayer. In a letter to one of his former students who, he says, had the requisite mental abilities to become a Roman lawyer or a Greek philosopher, Origen urges him to direct his intellectual gifts to the service of Christianity. The student's first love and basic work should always be the study and interpretation of Scripture. This must be done, however, in the context of prayer. Origen uses the saying of Jesus in Matthew 7:7 to impress upon his student that he must "knock" at Scripture's closed doors, "seek" for Scripture's hidden meanings, and, most importantly, "ask" or pray that understanding may be given him. Scripture yields its true meaning only to those who approach it in this way.[26] There is repeated evidence in Origen's biblical works that he practiced this himself. He frequently ends the prologue to a commentary or a homily with an allusion to prayer or a request for prayer to guide his understanding as he proceeds into the interpretation of the biblical text. This is evident in the following words from his earliest commentary on the book of Psalms, where he also alludes to Matthew 7:7: "Because," he says to his friend for whom

---

25. "The Second Conference of Abbot Isaac," *The Conferences of John Cassian* 1.10.11, *NPNF* 2 11:407–8.

26. *Letter of Origen to Gregory* 1, 3, *ANF* 10:295–96.

he is writing the commentary, "there is no possibility of good without God, especially when it comes to understanding the inspired Scriptures, I think you should approach the God and Father of the universe through our Savior and High Priest who became God. Ask him to allow me to seek in the right way because this opens the promise of finding to those who seek."[27] Or, as he says in his *Commentary on John*: "Since . . . we have come this far in the commentaries on the Gospel according to John . . . let us call on our perfect God who provides perfection through our perfect high priest Jesus Christ. We should ask him to open our mind to discover the truth in what we are investigating (*ComJn* 28.6)."[28]

Importance of the Psalms in Origen's Understanding of Prayer

One of Origen's early works was a treatise on the subject of prayer written at the request of his friends Ambrose and Tatiana. He does not speak of praying the psalms in this treatise but he often appeals to psalms in his discussions of the different points regarding prayer. He says, for example, that one should pray at least three times a day. His first argument for this comes from the prayers of Daniel, who prayed three times a day when he was in imminent danger (Dan. 6:10). He cites Peter going to pray at the sixth hour as evidence for prayer at midday (Acts 10:9–11). His remaining examples all come from psalms. The morning prayer is indicated by Psalm 5:3 ("in the morning you will hear my prayer") and the evening prayer by Psalm 141:2 ("the lifting up of my hands as the evening sacrifice"). There should also be prayer during the night, Origen adds, for David speaks of rising at midnight "to give thanks" (Ps. 119:62). The latter is further confirmed by a reference to Paul and Silas singing and praying at midnight in the jail at Philippi (Acts 16:25; *On Prayer* 12.2).[29]

When Origen offers a synopsis of the subjects he thinks should constitute prayer he again draws primarily on the psalms for his evidence.

27. These remarks of Origen are preserved in Epiphanius, *Panarion* 64.7.4.

28. *Origen: Commentary on the Gospel according to John, Books 13–32*, trans. Ronald E. Heine, FC 89 (Washington, DC: Catholic University of America Press, 1993), 202–3, revised. See also *ComJn* 1.89; 20.1; *ComRom* Prol.; *HomGn* 13.1; *HomEx* 1.1; 5.1; 8.1.

29. Translation in *Alexandrian Christianity*, trans. with intro. and notes by John Ernest Leonard Oulton and Henry Chadwick, Library of Christian Classics 2 (Philadelphia: Westminster, 1954), 262. It is worth noting that the practice of praying at least three times a day appears to have been a very old Christian practice. Tertullian, writing early in the third century, recognizes the same three hours for prayer (*On Prayer* 25). He grounds all three hours in the New Testament, citing some of the same passages Origen cites. The gift of the Holy Spirit was given to the disciples when they were assembled at the third hour (Acts 2:15); Peter went to pray at the sixth hour (Acts 10:9); Peter and John went to the temple at the ninth hour of prayer (Acts 3:1); and Daniel, Tertullian adds, prayed three times a day (Dan. 6:10).

Prayer should consist of four subjects, he says. It should begin with the glorification of God on the order found in Psalm 104:1–7: "O LORD, my God, you are greatly magnified; you clothe yourself with praise and majesty, and put on light as a garment." This should be followed, he thinks, by general thanksgiving for blessings received both by oneself and by others. David's response in 2 Samuel 7:18–22 to the promises of God concerning him and his house provide the evidence for this aspect of prayer. Confession should follow thanksgiving. Origen finds the model for confession in David's words, "Deliver me from all my transgressions" (Ps. 39:8) and, "My wounds stink and are corrupt, because of my foolishness. I am pained and completely bowed down; I go about mourning all day long" (Ps. 38:5–6). The fourth subject proper to prayer, Origen says, is one's request "for great and heavenly things." These requests should be offered in a general manner and for oneself, and should include requests for one's family and closest friends. Such requests should follow the example provided by Psalm 28:3, which states, "Do not draw me away with sinners nor destroy me with those who are unjust." Finally, Origen says, prayer should be concluded by glorifying God again on the order of the doxology found in Romans 16:27.

Origen bases his view that the requests addressed to God in prayer should be "for great and heavenly things" on two exhortations that do not appear in the Gospels but that he considers to be sayings of Jesus.[30] "'Ask for the great things, and the little things shall be added unto you'; and, 'Ask for the heavenly things and the earthly things shall be added unto you'" (*On Prayer* 2.2).[31] In his treatise *Against Celsus*, Origen alludes to and interprets these sayings in his remark that the prayer of a Christian "is not concerned with any everyday matters; for he has learnt from Jesus to seek for nothing small, that is, nothing perceptible to our senses, but only for things that are great and truly divine which, as God's gifts, help in the journey to the blessedness with Him attained . . . through His Son" (*Against Celsus* 7.44).[32]

An example of what Origen means by asking for "great" and "heavenly" things can be found in his discussion of the advantages that come to the person who prays. The first and greatest blessing of prayer, Origen argues, is that it focuses one's mind on God. Approaching God demands a certain disposition of the mind. Because God knows all the secrets of the soul, when we approach him our soul must compose "itself to please him who 'examines hearts and searches out our inner beings' (Ps. 7:9)."

---

30. See Oulton and Chadwick., *Alexandrian Christianity*, 331–32, for other places Origen cites this saying and for other church fathers who cite it.

31. Trans. in Oulton and Chadwick, *Alexandrian Christianity*, 240.

32. Trans. in *Origen: Contra Celsum*, trans. Henry Chadwick (Cambridge: Cambridge University Press, 1965), 432–33, modified.

Even if there should be no benefit in prayer beyond this, Origen says, this in itself would be an extraordinary gain. The book of Psalms is one of the places Origen turns to illustrate this blessing of prayer. The proper approach to God is shown in the words, "Unto you have I lifted up my eyes, O you who dwell in heaven" (Ps. 123:1) and, "Unto you have I lifted up my soul, O God" (Ps. 25:1). The person who approaches God with a mind that has been cleansed of such things as anger against those who have wronged him or her and all distracting thoughts "is made more capable of union with . . . 'the Spirit' of the Lord who fills the world." Furthermore, this purification for praying enables one to participate in the prayer of our advocate and high priest, the Son of God, "who prays to the Father along with him whose mediator he is" (*On Prayer* 8.1–9.2).[33]

One of Origen's most explicit statements about the use of the psalms in prayer appears in his treatise *Against Celsus*. Celsus had charged that Christians could not follow the higher reasoning of philosophy because their understanding was bound to things of the flesh and could "see nothing pure." Origen responded that we Christians "say in our prayer 'Create in me a clean heart, O God, and renew a right spirit within my being,' in order that we may see God with a pure heart which alone has the power to see him" (*Against Celsus* 7.45).[34] This statement suggests that Psalm 51:10 was a regular part of the prayers in the worship assemblies in which Origen participated. Had it not been, he would not have been able to say so confidently that this statement is a part of "our prayer." The predominance of references to various psalms in the instructions concerning prayer we have noted above also suggests that the psalms played a major role in both the public and private prayer life of Origen.

The Greater Church as the Praying Body

Origen did not believe that the individual Christian prayed in isolation, even if he might offer his prayer in private. We have already noted above that Origen believed the Word of God, our advocate and high priest with the Father, stands "praying on behalf of those who pray, [and] pleading along with those who plead" (*On Prayer* 10.2).[35] He also believed that God is surrounded with angels, the souls of the departed saints, and other spirits. This multitude of heavenly beings works "with people who wish to worship the supreme God." They are not themselves called upon in prayer by the persons praying, but "pray and intercede

33. Trans. in Oulton and Chadwick, *Alexandrian Christianity*, 255–58, modified.
34. Trans. in Chadwick, *Contra Celsum*, 433.
35. Trans. in Oulton and Chadwick, *Alexandrian Christology*, 258.

together with them." "Consequently," Origen says, when Christians pray "there are praying with them countless sacred powers who have not been invoked, assisting our mortal race." They do this, he adds, "because of the daemons whom they see fighting and working against" our "salvation" (*Against Celsus* 8.64).[36]

It is important to be aware of this larger body of beings engaged in prayer with the person praying on earth, for it is a part of Origen's concept of the church in which each person participates as a part of the body of which Christ is the head. It may be that Origen believed that the church existed in heaven with God prior even to the creation of the world.[37] It is certain that he understood the church to consist of all the saints of the Old Testament period along with all those who have embraced faith in Christ since the incarnation and, in addition, the angelic hosts of heaven.[38] He suggests, in fact, that when the church gathers for worship and prayer there may actually be two congregations assembled. One consists of those visible people who have come together and the other consists of an invisible assembly of angels. On the basis of Psalm 34:7, "The angel of the LORD will encamp around those who fear him and will deliver them," and Jacob's reference to an angel who delivers him from evil (Gen. 48:16), Origen concludes that when Christians assemble "genuinely for the praise of Christ" each one is accompanied by an angel (*On Prayer* 31.5). "[I]t may be," he says, that "angelic powers also stand by the gatherings of believers, and the power of the Lord and Saviour himself, and holy spirits as well, those who have fallen asleep before us, as I think, and clearly also those who are still in this life, although 'how' it is not easy to say."[39]

Origen takes this understanding a step further when he applies to the extended church sayings in the New Testament that speak of unity between the members of the body and unity between the body and Christ. Sayings such as, "If one member suffers, all the members suffer with it" (1 Cor. 12:26) apply, he believes, not just in this life but also to those no longer in this present life but who are animated by love for the suffering saints in the world. Furthermore, Christ's statement that he is sick when one of the saints is sick, or in prison or naked or hungry and thirsty when the saints suffer these things, shows that Christ considers what happens

36. Trans. in Chadwick, *Contra Celsum*, 501.

37. For a fuller discussion of this aspect of Origen's understanding of the church, see Ronald E. Heine, *The Commentaries of Origen and Jerome on St Paul's Epistle to the Ephesians*, OECS (Oxford: Oxford University Press, 2002), 48–53; H. J. Vogt, *Das Kirchenverständnis des Origenes* (Vienna: Böhlau Verlag, 1974), 205–10.

38. For this view, see F. Ledegang, *Mysterium Ecclesiae: Images of the Church and Its Members in Origen*, BETL 156 (Leuven: Leuven University Press, 2001), 649–55, 665–67.

39. Trans. in Oulton and Chadwick, *Alexandrian Christianity*, 325; cf. also *On Prayer* 11.1.

to the faithful to happen to himself (Matt. 25:31–45; *On Prayer* 11.2). It is this understanding that allows Origen to identify Christ as the speaker in some psalms even when the words seem inappropriate to him.

Christ as Speaker in the Prayers of the Psalms

Origen produced three commentaries on the book of Psalms as well as a large number of homilies. None of this extensive work has been preserved intact. We have only fragments from the commentaries that have been preserved in quotations in the works of later fathers and commentators and Latin translations of some of the homilies done in the fourth century.[40] Nevertheless, even given the fragmentary nature of the texts, it can be shown with certainty that Origen considered the person praying in many of the psalms to be Christ.

He begins a discussion of Psalm 71 by saying, "It is clear that Christ speaks the words in this psalm. He prays that God be his place of security. He who says, 'I am in the Father' (John 10:38) also says, 'Upon you was I cast from the womb; from my mother's womb you are my protector'" (Ps. 71:6). The contact point between this statement in Psalm 71 and the earthly life of Christ is God's deliverance of the infant Jesus from Herod's slaughter of the children of Bethlehem. Origen finds two additional contact points that help to confirm that Christ is the speaker in Psalm 71. The first is the words of Psalm 71:14, "And I shall add to all your praise."[41] "And who," Origen asks, "except for the Son, has added to all the praise of God found in the law and the prophets?" He argues that Jesus adds to the praise of God in the law and the prophets because he knows, in contrast to the understanding of the Jewish scribes, that "the letter which kills"—that is, the legal demands of the Old Testament—actually "teaches the words of the Spirit which makes alive." The second contact point Origen finds between Psalm 71 and the life of Christ is in verse 20. Here, after he has been resurrected and has thereby proclaimed the power of God, Christ says to the Father, "You brought me up again from the abyss of the earth."[42] These points of contact with the life of Christ establish for Origen that the words of the entire psalm are the prayer of Christ. The implicit reasoning behind this conclusion

---

40. For details on these works of Origen on the Psalms, see Ronald E. Heine, "Restringing Origen's Broken Harp: Some Suggestions concerning the Prologue to the Caesarean Commentary on the Psalms," in *The Harp of Prophecy: The Psalms in Early Christian Exegesis*, ed. Brian Daly (Notre Dame, IN: University of Notre Dame Press, forthcoming).

41. We must remember that Origen read the psalms in the Septuagint and that his text, consequently, sometimes differs from what stands translated from the Hebrew in our English Bibles. See "The Version of Scripture Read by the Early Church" in chap. 1.

42. *PG* 12:1517D–1520A.

is an extension of the kind of exegetical reasoning found in Acts 2:25–31. Here Psalm 16:8–11 is quoted and applied to Christ on the basis that the words could not apply to David but are appropriate to what happened to Christ. Origen is aware, however, that even in a psalm where it seems obvious that Christ is speaking, not every word should be ascribed to him. In Psalm 71, for example, he says that it is demons who speak the words of verse 11, "God has forsaken him; pursue him and seize him because there is no one to save him."[43]

Origen also considers Psalm 59 to be a prayer of Christ, citing as support the words "I ran without iniquity and kept my course straight" in verse 4, the words "I guard my strength in relation to you" in verse 9, and the words "Give attention to visit all the nations" in verse 5.[44] Psalm 3, however, is more complicated for Origen. The psalm has the title, "A psalm of David when he fled from Absalom his son." Origen notes that this seems to provide both the speaker and the occasion for the psalm. "But," he adds, "it is not possible to maintain that everything in this psalm relates to this story. For what do the words mean, if taken of David, 'I lay down and slept; I arose because the Lord will help me' (Ps. 3:5)?" Furthermore, "if someone wants to be a slave to the letter, and look for nothing beyond it, let him show how the following words of the prophet are true, 'You broke out the teeth of the sinners'" (Ps. 3:7). One must instead, Origen asserts, search out "who David is and who Absalom is," that is, who is represented by these two figures in the psalm. One also needs to ask what "the attack" of Absalom "against his father" is and what the "flight of the king is who meekly bears the uprising of the son who wants his kingdom, and commands those under him to spare the young man Absalom." "David," Origen notes, "is often used to mean the Christ in Scripture." The true identity of the attackers and their attack referred to in Psalm 3:1–2 is found in the story of the arrest, trial, and crucifixion of Jesus. The words of Psalm 3:3 are the words of Christ, who was not forsaken but through his resurrection was restored to the glory he had in the beginning. Likewise, the spiritual meaning of Psalm 3:5 is spoken "in the person of the Lord," who refers to the "sleep" he experienced at the time of his passion. Sleep is understood as the Pauline euphemism for death (1 Cor. 15:20, 51). "After this sleep," Origen says, "the Father helped him and raised him." The "teeth of sinners," which are broken out in Psalm 3:7, are not related directly to Christ. The clause is, instead, given a spiritual meaning applicable to all the saints. The teeth are the "senseless thoughts that occur to us contrary to nature" and that "the

43. *PG* 12:1520D.
44. *PG* 12:1477A.

adversaries" use "to devour our flesh," meaning "the things that arise by nature from the flesh."[45]

Origen must do some textual sleuthing before he can say that Christ is the speaker in Psalm 69. He finds the connection with Christ buried within a phrase that is interpreted in terms of the story of Christ in an earlier psalm. When he interprets the words of Psalm 69:2, "I was planted in deep mud and there was nothing substantial. I entered the depths of the sea and the hurricane swallowed me," Origen first applies the exegetical logic noted above in relation to Psalm 71. This logic, as noted earlier, goes back to the New Testament. But the logic doesn't appear to work this time. He considers whether David could make this statement and remarks, "We find David to have experienced nothing like this in the stories about him." When he rules out David as the referent, he then asks if these words might refer to Christ since the psalm contains the statement, "Zeal for your house has devoured me" (Ps. 69:9). The latter statement is related to Christ's cleansing of the temple in John 2:17. But, Origen says, "We do not know of even the Savior himself experiencing anything like this." There is nothing in the story of Jesus recorded in the Gospels, in other words, that appears to be an appropriate match for the words of Psalm 69:2.

Origen solves the mystery of the speaker in Psalm 69:2 by turning to the previous psalm, in which "the depths of the sea" are also mentioned: "I will return from Bashan; I will return in the depths of the sea" (Ps. 68:22). There Bashan is taken to refer to the "shame" that the Lord "despised" (Heb. 12:2) when he descended on our account, that is, in the incarnation. Since the speaker in Psalm 68:22 "teaches how he descended into Bashan and said, 'I will return in the depths of the sea,' it follows that the same person should be considered to speak the same words" in Psalm 69:2. The speaker of Psalm 69 can, then, be identified as Christ. Origen concludes: "Therefore, God the Word himself sends this prayer up to the Father, when he appropriates the sufferings related to the humanity that he assumed. And it is clear that he is referring to the regions of Hades where he alone descended and passed through."[46]

Determining When Christ Speaks in the Psalms

In the psalms considered so far Origen has identified Christ as the speaker in place of David, who is named in the title of the psalms. The process of identifying Christ begins, as we have shown above, by asking if particular words in the psalm are appropriate to David and his situation. When this is shown not to be the case the investigation then turns

45. *PG* 12:1117B–1132D.
46. *PG* 12:1512B; 1509A–B.

to Christ. First it is asked if the words in question relate to something in the literal life of Christ. If something is found, then it is concluded that Christ is the speaker. If nothing in the story of Jesus relates to the literal words in the psalm, the investigation proceeds to the spiritual significance of the words. The latter procedure is considered as valid a basis as the former for identifying Christ as the speaker in the psalm.

There is another way in which Origen sometimes identifies Christ as the speaker of words in a psalm that do not seem directly appropriate to him. We mentioned this in the conclusion to the preceding section when we noted that Origen saw an identity between Christ and the saints based on Jesus's parable in Matthew 25. In the prologue to his commentary on Psalm 4, he notes that this psalm is commonly attributed to David. It can, in a mystical manner, however, be attributed "to Christ, who assumes the person of the saints both when he considers their afflictions and their enlargement in these afflictions as his own . . . and when he turns his attention to those who are heavy-hearted and those who love vanity." When he discusses the opening words of the psalm, "The God of my righteousness heard me when I called on him," Origen says that "the person speaking is either the prophet," that is, David, "or Christ in the function that he took up on our behalf."[47] Psalm 22, in contrast, is clearly a prayer of Christ because of Jesus's use of the words of verse 1 in Matthew 27:46, "My God, my God, why have you forsaken me?" "This is the voice of the Lord Christ," Origen says, "when he was nailed to the cross." He adds:

> But it expresses our experience as well in a figurative way. For we, previously, were those who were forsaken and neglected, but now we have been accepted and saved in the sufferings of him who was not subject to suffering, when he took upon himself, as it were, our foolishness and sinfulness which he expresses in the following words of the psalm, "The words of my transgressions are far from my salvation." It is as if he said, "Sins make me far from salvation."[48]

Here Origen understands Christ to be praying but his words embrace the saints as well as himself, and some of the words, as they stand in the Septuagint at least, are appropriate only in relation to the saints.

Psalm 30, however, provides the clearest example of this aspect of Origen's understanding of the Psalms. The words of verse 3, "You brought my soul up from Hades," show "clearly" that "this psalm is spoken in the person of Christ." These same words, nevertheless, "can also be said in the person of a saint," Origen continues, because all saints "were in

47. *PG* 12:1133C–1136A.
48. *PG* 12:1253A–B.

Hades in a figurative sense when they were in sin and God brought them up when he helped them by means of his Word."[49] Marie-Josèphe Rondeau points out that Origen understands the words of Psalm 30:2, "O LORD my God, I cried to you and you healed me," to be Christ speaking in the person of his body.[50] "These words are spoken, on the one hand," Origen says, "in the person of the just person."

> But consider if it would not be just as proper to understand the words as follows with the Savior as the speaker. Believers are the body of Christ and members of one another. "If one member suffers, all suffer together. And if one member receives glory, all receive glory together" (1 Cor. 12:26). When the body of Christ, then, is suffering and standing in need of healing it would not be strange to say to him on behalf of our healing, "O LORD my God, I cried to you, and you healed me." For indeed he confesses our sins as his own in the twenty-second psalm when he says, "The words of my transgressions are far from my salvation," and in the sixty-ninth, "Lord, you know my foolishness, and my sins are not hidden from you."[51]

Here Origen has called on the identification of Christ with his church, based on the metaphor of the body that Paul uses in 1 Corinthians 12:26, to show that words that seem most appropriate to the saints can at the same time be understood as the prayer of Christ. We observed above that Origen used this same verse from 1 Corinthians with Jesus's parable in Matthew 25 in his treatise *On Prayer* to establish the unity between the saints still living and those who lived previously, and the unity between Christ and his body, the extended church of all time. Rondeau believes that this way of considering Christ to speak in the name of his body in the psalms is "one of the threads transmitting the ancient Christianization of the book of Psalms." She notes that this tradition culminates in Augustine.[52]

Jerome on the Prayers of the Psalms

Jerome produced a brief commentary and several homilies on the book of Psalms. In the prologue to his small commentary titled *Excerpts on the Psalms*, he acknowledges that he draws primarily on Origen for his comments.[53] Some scholars believe that the homilies are little more than

49. *PG* 12:1292B.
50. Rondeau, *Les commentaires patristiques*, 2:125.
51. *PG* 12:1292D–1293A.
52. Rondeau, *Les commentaires patristiques*, 2:25.
53. *S. Hieronymi Presbyteri Opera*, 1.1, CCSL 72, *Commentarioli in Psalmos*, ed. G. Morin (Turnholt: Brepols, 1959), 177–78.

translations of lost homilies of Origen on the psalms.[54] It will become evident in what follows that even if we are not dealing with translations of Origen's works on the psalms, we are never far from Origen when we listen to Jerome speak on this subject.

Jerome's homilies on the book of Psalms were delivered to the monks in his monastery in Bethlehem. "We are called monks," he says in his homily on Psalm 119 (120), "even though we are not all that we ought to be. We pray at the third hour, at the sixth, at the ninth; we say vespers at sunset; we rise in the middle of the night; then we pray again at cock-crow" (Hom. 41).[55] In the prologue to his homily on Psalm 9 he notes that this psalm had just been sung in the service (Hom. 4).[56] When he takes up Psalm 14 (15) Jerome comments on how opportune it was that this particular psalm had come up in the regular sequence of the liturgical reading on that particular day because it had a message of importance for his audience (Hom. 5).[57] The psalms, in other words, were not a part of the worship only when they provided the text for the day's sermon. They were regular fare in every worship service.

We noted earlier in this chapter that Rondeau has shown that the fathers pay particular attention to determining who the speaker is in each psalm,[58] and we observed Origen doing this. Jerome repeatedly notes in his expositions of the psalms that the interpreter must constantly be alert to the changing speakers in the psalms. "[T]he psalms are perplexing," he says, "because suddenly without any warning there is a change in person." There is sometimes, in fact, a dialogue between the praying person and God in the psalms. "Up to this verse the prophet has been speaking," Jerome continues, "now, all of a sudden, it is God who speaks to the people" (Hom. 13).[59] Jerome discusses this divine dialogue in his comments on Psalm 91:9 (90:9 LXX):

> The words above have been said *to the just man* in the name of the Lord; now, however, there is a change in persons and *the just person* in contemplation *answers* the Lord: "You, O LORD, are my hope." He who says this is a just person. "You have made the Most High your stronghold." Once more persons change, and it is this frequent change in persons that adds to the obscurity of the psalms. Now, *while the just person is praying* to the Lord and saying: "You, O LORD, are my hope," *he hears from the Lord the*

54. See Rondeau, *Les commentaires patristiques*, 1:54–55, where she discusses the work of V. Peri on this issue. See also Heine, "Restringing Origen's Broken Harp."

55. *The Homilies of Saint Jerome*, vol. 1, trans. Marie Liguori Ewald, FC 48 (Washington, DC: Catholic University of America Press, 1964), 312.

56. Ibid., 35.

57. Ibid., 38.

58. See note 14 above.

59. On Ps. 80; trans. in Ewald, *Homilies of Saint Jerome*, 1:97.

answer: "You have made the Most High your refuge." The following verse, therefore, continues appropriately. "No evil shall befall you, nor shall affliction come near your tent." (Hom. 68, italics mine)[60]

Jerome's Latin translation follows the Septuagint here, which differs somewhat from English renderings of the verse. In this prayer-dialogue he understands God to be addressed in prayer in the first line of verse 9 and God to respond to the prayer in the second line of the verse.

When he comments on the closing clause in Psalm 7:6, "Arise, O LORD my God, in the precept that you commanded," Jerome says, "We say this; we, the faithful, are uttering these words, for the psalms are constantly changing person." Two verses later, when he encounters the words, "Judge me, O LORD, on the basis of my justice and on the basis of the innocence that I possess," Jerome says, "David could not say this; these words properly belong to the Savior who has not sinned" (Hom. 3).[61] The latter comment exemplifies the exegetical logic we observed Origen using in the previous section and that we noted goes back to the New Testament itself in its application of various psalms to Christ.

Jerome identifies Christ most often as speaker in the psalms, in either his incarnate or exalted state. Occasionally the identification extends to include the saints as the body of Christ, as we also observed in Origen. When he refers to the words of Psalm 3:1, "many rise up against me," Jerome says that "this psalm can have reference both to David and to Christ, and through Christ to all the saints" (on Ps. 3:2).[62] The whole of Psalm 35 is about Christ, he says, but can "be referred to all the saints by means of Christ" (on Ps. 34:13).[63] When the speaker in Psalm 4:1 says, "You heard me, God of my justice," Jerome says that "it is unsuitable to take this of David." The statement would be audacious coming from the man who, in the previous psalm, "was nearly killed by his son because of the murder of Uriah." "The entire psalm, therefore, is to be referred to Christ and through Christ to the just" (on Ps. 4:2).[64] The whole of Psalm 31, Jerome says, "can be understood of David in a historical manner and of the Lord in a prophetic manner." When he comments on Psalm 31:20, however, he reverses the usual order of moving from David to Christ and starts with the assumption that the verse is about Christ but can also be understood of David. He says that this statement can be

60. *The Homilies of Saint Jerome*, vol. 2, trans. Marie Liguori Ewald, FC 57 (Washington, DC: Catholic University of America Press, 1966), 86, altered.

61. Ewald, *Homilies of Jerome*, 1:30–31.

62. *Excerpts on the Psalms*, CCSL 72:183. On the discrepancy between chapter and verse numbers given, see n. 9 above.

63. Ibid., 205.

64. Ibid., 184.

"understood as much of David as of the Lord, because God protected David from Saul and Absalom, and the Lord from the Pharisees and the Jews" (on Ps. 30).[65]

Yet Jerome is also willing to swim occasionally against the stream of the common Christian exegetical understanding and take a psalm only of David that previous exegetes had applied to Christ. He says, for example, that because of the words of the blind men at Jericho who called out to Jesus, "Son of David, have mercy on us," many take "David" in Psalm 132:1 to be a reference to the Savior. Jerome thinks this is not the case. "I am opposing this consideration," he says, "to those who construe David in this passage as Christ—not that we would deny that David is a type of Christ, in conformity with the scriptural texts; but that in this particular instance such exegesis does not make sense" (Hom. 44).[66]

Although Psalm 38 is spoken in the person of a penitent, "it can also be referred to Christ," Jerome says, because "the transgressions of the human race are the sin of Christ" (on Ps. 37).[67] The same is true of Psalm 69. Christ is understood as the speaker of the whole psalm even though, Jerome says, "some think that the words"—such as "O God, you know my foolishness, and my offences are not hidden from you" (Ps. 69:5)—"are not at all appropriate to him." Still, Jerome sees the words of Psalm 69:21, "They gave me gall for my food, and in my thirst they gave me vinegar to drink," as strong confirmation that Christ is the speaker in the psalm (on Ps. 68:2, 22).[68] Psalm 88 "is spoken in the person of the Savior, that is, in the person of the servant whom he considered it worthy to assume." "'Incline your ear to my prayer'" (Ps. 88:2) are the words "of the Son to the Father, speaking in our person" (on Ps. 87).[69]

Like Origen, Jerome gives careful attention to the identity of the speaker or speakers in each psalm. This holds the key, he thinks, to understanding a psalm. He sometimes identifies David as the sole speaker in a psalm; at other times he finds both David and Christ to be the speakers. In the latter cases, sometimes David and Christ speak in separate statements made in the psalm and at other times the same words are understood to be the words of both. They are David's words historically and Christ's words prophetically. When Christ speaks in the psalms, he may speak in his own person, since certain statements in the psalms seem to be especially relevant to particular points in his life. Or he may speak in our name. The latter is the case when Christ utters words that are not strictly

65. Ibid., 203.
66. Ewald, *Homilies of Jerome*, 1:329.
67. *Excerpts on the Psalms*, CCSL 72:206–7. He means that Christ took the sins of humanity on himself.
68. *Excerpts on the Psalms*, CCSL 72:215–16.
69. CCSL 78:400.

applicable to himself, such as confessing and asking for the forgiveness of sins. Some of the prayers of the psalms are also our own words spoken in our own person. Finally, Jerome finds God responding to some of the words addressed to him in the psalms in a kind of dialogue with the person praying. Jerome found a richness of prayer and praise in the Psalter. In fact, he considered our praise of God through the psalms to be an imitation of the praise of God that takes place in heaven.[70]

Augustine and the Prayers of the Psalms

Augustine is the undisputed master of using the psalms to lay one's soul bare before God in the praise and confession of prayer. "The very first sentence of Augustine's *Confessions* is a quotation from the Psalms," Rowan Williams observes, "and for the rest of the work hardly a page goes by without at least one such reference."[71] The psalms permeate everything Augustine wrote. Michael Fiedrowicz has noted that there are in excess of "ten thousand citations of the psalms" in the total collection of Augustine's writings.[72] He lived his entire Christian life in the context of the psalms. In his *Confessions* he relates how powerfully the psalms affected his thinking at the very beginning of his Christian faith (*Confessions* 9.4).[73] His ancient biographer, Possidius, points out that at the end of his life Augustine was still continually occupied with the psalms. He chose to be alone on his deathbed so that he could pray the penitential psalms in his final hours.[74]

Augustine produced a massive work on the Psalter called *Expositions of the Psalms*. The *Expositions* are homilies delivered to his congregation on each of the 150 psalms, with some psalms treated in multiple homilies. Although the work was spread over a period of thirty years, it was a unified plan in Augustine's mind. His goal was to bring the psalms into the Christian faith so that their words could "function fully as prayer" in the Christian era.[75]

It has been pointed out that there are two emphases found in Augustine's treatment of the psalms. The first is a "therapeutic" use of the psalms[76] similar to that noted earlier in Athanasius and other fathers,

---

70. Ibid., 392; trans. in Ewald, *Homilies of Jerome*, 2:47.

71. Rowan Williams, "Augustine and the Psalms," *Interpretation* (2004): 17.

72. *Expositions of the Psalms 1–32*, intro. Michael Fiedrowicz, trans. and notes by Maria Boulding, ed. John E. Rotelle, *WSA* 3.15 (Hyde Park, NY: New City, 2000), 13.

73. *Saint Augustine: Confessions*, trans. with intro. by R. S. Pine-Coffin, Penguin Classics (London: Penguin, 1961), 186.

74. Possidius, *Life of Augustine* 31.2, cited in Boulding, *Expositions of the Psalms 1–32*, 14.

75. Boulding, *Expositions of the Psalms 1–32*, 27–28.

76. Ibid., 39–43. Fiedrowicz uses the word "therapeutic" in his discussion of this feature but he does not use it as a category title. He refers to it, rather, as an "existential and

though their treatments lack the personal intensity of Augustine's. The second is the understanding of the psalms as the prayers of Christ.[77] This resembles the understanding we observed above in Origen and Jerome. Augustine, however, develops this concept further.

Augustine on the Psalms for the Healing of the Soul

In his *Confessions* Augustine indicates that Psalm 4 was especially important to the healing of his own soul at the time of his conversion. When he read the words of Psalm 4:1 he considered them to be the cry of his own heart in the presence of God. The words of Psalm 4:2 filled him with fear, for he thought he had done precisely what they condemned. He was moved to repentance and hope, however, by the words, "Tremble and sin no more" (Ps. 4:4), because he had come to regard his past with trembling and anticipated a future without sin. Verses 5 and 6 taught him that those who seek joy in external things "nibble at empty shadows" and starve their minds. When he came to the final verse of Psalm 4, Augustine says that he cried out in the confident anticipation of the resurrection that it conveyed (*Confessions* 9.4).

In this discussion in the *Confessions*, Augustine relates from his own experience what he later, in the *Expositions of the Psalms*, teaches his congregation to anticipate in praying certain psalms. Psalm 4 both diagnosed the condition of his soul and provided the therapy to heal it. This process filled him with joy and confidence (Ps. 4:7–8). In his exposition of Psalm 94 (93) Augustine applies this same understanding of both the chastening and the consoling aspects of the psalm to his congregation. This psalm speaks of the triumph of the wicked and of their crimes against the people of God. The righteous cry out to God in despair, asking how long this will continue. They are brought to the understanding that the Lord is aware of their situation and will deal with it and that they can rest in God as a rock of refuge. Augustine comments that if this situation upsets his congregation they may be assured that the psalm is grieving with them. It is asking their questions of life, not because it does not know the answer, but rather to help them find the answer. This, he adds, is the necessary process for anyone wishing to console another. First the consoler must grieve with the person suffering so that when the sorrow has been shared he or she may then bring comfort. This, Augustine concludes, is what the Spirit does in the psalms. He puts our thoughts into words for us (*Exp. Ps* 93.9, on

anthropological method of exposition . . . which treats the Book of Psalms as a mirror of the soul and a remedy for its healing" (43).

77. Ibid., 43–65.

94:3–4).[78] We must then bring ourselves into line with the emotions expressed in the psalm so that we can experience the healing that the psalmist experiences. "Look how the psalm corrects itself: allow yourself to be corrected along with it. It was to that end that the psalm adopted your complaint. . . . The psalm took on your words, so now you take on the words of the psalm" (*Exp. Ps* 93.27).[79]

Williams points out that Augustine believed that the words of the psalms released buried emotions in the person praying them. They involve the person praying in a conversation with God in which "the human speaker is radically changed and enabled to express what is otherwise hidden from him or her." In the discussion of the fourth psalm, which we considered above, Williams notes that "Augustine speaks of what the psalm . . . 'makes of him.'" "The act of recitation," Williams adds, "becomes an opening to the transforming action of grace."[80]

Like others before him, Augustine refers to the psalms as "a mirror" in which we see the reflections of our own souls. "If the psalm is praying, pray yourselves; if it is groaning, you groan too; if it is happy, rejoice; if it is crying out in hope, you hope as well; if it expresses fear, be afraid. Everything written here is like a mirror held up to us" (*Exp. 4 Ps* 30.1).[81] What I see may be a reflection of God's mercies in my life. This makes the psalms a source of joy as they stir my memories and bring to my consciousness the good things that God has done for me (*Exp. Ps* 106.1). The reflection of my soul that I see in the psalms may also, however, give me cause to fear as I see what Robert Frost called "my own desert places."[82] "Fear the evil within you," Augustine says, "your own unruly desires, not what God created in you, but what you have made of yourself." It is the perception of this interior of evil that wrings from my mouth the cry, "Cleanse me from my secret sins, Lord" (*Exp. 2 Ps* 18.13, on Ps. 19:12).[83] We must discover the situation of the person praying in each psalm, Augustine says, so that we may know that it is our situation as well. Then, he adds, as we share his situation, "we may unite our prayer with his" (*Exp. Ps* 54.4, on Ps. 55:1).[84]

78. *Expositions of the Psalms 73–98*, trans. and notes by Maria Boulding, ed. John E. Rotelle, *WSA* 3.18 (Hyde Park, NY: New City, 2002), 385–86; also cited in the introduction by Fiedrowicz in *Expositions of the Psalms 1–32*, 39–40.

79. As quoted by Fiedrowicz in *Expositions of the Psalms 1–32*, 40.

80. Williams, "Augustine and the Psalms," 18; cf. Fiedrowicz in *Expositions of the Psalms 1–32*, 40.

81. Boulding, *Expositions of the Psalms 1–32*, 347.

82. "Desert Places," in *The Poetry of Robert Frost*, ed. Edward Connery Lathem (New York: Hold, Rinehart, and Winston, 1969), 296.

83. Boulding, *Expositions of the Psalms 1–32*, 212.

84. *Expositions of the Psalms 51–72*, trans. and notes by Maria Boulding, ed. John E. Rotelle, *WSA* 3/17 (Hyde Park, NY: New City, 2001), 55–56.

True prayer, Augustine emphasizes in his comments on Psalm 34, seeks nothing but the Lord himself. He notes that the psalmist does not ask for wealth, health, or any other personal advantage. He asks only for the presence of the Lord in his life. Prayer, in other words, is not a Christmas list one presents to God. Its one overriding motivation should be to have the presence of the Lord himself in one's life. When this is true, Augustine adds, then lesser favors will follow. If one's prayer asks only for the Lord to be present, then, Augustine adds, even while one prays the Lord will say, "Look, I am present; what do you want? What are you asking of me? Whatever I give you, it will be of far less worth than myself. Have me, have me myself, enjoy me, embrace me" (*Exp. 2 Ps* 33.8–9).[85]

Augustine on Identifying the Speakers in the Psalms

Like Origen and Jerome, Augustine recognizes various speakers in the psalms. Also like them, he recognizes that the speaker in the psalms may change suddenly and unexpectedly. These changes are not signaled in any way by the author. It is only the wording of the text itself that reveals whether the speaker is human or divine (*Exp. Ps* 44.8).[86] Augustine's process for identifying Christ as speaker in a psalm follows the same techniques we previously observed Origen using.

David himself, often referred to as the prophet, is sometimes the speaker (*Exp. Ps* 11.6; *Exp. 1 Ps* 30.20). At other times David may speak as the church or as Christ (*Exp. Ps* 59.1). Occasionally Augustine points out that a particular psalm must be understood as spoken by Christ rather than David because the words do not fit David's situation as suggested by the title of the psalm. The words of Psalm 3:6 (LXX), for example, about resting, sleeping, and arising, must be spoken by Christ concerning his death and resurrection because they are not proper to the time of David's flight from Absalom, to which the title assigns the psalm. More often, however, it is simply the words themselves that suggest the speaker. Sometimes the words are equivocal, suggesting a divine speaker but demanding that they be our own words. Psalm 27 presents such a case. It is not correct to say that the words of this psalm are our words and not those of the Spirit for they seem to belong more appropriately to the Spirit than to ourselves. But, Augustine remarks in strong language, "If we deny that they are ours, we are lying." This psalm is filled with groans and tears. It is the prayer of one who is miserable. The Lord, however, cannot be miserable. It is a case of the merciful Lord address-

---

85. *Expositions of the Psalms 33–50*, trans. and notes by Maria Boulding, ed. John E. Rotelle, *WSA* 3/16 (Hyde Park, NY: New City, 2000), 29–30.
86. Ibid., 288.

ing the miserable in their own voice. Consequently, Augustine adds, "[I]t is our voice here and not our voice," and, "it is the voice of the Spirit of God and not his voice" (*Exp. 2 Ps* 26.1).[87]

In other psalms Christ is unquestionably the speaker because words from these psalms are connected with Jesus in the Gospels. Psalm 31:5, for example, is quoted as Jesus's dying words on the cross (Luke 23:46), and verses from Psalm 22 are connected with the crucifixion of Jesus in the Gospels (Matt. 27:46; John 19:24). When the words of a psalm appear in the Gospels it is clear that Christ is speaking in the psalm (*Exp. 2 Ps* 30.11).[88] Psalm 16 is used in the New Testament as a proof that Jesus was the Messiah (Acts 2:25–31; 13:35–37). Augustine can, therefore, confidently connect it with Christ. It is not a messianic proof for him, however, but a prayer of Christ speaking "from the standpoint of the human nature he assumed" (*Exp. Ps* 15.1).[89]

Christ Speaks in Every Psalm

In one sense, it is proper to say that Augustine understood Christ to be the speaker in every psalm. He refers to the Christ who speaks in the psalms as the whole Christ. By this Augustine means both head, that is, Christ himself now ascended into heaven, and body, which he understands to be the church on earth from the earliest saints of the Old Testament through the end of time.[90] The church that speaks in the psalms as the body of Christ, in other words, is the church universal and eternal. He asks his congregation, for example, if they think they alone are the body of Christ to the exclusion of all the saints who have preceded them. He replies that the body of Christ embraces all the righteous from the beginning of creation. Those earlier saints "believed that he would come, and we believe that now he has come. They were healed by faith in him, just as we were" (*Exp. 3 Ps* 36.4).[91] In another homily, Augustine asserts that Christ's "body is the Church: not this or that local church, but the Church that extends throughout the world." This is the dimension of space. Then he adds that of time: "It is made up not only of people alive today, for those who have gone before us belong to the Church too, and so do those who will come after us, even to the end of time" (*Exp. Ps* 56.1).[92]

---

87. Boulding, *Expositions of the Psalms 1–32*, 274.
88. Ibid., 330–31.
89. Ibid., 182.
90. This has been observed by many scholars of Augustine. See for example, Rondeau, *Les commentaires patristiques*, 2:365–88; Fiedrowicz in *Expositions of the Psalms 1–32*, 57–65; Williams, "Augustine and the Psalms," 18–20.
91. Boulding, *Expositions of the Psalms 33–50*, 131.
92. Boulding, *Expositions of the Psalms 51–72*, 104.

This concept of the body of Christ speaking in the psalms gives a powerful dynamic to Augustine's understanding of the psalms as prayer. His comments on the words of Psalm 86:3, "Have mercy on me, Lord, for I have cried to you all day long," show the dynamics of this understanding in action.

> You have cried out during your days, and your days have expired; someone else took your place and cried out in his days; you here, he there, she somewhere else. The body of Christ cries out all day long, as its members give place to each other and succeed each other. One single person spans the ages to the end of time, and it is still the members of Christ who go on crying out, though some of them are already at rest in him, others are raising their cry now, others will cry out when we have gone to rest, and others again after them. God hears the voice of Christ's entire body saying, *I have cried to you all day long.* (*Exp. Ps* 85.5)[93]

In discussing Psalm 22 Augustine wrestles with how the words, "My God, my God, why have you forsaken me?" which are clearly the words of Christ because he speaks them on the cross, can be followed immediately by the words, "The tale of my sins leaves me far from salvation." The confession of sins does not seem appropriate to Christ. But surely the whole psalm should be understood as the words of Christ, for other statements, such as, "They shared out my garments among them, and cast lots for my tunic" (Ps. 22:18), sound as though one is reading the crucifixion narrative in the Gospels. The solution to this mystery is that Christ speaks in this psalm as both body and head (*Exp. Ps* 37.6).[94]

It is we, who constitute the church, who say in Psalm 38:3, "There is no peace in my bones in the face of my sins," even though later in the psalm the voice is that of Christ speaking of his passion. It is the "whole Christ" who speaks in this psalm. We are "members" of his body, as Paul says in Ephesians 5:30 and repeats "in many of his letters" (*Exp. Ps* 37.6).[95] Again, it is "Christ in his totality" who speaks in Psalm 3, Augustine says. This means Christ as head and body, in accordance with Paul's words in 1 Corinthians 12:27. Psalm 3, therefore, is the prayer of the persecuted church throughout the world. But it can also be the words of the individual beset with temptations: "Lord, how numerous are they who afflict me! Look how many rise up against me!" In either case the words of Psalm 3 are the words of the whole Christ, for the devil and his angels rage not only "against

93. Boulding, *Expositions of the Psalms 73–98*, 225.
94. Boulding, *Expositions of the Psalms 33–50*, 150–51.
95. Ibid., 150.

the body of Christ as a whole, but also against each one individually"
(*Exp. Ps* 3.9–10).[96]

It is evident that Augustine's understanding of the psalms as the prayers of the church is the culmination of the teachings of the church fathers on this subject. The early church consistently worshiped and addressed God in the prayer language of the psalms. The psalms brought before God not only all of the church's needs but also the needs and concerns of the individual members of the church.

Praying the Psalms Today

There has been a rebirth of interest in the ancient practices of the church, and this has included an interest in how the church prayed. In 2001, Arthur Paul Boers published an article in *Christianity Today* titled "Learning the Ancient Rhythms of Prayer."[97] In this article Boers discusses the worship centers at Taizé in France, Lindisfarne in England, and Iona off the coast of Scotland. These centers attract thousands of young people each year. The practice of the ancient modes of Christian prayer is one of their major attractions. These centers emphasize gathering, usually at morning, noon, and evening, to chant prayers corporately. The prayers include the Lord's prayer, numerous psalms, and other traditional prayers of the church.

It is not practical, of course, to imagine that the average working Christian is going to be able to assemble with the church three times a day to pray. Even in the ancient church those who assembled daily for three or more times of prayer must have been a relatively small portion of the Christians. It is possible, however, for the majority of Christians to find a regular time to pray the words that the ancient church prayed in the psalms, if not corporately, at least individually.

Praying the prayers of the ancient church could greatly enrich the average Christian's prayer life. Many feel inadequate, or even ignorant, when it comes to prayer. Dietrich Bonhoeffer once said in his book *The Psalms: The Prayer Book of the Bible* that we learn to pray like a child learns to speak. The father speaks to the child and the child repeats the father's speech after him. "We should speak to God," Bonhoeffer says, "not in the erroneous and confused language of our own hearts, but in the clear and pure language that God has spoken to us in Jesus Christ."[98]

---

96. Boulding, *Expositions of the Psalms 1–32*, 81–84.

97. Arthur Paul Boers, "Learning the Ancient Rhythms of Prayer," *Christianity Today*, January 8, 2001, 38–45.

98. Dietrich Bonhoeffer, *Die Psalmen: Das Gebetbuch der Bibel* (Giessen: Brunnen Verlag, 1995, reprint; 1940), 10–11.

The psalms can become our instruction book in prayer, teaching us how to lay our souls bare before God in God's own words. They can also give a whole new agenda to our prayer life. When we begin to use the psalms as our own prayers we will find our prayers lifted out of the narrow personal ruts they tend to run in and expanded to the farthest horizons of God's concerns.

The conversational aspect of prayer in the psalms may, in fact, be more pronounced when we pray them as individuals than when we pray them with the gathered church. When I read the psalms prayerfully alone, sometimes I am instructed or exhorted by the voice of the ancient author as he relates the stories of Israel; sometimes I myself am speaking, addressing God directly in the words of the psalmist; at other times I am directly addressed by God in the words of the psalm. The conversation may move back and forth within a single psalm.

We can also learn from the fathers that even if we must pray the psalms in private, we still pray them in community. When I pray the psalms my voice blends in praise, petition, and confession with that of the whole people of God, whether my contemporaries or my predecessors in faith, who have lifted and who continue to lift up these prayers to God. This solidarity with the whole church in prayer includes even Christ himself, the head of the church. In this communal sense all the words of the psalms become my prayer even if I am not at the moment experiencing the joys or sufferings they express. I can lift up even the words of Psalm 22:1, which Jesus prayed on the cross, "My God, my God, why have you forsaken me?" for I am one with the whole body of Christ, and where "one member suffers all suffer together." My prayer is one with those in seemingly God-forsaken situations who cry out for deliverance but none comes, even as Jesus cried out for deliverance in Gethsemane, when none was forthcoming.

LIVING IN THE TEXT

"But we have the mind of Christ."

1 Corinthians 2:16

IN A REVIEW of the television movie "Out of the Ashes," about a Jewish gynecologist at Auschwitz, Robin Pogrebin refers to Christine Lahti, who played the leading role, as "inhabiting" her character. Achieving such an identification with a character demands much more than learning lines. It demands time and effort on the part of the actress or actor to enter the mind of the character. Pogrebin says that to prepare for her role, Lahti "steeped herself in the history of the Holocaust, reading books and testimonials, watching films about the period and visiting museums." This immersion in the circumstances of her character's life affected Lahti's own life to the extent that she began to feel a kind of anxiety that she had never felt before. The whole process continued to affect her even after the filming finished. "When I got back to my life," Lahti said, "I could take nothing for granted ever again."[1]

It might be said that the church fathers did something similar with the Old Testament. They did not usually choose characters in the Old

1. Robin Pogrebin, "A Survivor's Story: Choosing When There Are No Choices," *New York Times*, April 13, 2003, 12.

175

Testament and attempt to identify with them. Nor were they concerned with being convincing in performing a role. The one character they consciously wanted to inhabit was Christ, whose image and mind they sought in the pages of the Old Testament as well as, if not more than, in the New. It is not, however, simply an imitation of Christ that is under consideration here, though that is always present. It involves also the broader issue of looking at oneself and the world through eyes that have been focused by the biblical story. Robert Jenson refers to Karl Barth's discovery of what Barth called a "'strange new world'" in the Bible as "a reality one could understand only by *inhabiting* it."[2] While the world of the Bible was certainly not as strange to the church fathers as it was to the nineteenth-century liberal mind of Karl Barth, they did consider it something to be inhabited.

It is important here, for both the ancients and moderns, to make a distinction between the story of the Bible and biblical, or Near Eastern, history. Neither Barth nor the church fathers thought they could relive biblical history. We noted in chapter 3 that although Gregory of Nyssa set forth the life of Moses as a model of the spiritual life, he was well aware of the temporal and cultural differences separating his readers from Moses. Gregory knew that his readers could not reenter the historical world of ancient Egypt or share in the nomadic life of the Israelites in the wilderness.[3] It is the *story* conveying the divine message that is the subject of living in the text. This is not to say that the biblical story is devoid of history. It is to say, rather, as Northrop Frye has said, that what is historically true in the Bible is not there "because it is historically true but for different reasons," which have to do "with spiritual . . . significance."[4] Or, as Henri de Lubac put it, "Everything in Scripture is 'spiritual.' . . . All that Scripture recounts has indeed happened in history, but the account that is given does not contain the whole purpose of Scripture in itself. This purpose still needs to be accomplished and is actually accomplished in us each day."[5] Living in the text means living in the *story* of the text, not trying to live in the *ancient history* of the text. This may be an important element that post-Enlightenment Christians need to discover. Simply reconstructing the history in the text may help us understand the text better, but it does not call the believer to "live in the text."

2. Robert W. Jenson, "Karl Barth," in *The Modern Theologians*, ed. David F. Ford, 2nd ed. (Cambridge, MA: Blackwell, 1997), 21.

3. See "Gregory of Nyssa: Reimagining the Life of Moses as a Model of Christian Virtue" in chap. 3 above.

4. Northrop Frye, *The Great Code* (San Diego: Harcourt Brace, 1982), 40.

5. Henri de Lubac, *Medieval Exegesis*, vol. 1, *The Four Senses of Scripture*, trans. Mark Sebanc (Grand Rapids: Eerdmans, 1998; original edition 1959), 227.

Coming to Live in the Text

The biblical story functions somewhat like a paradigm into which one fits the circumstances of one's own life. But, like the Greek student who needs to identify the ending of a noun, the paradigm must be internalized if it is to function properly. This paradigmatic function of Old Testament story appears to be the reason the author of the epistle to the Hebrews introduces in Hebrews 11 a list of faithful sufferers from the Old Testament. A few lines before introducing the list, he refers to the suffering that the recipients of his letter have experienced, and perhaps were still experiencing, and exhorts them to faith and endurance (Heb. 10:32–36). Then he leads them into the world of the Old Testament, into the stories of the faithful from Abel to the Maccabean martyrs. The characters in these Old Testament stories, the author suggests, are witnessing the life his readers are living (Heb. 12:1). His purpose in recalling these stories is not to relate history but to encourage his readers to run the race before them with endurance (Heb. 12:1) in the same way that these previous saints ran their race with endurance. These saints are a paradigm for his readers. He is encouraging them to imitate the faithfulness conveyed in the stories of these Old Testament characters in order to live faithfully in their own day. The individual stories of the readers of the epistle to the Hebrews will, in their turn, be blended into the overarching story of human faith and God's faithfulness, for the Hebrew writer goes on to say that those earlier faithful heroes will not "be perfected apart from us" (Heb. 11:39–40).

Deep Familiarity with the Text

For the church fathers, living in the text involved two related but separate aspects. The first was a thorough knowledge of the text gained from years of reading and hearing its stories. This was the sine qua non. Augustine believed that the first step the person who wanted to investigate the meaning of the Scriptures must take was to read them in their entirety, even to memorize them, although parts would not yet be fully understood (*On Christian Doctrine* 2.8.12–9.14). Jerome counseled his friend Paulinus of Nola "to live among" the books of the Bible, "to meditate upon them, to know nothing else, to seek nothing else" (*Epistle* 53.10). This thorough knowledge of the biblical text is evident in the writings and sermons of all the major church fathers.

Ambrose, in the following example from his *Flight from the World*, can weave together passages with common words or themes and expect his readers to grasp the larger pictures on which he has drawn.

> Therefore let us flee from here, where there is nothing, where all that is reckoned noble is empty, and where the one who thinks himself to be

something is nothing, yes, nothing at all. "I have seen the wicked man highly exalted and lifted up beyond the cedars of Libanus, and I passed by, and behold, he was not" [Ps. 37:35–36]. And do you pass by like David. . . . Pass by like Moses, that you may see the God of Abraham and of Isaac and of Jacob and that you may see a great vision [cf. Exod. 3:6; Matt. 22:32]. This is a great vision, but if you wish to see it, remove the sandals from your feet [Exod. 3:5], remove every bond of iniquity, remove the bonds of the world, leave behind the sandals which are earthly. . . . For the man who seeks the good is praised, not for his sandals, but for the swiftness and grace of his feet, as Scripture says, "How beautiful are the feet of those who preach the gospel of peace, of those who bring glad tidings of good things!" [Isa.52:7; Rom. 10:15]. Therefore remove the sandals from your feet, that they may be beautiful for preaching the Gospel. "Remove" [Exod. 3:5], the text says, not "bind." "Remove," so that you may pass by and may find that the unholy man whom you admired on earth is nothing and can be nothing. Pass by, therefore, that is, flee from earth, where there is evil and where there is avarice.[6]

Ambrose's point in this exposition, which is a meditation on the biblical verb "to pass by," is the simple exhortation to turn away from the lure and vanity of worldly things and fasten one's attention on the divine. His approach reveals that he himself lives in the biblical text and assumes that his readers do the same. For his presentation to work, the fragmentary allusions in his address must pull up for his readers the biblical stories in which they are embedded. They can do this only if the minds of the readers are soaked in the stories of the Bible. His readers must know of Lebanon's fame for its magnificent cedars and of the biblical usage of this phrase as a metaphor for the proud. They must know the story of Moses's encounter with God at the burning bush and the demand that he remove his sandals in the presence of the holy. And they must know Isaiah's words to the exiles, who longed for a message of deliverance, words that Paul would later take up and apply to the messengers who announce deliverance in Christ. I have inserted the biblical references in the quotation. Ambrose makes no reference to the sources of his allusions because he assumes that they will resonate in the minds of his readers. This living in the text in the sense of living *with* the text intensely and for a prolonged period of time will be evident in each of the people we will consider in this chapter.

Molding Life by the Text

The other aspect of living in the text that is found in the church fathers stands squarely on the shoulders of the first and is impossible

6. *Saint Ambrose: Seven Exegetical Works*, trans. Michael P. McHugh, FC 65 (Washington, DC: Catholic University of America Press, 1972), 300–301.

without it. The biblical text, in both its vision and vocabulary, shaped the vision, discourse, and life of the fathers. Robin Darling Young has pointed out that the fourth-century monk Evagrius "understood the monk to be just as much an inhabitant of the biblical world as the characters who appeared in the text." Monks were the "virtual contemporaries" of "the patriarchs, prophets, and apostles" and shared the same "understanding of the inner structure of created reality as had" these earlier saints.[7] Averil Cameron considers the culmination of this process to have been the primary factor that "enabled Christianity to prevail in the medieval culture of Byzantium and the West." "Christian discourse," she says, "provided both the framework within which most people looked at the world and the words that they used to describe it."[8]

The church fathers did not view the story of Scripture as something that needed to be brought into line with life as they knew it in their particular age. Rather, they looked at their own lives and times from the viewpoint of Scripture. They saw the conflicts they experienced both in their souls and in their societies as the conflicts depicted in Scripture. They experienced as their own the struggles, defeats, and victories in Scripture. And they described these experiences in the language and concepts of Scripture. Their desire was to view and live life as Christ had done. This was an intense desire in most of them and they stressed that such an intensity of desire was necessary, alongside the time spent in study, to find Christ in Scripture. The ultimate goal in this pursuit was not intellectual, of course, but the practical goal of imitating Christ in the everyday activities of life; it was the acquisition and practice of the virtues set forth in Scripture. These virtues were especially connected with Christ. Origen and Gregory of Nyssa, as we will see later in this chapter, could say that to become identified with Christ is the same as acquiring and practicing all the virtues, for Scripture equates the virtues with Christ. Living in the text was not an intellectual exercise for the church fathers but was a practical and, sometimes no doubt, painful molding of their own lives into the image of Christ. Let's look at some specific examples of early Christians who lived in the text.

7. R. D. Young, "Appropriating Genesis and Exodus in Evagrius's *On Prayer*," in *In Dominico Eloquio—In Lordly Eloquence*, ed. P. M. Blowers, A. R. Christman, D. G. Hunter, and R. D. Young (Grand Rapids: Eerdmans, 2002), 243–44. See also Paul Blowers, "The Bible and Spiritual Doctrine: Some Controversies within the Early Eastern Christian Ascetic Tradition," in *The Bible in Greek Christian Antiquity*, ed. and trans. Paul M. Blowers (Notre Dame, IN: University of Notre Dame Press, 1977), 230–31.

8. Averil Cameron, *Christianity and the Rhetoric of Empire: The Development of Christian Discourse* (Berkeley: University of California Press, 1991), 222.

Ephrem the Syrian and Engagement with the Biblical Text

Ephrem was appointed to a teaching position by his bishop in the church in Nisibis on the eastern frontier of the Roman Empire (in modern southeastern Turkey) shortly after the Council of Nicaea in AD 325. He continued in this position until Nisibis became a part of the Persian empire in AD 363, at which time he, along with the entire Christian population of Nisibis, was forced to leave. He migrated to Edessa, approximately one hundred miles to the west, where he spent the last ten years of his life.[9]

Ephrem's native language was Syriac. He read the Bible in Syriac translations, and he produced his works in the Syriac language. He was also a poet and wrote most of his theological works as poetry. He lived with the text of the Bible his entire life. He says in his *Hymns on Virginity*:

> Your truth was with me in my youth,
> Your faithfulness is with my old age. (37.10)[10]

Sebastian Brock describes Ephrem's approach to theology as "essentially Biblical and Semitic in character," without ties "to a particular cultural or philosophical background," and says that it "operates by means of imagery and symbolism which are basic to all human experience."[11]

Ephrem believed both creation and Scripture witness to God. He says in his *Hymns on Paradise*:

> In his book Moses
>   described the creation of the natural world,
> so that both Nature and Scripture
>   might bear witness to the Creator. (5.2)[12]

Both nature and Scripture contain spiritual reality embedded in the material medium. Both, therefore, must also be read with the eye of faith to perceive their witness.[13]

Ephrem considered God to be incarnate in the language of Scripture in much the same way that he was incarnate in Jesus of Nazareth. Brock refers to Ephrem's frequent statement that in the Scriptures God "puts

---

9. *Saint Ephrem: Hymns on Paradise*, intro. and trans. Sebastian Brock (Crestwood, NY: St. Vladimir's Seminary Press, 1990), 9–11.
10. Ibid., 9.
11. Ibid., 40.
12. Ibid., 102.
13. Ibid., 39.

on names." This is a condescension on God's part to the limitations of our human abilities.[14] The "Creator," Ephrem says,

> has clothed His majesty
>   in terms that we can understand.
>
> (*Hymns on Paradise* 11.5)

The person who forgets, however, or ignores that the terms in which God is clothed in Scripture are metaphors,

> abuses and misrepresents that majesty
>   and thus errs
> by means of those metaphors
>   with which God clothed Himself for his benefit.
>
> (*Hymns on Paradise* 11.6)[15]

It is not God the Father alone, however, whose image lies embedded in the metaphors and symbols of Scripture. The image of Christ is to be found there as well. In his *Hymns on Virginity* Ephrem uses the striking metaphor of Christ painting his own portrait in the writings of the law and prophets.

> Scattered symbols you have gathered up
>   from the Torah for your comeliness.
> You have published the models . . .
>   which are in your Gospel,
>   along with the prodigies and signs of nature.
> You have mixed them together as the paints for
> your portrait; you have looked at yourself,
> and painted your own portrait.
> . . . .
> The prophets, the kings, and the priests,
>   who were creatures, all of them painted
>   your portrait, but they themselves bore no resemblance.
> . . . .
> They indeed drew the lines of your portrait;
>   you in your coming brought it to completion.
> The lines then disappeared due to the strength of the paints,
>   the most brilliant of all colors.
>
> (*Hymns on Virginity* 28.2–3)[16]

---

14. Sebastian Brock, *The Luminous Eye: The Spiritual World Vision of Saint Ephrem*, Cistercian Studies Series 124, rev. ed. (Kalamazoo, MI: Cistercian Publications, 1992), 42.

15. Brock, *Hymns on Paradise*, 155–56.

16. Sidney H. Griffith, *"Faith Adoring the Mystery": Reading the Bible with St. Ephraem the Syrian*, The Père Marquette Lecture in Theology 1997 (Milwaukee: Marquette University

Sidney Griffith has argued that Ephrem understood the symbols and names in the Old Testament narratives to be paradigmatic "for the Christian's own understanding of God and the world." There was, in fact, a kind of transposition that took place in the reading process. "Ephrem read the Scriptures in terms of these symbols, types, names and titles, and they in turn became the terms of his own thought."[17] Ephrem's relationship with the biblical symbols was a delicate one. They were neither destroyed in order to discover and expound their meaning nor forced into the mode of thought of the eastern Roman Empire of the fourth century AD. Ephrem recognized that the biblical language symbolized something greater, but he also recognized that the particular forms of expression were essential for understanding that greater entity.

Sebastian Brock has called Ephrem's approach to the biblical text an approach of "engagement," and especially "an engagement . . . of love and wonder." He contrasts it to both the scientific approach inherited from Francis Bacon, in which the mind attempts "to dominate and subjugate the object of its enquiry," and the detachment from the text that was the ideal of much twentieth-century interpretation of the Bible. For Ephrem, the interpreter must engage in a dialogue of love with the divine voice in the text if he or she is to ascertain its meaning (*Hymns on Faith* 32.1). Ephrem says:

> Your fountain, Lord, is hidden
> from the person who does not thirst for You;
> Your treasury seems empty
> to the person who rejects You.
> Love is the treasurer
> of Your heavenly treasure store.
>
> (*Hymns on Faith* 32:2–3)[18]

To know the divine through Scripture, Ephrem insists, we must become participants in the textual symbols that both hide and disclose the mystery.[19]

Origen on Inhabiting Christ through Scripture

Origen lived in Scripture as few others in the history of the church have. While he was certainly well educated in the intellectual disciplines

Press, 1997), 31–32. I have substituted "symbol" in the first line where Griffith has *râzê*, which he defines as "symbol" in the preceding paragraph.

17. Ibid., 28–29.

18. Brock, *Luminous Eye*, 43–44.

19. Ibid., 44.

of his age and thoroughly versed in the philosophy of his time, his discourse was determined far more by the language of Scripture than by that of philosophy. He spoke of philosophy in scriptural metaphors rather than vice versa. When he wanted to advise his student Gregory to learn all he could from philosophy and use it for Christian purposes, he did it in a scriptural metaphor. "Spoil the Egyptians," he counseled Gregory (*Epistle to Gregory* 1). He says in his defense against the Platonist Celsus's attack on the teachings in the Scriptures that "the sacred writings of the prophets have something more profound about them than the words of Plato admired by Celsus" (*Against Celsus* 6.17–18).[20] Origen knew the writings of the philosophers, but he lived in the Scriptures.

Eusebius tells us that when Origen was a boy his father insisted that he put study of the Scriptures before his normal school studies. His father required the boy, Eusebius says, to memorize passages of Scripture daily and repeat them aloud. Origen threw himself into this study, not only memorizing Scripture, as his father demanded, but continually pestering his father with questions about the meaning underlying the words he was memorizing (*Ecclesiastical History* 6.2.7–9). Eusebius adds that after Origen had assumed the leadership of a school connected with the church in Alexandria, he would put in a strenuous day teaching and then spend most of the night studying Scripture (*Ecclesiastical History* 6.3.9). Eusebius's stories may have been embellished to enhance his depiction of Origen's godliness, but Origen's versatility in handling the Scriptures, as demonstrated throughout his writings, suggests that his study of them had been long and intense. Origen said later in his life that Christ appears to those "who think about him and meditate on him and live 'in his law day and night'" (*HomGn* 11.3).[21]

Origen speaks of his experience with Scripture from the perspective of standing within the text. He treats his hearers or readers in the same way. Origen's homilies, especially, address his hearers as people who stand within the scriptural text and experience the trials and victories depicted there. They have come out of Egypt; they have struggled in the wilderness; they have crossed the Jordan; and they battle daily against the inhabitants of the land of Canaan. They are to view their own lives, with their particular conflicts, within the conceptual framework provided by the biblical text. This injects a note of immediacy and urgency into the reading of Scripture. One is reminded of Karl Barth's assertion that

20. *Origen: Contra Celsum*, trans. Henry Chadwick (Cambridge: Cambridge University Press, 1965), 331.

21. *Origen: Homilies on Genesis and Exodus*, trans. Ronald E. Heine, FC 71 (Washington, DC: Catholic University of America Press, 1982), 175.

every verse in the Bible is virtually a concrete faith-event in my own life. . . . Have I experienced anything more important, incisive, serious, contemporary than this, that I have been personally present and have shared in the crossing of Israel through the Red Sea but also in the adoration of the golden calf, in the baptism of Jesus but also in the denial of Peter and the treachery of Judas, that all this has happened to me here and now?[22]

Origen reads the Old Testament narratives as a kind of typology of ongoing Christian experience. If, he argues, the author of Hebrews can claim the tabernacle and its system of worship as a representation of heavenly things (Heb. 8:5), then the wars described in the book of Joshua that Jesus[23] wages in conquering the land can be understood as representations of the wars our Lord Jesus wages against Satan and his angels (*HomJos* 12.1). The Canaanites, Perizzites, and Jebusites are within us. They are the vices against which we struggle (*HomJos* 1.7). The crossing of the Jordan is our baptism into Jesus (*HomJos* 5.1). Paul informs us of the battles awaiting us after crossing the Jordan, battles "against rulers and authorities, against world rulers of this darkness, against wicked spiritual beings in the heavens" (Eph. 6:12). These enemies arise within our own hearts (*HomJos* 5.2). They are the kings in Canaan enthroned on our vices in fortified cities that we must overthrow (*HomJos* 13.1; 14.1). Origen often uses Ephesians 6:12 as a template for speaking of the wars recorded in Joshua (*HomJos* 1.5; 11.4; 12.1; 15.1, 5).[24] This verse and others, such as 1 Corinthians 10:11 and Ephesians 2:2 (see *HomJos* 13.1; 14.1), provide the means for Origen to place his audience into the middle of the action in the biblical text. These verses allow his audience to live in the text of the Old Testament from a Christian perspective.

For Origen, however, the higher goal of living in the biblical text is to inhabit the mind of Christ himself.[25] He is aware that only a relatively few people will achieve this because most will neither have the kind of desire nor spend the amount of time with the biblical text that this demands. It is a goal that can be attained only by living with the biblical text for a

22. Karl Barth, *Church Dogmatics*, 1/2, ed. G. W. Bromiley and T. F. Torrance, trans. G. T. Thomson and H. Knight (Edinburgh: T&T Clark, 1980), 709.

23. Jesus is the Greek rendering of the Hebrew name Joshua. In his first homily on Joshua, Origen treats the name Jesus, which is the LXX rendering of Joshua. The book of Joshua is not about the accomplishments of the son of Nun, he argues, but about Jesus the Son of God. See *Origen: Homilies on Joshua*, trans. Barbara J. Bruce, ed. Cynthia White, FC 105 (Washington, DC: Catholic University of America Press, 2002), 26–36.

24. See also, Ronald E. Heine, *The Commentaries of Origen and Jerome on St. Paul's Epistle to the Ephesians* (New York: Oxford University Press, 2002), 66–69.

25. See Ronald Heine, "Reading the Bible with Origen," in Blowers, *Bible in Greek Christian Antiquity*, 141–44.

prolonged period of time with an intense love for Christ and a desire to know him through the text. By Origen's time the term Scripture included the New Testament[26] as well as the Old, and Origen certainly included the text of the New Testament when he spoke of acquiring the mind of Christ through Scripture. It will become apparent in the following discussion, however, how important Old Testament texts were for Origen's understanding of acquiring the mind of Christ through Scripture.

When he discusses the story of the Samaritan woman at Jacob's well, Origen equates the well with the Scriptures, and the water that Jesus refers to as a spring of water "leaping into eternal life" with a higher knowledge given by Christ himself. This higher knowledge of Christ cannot be attained, Origen asserts, unless one has come regularly over an extended period of time to Jacob's well, thirsting like the deer of Psalm 42. The majority of people, he concludes, are very deficient in this practice (*ComJn* 13.20–42). In other places Origen uses food analogies to refer to Scripture. Discussing the words "In the evening you will eat flesh and in the morning you will be filled with bread" (Exod. 16:12), he takes the "bread" to be the "books of the Law and prophets," which Jesus delivered to the church after his resurrection (see Luke 24:27, 44–45). We are incapable of understanding higher doctrine, which Origen equates with eating flesh, until we have spent the day of our life feeding on the bread. Then, in the evening, "after long exercises . . . [and] much advance," we can feast on the flesh (*HomEx* 7.8).[27] Notice again the emphasis on the necessity of an extended period of time with Scripture in order to enjoy its intended purpose.

Origen's most profound statements concerning acquiring the mind of Christ are found in two passages in his *Commentary on John*. One is in his discussion of Jesus and the Samaritan woman at Jacob's well (John 4:7–16), to which we referred above, and the other is in the prologue to the commentary. In the former, Origen draws on Paul's enigmatic allusion to "the things beyond those that have been written" (1 Cor. 4:6) to interpret the "water that leaps into eternal life" of John 4:14. Origen stresses in this discussion that this more mysterious understanding rests squarely on an understanding of the things that have been written, that is, the Scriptures. In a homily on 1 Corinthians he says that the heretics, who ignore the teachings of Scripture, take this phrase in 1 Corinthians to justify their claim that they have secret teachings from the Savior. Origen dismisses this as a deceptive mythology. One cannot go up to the things that have not been written before one has thoroughly understood

---

26. In a discussion of Scripture, Origen uses the term "New Testament" (*kainē diathēkē*) and says it consists of four Gospels, the Acts and the epistles of the apostles, and the apocalypse (*ComJn* 1.15–22).

27. Heine, *Homilies on Genesis and Exodus*, 312–13.

those things that are written. He compares it to climbing a ladder—one must begin at the lower rungs and proceed upward from there.[28]

We must go up, Origen says, from the Scriptures to Jesus that he may give us the "water that leaps into eternal life" (*ComJn* 13.37). It is not possible to say with certainty whether Origen here meant by the term Scripture the Old and New Testaments together, or whether, as Rolf Gögler assumes, he meant specifically the Old Testament.[29] The latter certainly fits Origen's understanding of the Old Testament Scriptures. We truly go up from them to Jesus. Going up from the Scriptures to Jesus means, for Origen, attaining the mind of Christ, for only those who have the mind of Christ can receive the water Jesus gives.

In the prologue to the *Commentary on John* Origen offers another important discussion of attaining the mind of Christ by living with Scripture. In the early sections of the prologue, he constructs a pyramid of the scriptural books beginning with the law of Moses at the bottom and climaxing with the Gospel of John at the top. The whole of Scripture speaks of Christ, he says, but the four Gospels do so with a unique clarity. Among the Gospels themselves, Origen claims, the Gospel of John stands at the peak because it presents Jesus's divinity more fully than the others (*ComJn* 1.14–22).[30] Origen asserts that one must share the experience of John and Mary at the cross to be able to understand "the mind" of this Gospel, for at the cross Jesus says of John to Mary, "Woman, behold your son" (John 19:26). Origen believes that Mary had no son except Jesus. He argues on this assumption that Jesus's statement is equivalent to saying, "Behold, this is Jesus whom you bore." Origen juxtaposes Paul's assertion in Galatians that he "no longer lives, but Christ lives in him" (2:20) and concludes that because Paul's statement could be said of John as well, Jesus can refer to John as Mary's son, the Christ.

This leads Origen to reflect on the responsibility laid on us to understand the treasures of Scripture in a worthy manner. The Scriptures contain everyday language that anyone who so desires can read. But the treasure contained in the ordinary words can be known only by the person who can truthfully say, "But we have the mind of Christ, that we

28. Fragment 19 on 1 Cor. in Claude Jenkins, "Origen on 1 Corinthians," *JTS*, o.s. (1905): 357.

29. Rolf Gögler, *Origenes: Das Evangelium nach Johannes* (Einsiedeln: Benziger Verlag, 1959), 245. As I noted earlier, the term "Scripture" had come, by Origen's time, to include the New Testament as well as the Old. Origen sometimes uses it both ways. He has twice referred to "all Scripture" in this particular discussion, which may suggest that he is thinking of the Old and New Testaments together.

30. See Ronald E. Heine, "The Introduction to Origen's *Commentary on John* Compared with the Introductions to the Ancient Philosophical Commentaries on Aristotle," in *Origeniana Sexta*, ed. Gilles Dorival and Alain Le Boulluec, BETL 118 (Leuven: Leuven University Press, 1995), 8–11.

may know the things that have been given us by God" (*ComJn* 1.23–24). The treasures of Scripture, in other words, are discovered by those who have lived with them long enough and seriously enough that they have come to inhabit Christ. Origen obviously believed that he had experienced this just as he asserts that John had, for the point of his argument in the prologue to his *Commentary on John* is that only the person who has done so can understand the meaning of John's Gospel.

Inhabiting the mind of Christ is not limited for Origen to an intellectual or spiritual understanding of Christ and Scripture. It results in taking on the virtues that Scripture associates with Christ. "To 'learn Christ,'" Origen can say in explaining Paul's words in Ephesians 4:20, "is the same as learning virtue" (*ComEph* 4:20).[31] "We have often said," Origen comments on Romans 13:14, "that Christ is at the same time wisdom, righteousness, sanctification, truth, and all the virtues. Assuredly the one who has received these is said to have put on Christ. For if Christ is all these things, the one who has them necessarily has Christ as well" (*ComRom* 9.34).[32] Inhabiting the mind of Christ, therefore, affects the way one lives in the world. To be dishonest or unjust is to join the soldiers who struck Christ and spat on him. Christ is honored by showing "honor and devotion to wisdom, justice, and truth, and to all things which Christ is said to be" (*ComRom* 2.5).[33]

For Origen, the end result of inhabiting Christ is that each person who does so becomes, in a way analogous to Christ, a means whereby God reveals himself in the world. In a homily on Jeremiah 16 Origen combines the story from Exodus 33:22–23 about Moses seeing God's back through a cleft in a rock with Paul's statement in 1 Corinthians 10:4 that "the rock was Christ." Just as Jesus "was a rock, so all who are imitators of Christ become rocks." Furthermore, just as Jesus's presence on earth provided a cleft through which God's back was seen, so his imitators, through their words, provide a cleft in themselves through which God is contemplated (*HomJer* 16.2–3).

Gregory of Nyssa and the Sculpturing of the Soul by Scripture

Gregory of Nyssa's understanding of Scripture and the Christian life is structured around two central concepts. He understands the sequence

---

31. Heine, *Commentaries of Origen and Jerome on Ephesians*, 185; see also pp. 190 and 252–53 on Eph. 4:24a and 6:11.

32. *Origen: Commentary on the Epistle to the Romans, Books 6–10*, trans. Thomas P. Scheck, FC 104 (Washington, DC: Catholic University of America Press, 2002), 233, modified.

33. *Origen: Commentary on the Epistle to the Romans, Books 1–5*, trans. Thomas P. Scheck, FC 103 (Washington, DC: Catholic University of America Press, 2001), 116–17.

of things related in Scripture to determine Scripture's meaning, and he understands the Christian life to be controlled by a constant "straining forward," a concept borrowed from Paul in Philippians 3:13.[34] The first refers to progress in the order of the biblical text and the second refers to progress in the development of the soul. The two blend into each other as Gregory depicts the shaping of the soul through Scripture.

Gregory believes that the order of the biblical text itself is significant. The fact that something precedes or follows something else in Scripture points to the intention the Holy Spirit had in ordering the text in that particular way. In his study of the titles of the psalms Gregory notes that the historical circumstances of David's life alluded to in the titles of the various psalms are not in historical order. He raises the question of why the psalms are "at variance with the sequence of history" (*Inscriptions of the Psalms* 2.11). To answer this question Gregory refers to the approach he had defined at the beginning of the study.

> First, one must understand the aim to which this writing looks. Next, one must pay attention to *the progressive arrangements of the concepts* in the book under discussion. These are indicated both by *the order of the psalms*, which has been well arranged in relation to knowledge of the aim, and by the sections of the whole book. (*Inscriptions of the Psalms*, preface, italics mine)[35]

The aim of the Psalter, Gregory contends, has nothing to do with history. Its aim is to attract "those wandering in the vanity of life . . . to the true life" (*Inscriptions of the Psalms* 2.11). It accomplishes this aim by "a skilful and natural sequence in teaching" (*Inscriptions of the Psalms* 1.1).

The Spirit as Sculptor

Gregory compares the way the Holy Spirit shapes our souls through the Psalter to the way a sculptor goes about his work. The sculptor begins with a concept of what he wants to produce. There is then a necessary order to how he goes about accomplishing his aim. First the stone must be broken away from the larger rock to which it is attached and trimmed of all unnecessary protrusions. After this follows a process of carving,

---

34. For the first understanding, see Jean Daniélou, "Akolouthia chez Grégoire de Nysse," *Revue des sciences religieuses* (1953): 219–49; for the second, see Jean Daniélou, "La colombe et la ténèbre dans la mystique Byzantine ancienne," *Eranos Jahrbuch* 23 (1954): 409–18; and Jean Daniélou, *From Glory to Glory*, trans. Herbert Musurillo (New York: Charles Scribner's Sons, 1961), 56–71.

35. Ronald E. Heine, *Gregory of Nyssa's Treatise on the Inscriptions of the Psalms*, introduction, translation, and notes, OECS (Oxford: Clarendon, 1995), 83.

smoothing, and polishing with ever more delicate instruments as the sculptor "imposes the likeness of the model's form on what remains" (*Inscriptions of the Psalms* 2.11). Finally, he polishes the finished product to a smooth surface. All these actions must follow in their proper order to accomplish the goal.

The aim of the sculptor of our souls is to hew us "to the divine likeness." First, the Psalter breaks us away from the rock of evil to which we have attached ourselves. Then it trims off the excesses and begins forming us by stripping away the hindrances to our achieving the goal. Finally, "by means of the forms of virtue, it forms Christ in us, in whose image we existed in the beginning, and in which we again come to exist" (*Inscriptions of the Psalms* 2.11). The sequence of the historical events alluded to in the psalms is irrelevant to this process. The sequence of the psalms is "the sequence related to salvation." Gregory gives a brief example of how he perceives this working. The first psalm, he says, removes us from our "cohesion with evil." The second shows us that we should trust in the Lord, and the third indicates the temptation that the enemy puts before us as soon as we align ourselves with the Lord (*Inscriptions of the Psalms* 2.11).[36] Gregory notes that most of the psalms that contain in their titles the word "alleluia," which means "praise the Lord," appear near the end of the book. This is because "praising God is appropriate for those who have already arrived at the goal of the virtuous way of life and have been purified through the preceding sections of the Psalms" (*Inscriptions of the Psalms* 2.7).[37]

The Formation of the True Human Being

The goal of the whole process for Gregory, as we noted above, is "to form Christ in us, in whose image we existed in the beginning, and in which we again come to exist" (*Inscriptions of the Psalms* 2.11). He develops the formation of Christ in the soul in his study of the psalms with several images drawn from the psalms on which he comments. When the Psalmist refers to the "shadow" of God's "wings" (Ps. 57:1), Gregory understands the shadow to refer to the virtues. God's nature itself is "unattainable and incomprehensible to human nature," flying high "above the thought of humanity." The virtues, however, impress the shadow of his nature on us (*Inscriptions of the Psalms* 2.14).[38] Gregory says the same thing more prosaically in his treatise *On the Profession of Christianity*. Humanity began, as Genesis 1:27 teaches, in the likeness of God. The goal of Christianity is to restore humanity to this original state. But how, Gregory wonders,

36. Ibid., 163–65, some modified.
37. Ibid., 142.
38. Ibid., 196.

can humanity strain forward and become like God. Scripture does not demand, he claims, that human nature become like the divine nature. What it demands instead is that human nature imitate the activities of God, which are the virtues.[39] When the Psalmist says, in the Septuagint translation that Gregory read, "The light of your face has been imprinted on us, Lord" (Ps. 4:6), Gregory understands the face of God imprinted on us to be the virtues, "for the divine form is imprinted in these" (*Inscriptions of the Psalms* 1.4).[40]

The order of the Psalms, Gregory claims, follows the progress of those being perfected through virtue. He calls this order the "logic of virtue" (*Inscriptions of the Psalms* 2.14).[41] The conclusion of this "logic" in the psalms is the formation of "the true human being" (*Inscriptions of the Psalms* 2.16).[42]

The true human being is the person who lives in the world as the image of God. This person is the final product of the divine sculptor's work. By practicing the virtues, this person has given form to that "imprint . . . imposed on our nature in the beginning" (*Inscriptions of the Psalms* 2.16).[43] Gregory understands the image of God, as Paul did (2 Cor. 4:4; Col. 1:15), to be Christ (*Inscriptions of the Psalms* 2.11). The true human being, therefore, is the person who has inhabited Christ to the point that his life is a Christ-shaped life.

The Practical Goal of the Intellectual Exercise

The church fathers lived in the text of the Bible. They knew its stories, its words of praise and condemnation, its instructions and warnings, its promises and fulfillments. They read its words, listened to its words, thought in its words, spoke its words, and lived by its words. Scripture defined their lives. The intellectual task of knowing Scripture, however, neither began nor ended as an intellectual task. It began in the passionate desire to know Christ and reached its end in being formed in his image. This was not a self-centered circle. To be formed in the image of Christ meant for them to live among their fellow humans in justice, truthfulness, fidelity, and love.

39. On the importance that the early Christians attached to imitation in the formation of the virtuous life, see Robert L. Wilken, *Remembering the Christian Past* (Grand Rapids: Eerdmans, 1995), 121–44.

40. Heine, *Gregory of Nyssa*, 93.

41. Ibid., 193.

42. Ibid., 211.

43. Ibid., modified.

Origen best sums up the process in the metaphorical language of constructing a library within oneself as he concludes his homily on Noah's ark. Just as Noah heard the word of God in a world that was becoming ever more evil and, in obedience to that word, built an ark that saved all who listened to him, so anyone who hears "the word of God" as Noah did "is building an ark of salvation within his own heart and is dedicating a library . . . of the divine word within himself." The dimensions of this ark or library of salvation, Origen says, are "faith, hope, and love"; faith in the Trinity, love expressed in gentleness and kindness, and hope exalted to heaven. Then he turns to counsel.

> If, therefore, you build an ark, if you gather a library, gather it from the words of the prophets and apostles. . . . From this library learn the historical narratives; from it recognize "the great mystery" which is fulfilled in Christ and in the Church. From it also learn how to correct habits, to curtail vices, to purge the soul and draw it off from every bond of captivity, setting up "rooms" in it . . . for the various virtues and perfections. (*HomGn* 2.6)[44]

44. Heine, *Homilies on Genesis and Exodus*, 86–87, modified.

Epilogue

Jesus of Nazareth was and is the foundation on which the Christian faith stands. This foundation, however, has never been Jesus alone. The Christian faith was built on the foundation of Jesus of Nazareth as understood in relation to the Scriptures of the Old Testament. These Scriptures defined who he was for Christian faith. They provided the framework in which his birth, ministry, passion, resurrection, and exaltation were viewed. His earliest followers proclaimed the story of his life in conjunction with the little phrase, "It is written." That phrase always introduced a text from the Old Testament that was seen to give validity to what Jesus had done and experienced. The Old Testament is intertwined in the church's gospel in such a way that it cannot be extricated without destroying the gospel. The church fathers continued the practice of understanding Jesus in this Old Testament framework and expanded it. Not only did Old Testament texts validate for them who Jesus was, these texts also served to interpret what he had accomplished for humanity, especially through his passion and resurrection.

Because they found Christ in the Old Testament, the church fathers also found their own lives as his followers prefigured there. The historical narratives of Israel's enslavement, deliverance, temptations, defeats, and victories reflected the experiences of their own souls. They looked to the precepts and examples found in the Old Testament so that their lives might be shaped into the image of Christ. They praised God, confessed their sins, and petitioned God for help in the words of the psalms of David. The Old Testament was their prayer book as well as their primer in the faith. But it was never used in any of these capacities in isolation from Christ. They looked at Christ through the Old Testament and they looked at the Old Testament through Christ. The two were inseparable in the minds of the church fathers.

In the understanding of the church fathers, the Old Testament is dependent on Christ for its meaning in the way that a compass is dependent on the magnetic field of the North Pole. The latter is not a part of the compass but all its readings depend on it. The church fathers understood the law, the prophets, and the psalms to point toward Christ. They approached the Old Testament with the assumption that its overarching purpose was to communicate a message about Christ. Tertullian refers to Christ as "the illuminator of the ancient writings" (*Against Marcion* 4.40). Hilary states that all prophecy is "about Christ and through Christ."[1] Origen said that "statements about Christ . . . have been recorded in the Pentateuch, and . . . in each of the prophets and in the Psalms, and in general 'in all the Scriptures,' as the Savior himself says when he sends us back to the Scriptures and says, 'Search the Scriptures for you think you have eternal life in them. And it is they that testify of me'" (*ComJn* 5.6).[2]

We have observed a variety of approaches taken by the church fathers to understanding the Old Testament. They sometimes wrestled with the proper reading of the text; they paid attention to the nuances of grammar and vocabulary; they noticed geographical and topographical points; they took account of historical aspects in the text. These were, however, only the basics for perceiving the significance of the text. Each served to point toward a deeper meaning hidden from all whose minds Christ had not "opened . . . to understand the scriptures" (Luke 24:45) or from all from whose eyes he had not removed the veil (2 Cor. 3:14). The fathers meant by this that faith in Jesus of Nazareth as the promised Christ affects the way one understands what has been written in the Old Testament. Henri de Lubac has observed that ancient "Christian exegesis is an exegesis in faith. . . . Taken in its entirety, not in its details, and in its substance, not in its embroideries, it is an act of faith in . . . the Incarnation."[3] Or, as others have described Christian exegesis using the words of Paul, it is an exegesis that moves "from faith to faith" (Rom. 1:17), that is, it begins in faith and ends in faith. The focus on Christ as the interpretive center of the Old Testament is the true heritage of the church fathers' reading of the Old Testament. In this they perpetuated the understanding of the Old Testament found among the earliest Christians in the New Testament. This heritage, as I noted in the introduction, was continued by the leaders of the Protestant Reformation. It remains the heritage of all Christians.

1. Hilary of Poitiers, *Commentary on the Psalms* 147 (on Ps. 54.2).

2. *Origen: Commentary on the Gospel according to John, Books 1–10*, trans. Ronald E. Heine, FC 80 (Washington, DC: Catholic University of America Press, 1989), 163–64.

3. Henri de Lubac, *Medieval Exegesis*, vol. 1, *The Four Senses of Scripture*, trans. Mark Sebanc (Grand Rapids: Eerdmans, 1998; original edition 1959), 260.

English Sources for
Exegetical and Homiletical
Works of the Church Fathers

Translation Series

There is no series devoted exclusively to the exegetical and homiletical works of the fathers. The following series all contain some of these works. It should be remembered that much of the fathers' exegetical work was done in the context of their theological writings so that writings that are neither commentaries nor sermons will usually contain significant amounts of exegetical work.

The Ancient Christian Writers. New York/Mahwah, NJ: Paulist Press, 1946–. This excellent series contains the most comprehensive annotations of any of the series in English.

The Ante-Nicene Fathers. Peabody, MA: Hendrickson, reprint of the 1885–96 publication. These volumes can be difficult reading because of their nineteenth-century English. The series is still useful, however, because it contains works that have been translated nowhere else. Selections from this series often appear in online translations of the fathers.

The Classics of Western Spirituality. New York/Mahwah, NJ: Paulist Press, 1946–. This series contains only a few writings of the church fathers. They are lively, modern translations, however, and some are works not available elsewhere.

The Early Church Fathers. London/New York: Routledge, 1996–. This is a very new series and contains many works not previously available in English.

The Fathers of the Church. Washington, DC: The Catholic University of America Press, 1947–. This is the largest collection of works of the fathers in modern English and contains numerous exegetical and homiletical works.

The Library of Christian Classics. London: SCM/Philadelphia: Westminster Press, 1953–1966. These are excellent translations but only the first eight volumes contain works of the church fathers.

Oxford Early Christian Texts. Oxford: Clarendon Press, 1970–. This series has the Greek or Latin text on one page with an English translation on the facing page. It is intentionally limited in the scope of works that it will include. These texts are helpful for those who can make their way, at least a bit, with the original texts.

The Nicene and Post-Nicene Fathers, First and Second Series. Peabody, MA: Hendrickson, reprint of the 1886–1900 edition. The first series contains works of Augustine and John Chrysostom and the second series contains the writings of the other fathers who wrote after the Council of Nicaea in AD 325. See my comments above on *The Ante-Nicene Fathers*.

Popular Patristics Series. Crestwood, NY: St. Vladimir's Seminary Press, 1977–. This series largely comprises works that have not been previously translated and offers a lively modern translation.

The Works of Saint Augustine. A Translation for the 21st Century. Hyde Park, NY: New City Press, 1990–. This is an excellent translation of Augustine's works into modern English idiom.

Commentary on the Bible Series Based on the Church Fathers

Two series of commentaries are in process that draw their exegetical comments from the church fathers. Both are producing commentaries on the Old and New Testaments. Comments are drawn from various fathers and are arranged in relation to the chapter and verse of the biblical book being exegeted.

Ancient Christian Commentary on Scripture. Downers Grove, IL: InterVarsity Press, 1998–.

The Church's Bible. Grand Rapids: Eerdmans, 2003–.

Online Sources of Translations of the Fathers

Christian Classics Ethereal Library: http://www.ccel.org (translations from *The Ante-Nicene Fathers* and *The Nicene and Post-Nicene Fathers*, First and Second Series. See the descriptions of these works above.)

Early Church Fathers

> Additional Texts: http://www.tertullian.org/fathers/

> Augustine: http://personal.stthomas.edu/gwschlabach/aug.htm

> The North American Patristics Society: http://moses.creighton .edu/NAPS/ (By clicking "Links" at this web site you will have access to a number of additional online textual sources.)

INDEX